brae

W9-BGL-029

THE CYCLIST WHO WENT OUT IN THE COLD

ALSO BY TIM MOORE

French Revolutions
Do Not Pass Go
Spanish Steps
Nul Points
I Believe in Yesterday
You Are Awful (But I Like You)
Gironimo!

THE CYCLIST WHO WENT OUT IN THE COLD

ADVENTURES RIDING THE IRON CURTAIN

TIM MOORE

PEGASUS BOOKS
NEW YORK LONDON

THE CYCLIST WHO WENT OUT IN THE COLD

Pegasus Books Ltd
148 West 37th Street, 13th Floor
New York, NY 10018

Copyright © 2017 by Tim Moore

First Pegasus Books hardcover edition January 2017

All rights reserved. No part of this book may be reproduced in whole or in part
without written permission from the publisher, except by reviewers who may quote brief
excerpts in connection with a review in a newspaper, magazine, or electronic publication;
nor may any part of this book be reproduced, stored in a retrieval system, or transmitted
in any form or by any means electronic, mechanical, photocopying, recording, or other,
without written permission from the publisher.

ISBN: 978-1-68177-299-8

10 9 8 7 6 5 4 3 2 1

Printed in the United States of America
Distributed by W. W. Norton & Company, Inc.

Thanks to the wondrous Raija Ruusunen, Ed Lancaster and the ECF, Stephen Hilton, the saintly and several Samaritans of Hossa, Peter Meyer and everyone else at MIFA, Matt, Fran and Nick at Yellow Jersey, Peter Milligan, my entire family, Comrade Timoteya and Lieutenant Colonel Stanislav Petrov.

1. TO THE NORTH

'You understand how it is here, the weather?'

The elderly Norwegian in a Charlie Brown earflap hat was the first pedestrian I had encountered since leaving Kirkenes, a little port hunkered pluckily up in Europe's furthest top-right corner. On his third and loudest attempt, he had at last penetrated a howling blizzard and the many thermal layers that swaddled my head.

It was a disappointing response to my own snood-muffled enquiry: the distance to Näätämö, across the border in Finland, the European Union's northernmost settlement and the only place for hours around that offered an overnight alternative to a hunched and lonely death in the sub-Polar darkness. My understanding of how it was there, the weather, had, I felt, been pretty solid for a graduate from the No Shit Sherlock School of Climate Studies: our conversation was taking place 400km above the Arctic Circle, in winter. Nonetheless, this knowledge base had broadened memorably over the previous eighteen hours, and in ways that left the tiny exposed parts of my face encrusted with frozen tears of pain and terror. I nodded feebly, expending around 8 per cent of my physical reserves.

'So why you are WITH BICYCLE?'

The road to forsaken hypothermia had begun in cruelly different circumstances. The August before, I was outside a café in Florence, winding down after another day at the coalface of Offbeat Travel Writing – in this instance, failing to catch giant catfish beneath a city-centre bridge, under the watchful gaze of a hundred loudly critical onlookers. My phone rang: it was the *Guardian*'s Germany correspondent, who had my contact details from a commission related to a distant misadventure that had left said coalface deeply imprinted with my own screaming death-mask. 'Hello,' I said. 'Please tell me this has absolutely nothing to do with the Eurovision Song Contest.'

Having reassured me, he requested my opinion on something I had never heard of, rather than simply wished I hadn't. Our conversation was correspondingly brief, just long enough for my interviewer to imagine a story headlined, 'Part-time cyclist knows nothing of new Iron Curtain bike trail.'

I set off home the next day, having for this trip exchanged my usual budget airliner for the four-wheeled fruit of a cheapskate's midlife crisis: a two-door, eighteen-year-old BMW, recently acquired as it bumped noisily along the bottom of its depreciation curve. It was a ruminative drive, partly because of my dilatory chosen route, and partly because the radiator hose blew off whenever I put my foot down. Across northern Italy I found myself on big, winding chunks of the roads I had cycled two years earlier when I had retraced the 1914 Giro d'Italia on a ninety-nine-year-old bike with wooden wheels. Crossing into France I sought out Alpine climbs remembered, more fuzzily, from my ride around the 2000 Tour de France route. And all the while my thoughts were snagged by the idea of tackling this Iron Curtain Trail.

What a deliciously cool and breezy antidote such a ride would be to my current, wilting south-European summer, periodically enhanced as it was by an antifreeze steam facial whenever I raised the bonnet in a lay-by. Then there were nostalgic memories of a three-month journey my wife and I had made in 1990, driving across Scandinavia and a great swathe of the Eastern Bloc, just weeks after the Berlin Wall came down. This over-ambitious, under-budget epic had, I now realised, set the template for my subsequent travels. We survived on stolen bacon and took turns at the wheel of – hmmm – a two-door, eighteen-year-old Saab.

Reflecting on that trip, my mind's eye offered up repeated images of yawning flatlands viewed through a grubby windscreen. The prospect of freewheeling along such gloriously prone landscapes held immense appeal to a man gazing through another grubby windscreen at some of our continent's most merciless inclines, ones he had ridden up when he was either slightly too old to be doing so or much too old. Then again, he was now two years older than much too old, and 6,700km – the Iron Curtain Trail's total distance as gleaned by the *Guardian* man from the press release in front of him – was twice as far as he had ever previously managed in one go.

I came home with a new obsession, along with the facility to ask for five litres of demineralised water in a selection of continental languages. As a child of the Cold War – in fact, for many years a proper grown-up – I still couldn't get my head round the fact that one could now traipse gaily hither and thither across the death-strip. How unthinkable that would have seemed to my younger self. At the age of twelve I'd acquired a wooden-clad, Russian-built short-wave radio, and spent long hours twiddling through eerie interval signals broadcast by Soviet-satellite propaganda stations, loop tapes of ten-note trumpet fanfares interspersed with some fruity-voiced defector announcing: 'This is Radio Prague, Czechoslovakia.' I was enthralled and petrified in equal measure. Back then you'd be packed off to the gulag for smuggling Wrigley's Juicy Fruit in through the Iron Curtain, or shot dead trying to climb out over it. Now I could ride a bike across it at will.

And beyond all that, this Iron Curtain Trail tracked the full length of what I think we can all agree is our planet's most splendid continent, an unrivalled diversity of culture, history, climate and geography – all in one fun-sized package! Infected to the point of delirious commitment, I contacted the European Cycling Federation, bureaucratic overlords of this new trail and a dozen other long-distance 'Euro Velo' routes that traverse our fair continent. The ICT, I soon learned, was more properly known as Euro Velo 13, which travelled through no fewer than twenty countries between Kirkenes and its terminus at Tsarevo, on Bulgaria's Black Sea coast.

Online investigation revealed some exciting truths about the route I was by now emotionally obligated to tackle. Long stretches of EV13's 6,700km were as yet unsignposted, beginning with its entire 1,700km passage through Finland. Other sections were no more than vaguely mapped with dotted lines – most notably through Russia, where it wandered distantly inland to avoid a long section of Baltic coast that was closed to foreigners, on account of an embarrassment of military and nuclear facilities. No less exhilarating was the revelation that nobody had yet conquered the virgin EV13 in its entirety – assuming you were happy to exclude a lavishly supported corporate team of electric cyclists, which I was, and to heartlessly dismiss a middle-aged German for not starting in quite the right place, which I did.

I convinced my editor and cleared my diary. Then I emailed the ECF to impress them with my trailblazing intention, and to enquire if any of EV13's missing links had been recently filled in. In the weeks ahead, the ECF's Ed Lancaster would humble me with his kind and invaluable assistance. It is fair to say, though, that Ed's initial response filled my heart with uglier emotions. 'I thought it was important to highlight at this stage that we are now putting the total distance of the route at 10,000kms,' I read, my jaw settling at full gape, 'so maybe a bit more than you were calculating.' A bit more. Like almost precisely 50 per cent more. Not twice as far as I'd ever ridden in one go, then, but three times. I'd barely turned a pedal in a year, and my, um, forty-eleventh birthday lay just a few months ahead.

My wife had for some time been cheerily introducing my adventure to friends and relations as 'a ride too far'. The gently corrosive drip of this billing now abruptly swelled into an acrid torrent of concentrate that burned a ragged, smoking hole straight through my morale. Ten thousand kilometres was a ride and a half too far, the ride to end all rides with an extra ride on the side. Yet there was nothing to be done: my obligation had recently progressed beyond the emotional to the rigidly contractual. More than that, I'd already bought the bike. And what a bike it was.

The MIFA 900 series made its debut at the Leipzig Trade Fair in 1967, accompanied by whatever passed for a publicity fanfare in the German Democratic Republic – I'm seeing an encirclement of grey-suited men in horn-rimmed spectacles clapping expressionlessly, while a Stasi officer poorly disguised as a podium dolly-bird takes careful note of the cadence and intensity of every individual's applause. Superficially, this little 20-inch wheeler with its folding, step-through frame was a match for the new wave of compact urban bicycles then being launched in the West – it was only two years since the Dawes Kingpin had spawned the shopping-bike genre, and MIFA's 900 actually beat the famous Raleigh Twenty to production by eighteen months.

But take that first 900 – more specifically a 901 – off its jerkily revolving Leipzig rostrum, and you would note the odd shortcoming. For one, the bike had no gears whatsoever. It lacked the supportive strut that bolstered the vulnerable open frames of its Western counterparts, and was fitted with a visibly inadequate folding hinge-lock. Most conspicuously, the single brake lever operated a metal rod that depressed a stout rubber pad onto the top of the front tyre, via a big hole in the mudguard. This startlingly shit 'spoon brake' was a throwback to the age of the penny-farthing – an age when deceleration issues were the principal cause of 3,000 annual cycling deaths, and when about 3,012 people owned bikes.

The Central German Bicycle Works, whose native acronym gave MIFA its name, manufactured the 900 series until the Wall came down. The model's development over those twenty-two years is a handy metaphor for the progress of Soviet-model state socialism: there were no developments. Actually, that isn't quite true. From 1973 the decorative stripes on the mudguards, hitherto colour-coded to the frame, were all more economically painted in Comrade Red. From 1986, they switched to the less comradely but even more economic black. A 'flagship' 904 model was also introduced in 1977, with shopping racks fore and aft, a 29mm armour-piercing cannon and a normal, non-Victorian front-wheel caliper brake. But the vast majority of 900s still came with spoon brakes, and none offered gears or a frame that didn't buckle in two if you liked your bratwurst.

On the face of it, such archaic shonkiness should have guaranteed commercial failure – especially as the cannon never existed.

But in the GDR, commercialism wasn't a factor. To paraphrase Henry Ford, East Germans could have any bike they wanted, as long as it was a MIFA 900. And not just East Germans – the 900 was offered to/foisted upon comrades right across the Soviet world, becoming the default pedal-powered runabout from Vietnam to Cuba.

The consequence of this international monopoly can be considered astonishing. In 1977, 150,000 Raleigh Twentys were built – the *annus mirabilis* of the British bike industry's final mass-market, global success, which sold just over a million in its production run. In 1978 alone, the MIFA plant in Sangerhausen churned out 1.5 million 900s. By the time the last one rolled off the line in 1990, over three million had been built. Take China out of the equation, and you will struggle to find any machine in the history of bicycle manufacture that betters this total. I did, and failed.

And having failed, I wanted one. It had been the same during that 1990 trip, when I developed a deep maternal affection for the Trabants abandoned on every East European street, headlights shattered and Bakelite doors ajar, sneered at by their VW and Audi replacements speeding sleekly past. Three million Trabants were built, too: another ubiquitous but unloved ugly duckling, another semi-functional, jerry-built anachronism. And each one a little piece of big-ticket history, a symbol of the one-size-fits-all Communist experiment, which at its peak encompassed a third of the world's population. I'd been brought up to regard East Europeans with fear or pity, depending on whether they were saluting at an endless parade of missile launchers or being pistol-whipped for wearing Levi's. But as we drove past all those oatmeal Trabants, how histrionic my adolescent emotions seemed. That gormless radiator-grille smile was the true face of an evil empire. Who could not warm to such a goofy, hopeless, squat little underdog, other than perhaps anyone who had ever owned one? Anyway, let's just agree that the MIFA 900 was a Trabant on two wheels, and that this was why I came to be hauling a black-trimmed mudguard through the snow-bound reception door of Europe's northernmost hotel.

I'd booked the hotel long in advance with a view to spending the night there, but Kirkenes was on its well-clad, steamy-breathed way to work as I dragged my bike, mummified in plastic sheeting, past fridge-faced council offices and warehouses. The overnight blizzard had cleared but its fallout lay deep and crisp and even, the thick topcoat to an archetypally Scandinavian study in bleak but bland prosperity. My heavy Arctic boots struggled ominously for purchase: if I could barely stay upright walking 100 yards in great big wellies, what hope of riding 100 kilometres on two thumb-sized patches of rubber?

How my body had whimpered for rest, having been repeatedly hauled from slumber during an all-night coach ride by the violent fishtailing of our driver's latest attempt to regain control as we careered through the white-out. But the minute I lay down on the hotel bed for a money's-worth doze, my brain buzzed into life: *mission-mode activated!* Robotically I rose to my feet and submitted to some clip-board-wielding internal master of destiny, and his stridently delivered checklist. Shower! Very good, sir. Don body layers! Very good, sir. Swish noisily to breakfast, lay waste to buffet, unwrap and reassemble bicycle, mount panniers, don head layers, unnerve Australian Northern Lights watchers, conquer Arctic! Typically, the minute I heaved the bike outside and down the hotel steps, this sir character smartly buggered off, leaving me bereft of vigour and discipline.

The manager poked his head through the door, blew his cheeks out in response to the conditions, then encapsulated my riding companion with commendable efficiency.

'Small bicycle.'

The principal failing of my itinerary was afforded similar shrift.

'Summer is good for bicycle. Now is not good.'

I knew my first waypoint was the road past the airport, and asked him to direct me. He did so with palpable reluctance, then slipped into a more urgent, pleading tone.

'Too cold. Take taxi, please, to airport is just few kilometre!'

I watched his shaking head disappear, then turned my pasty, hopeless face towards the beanie-hatted young JCB drivers busily pushing snow into giant spoil heaps around the car park opposite. Somewhere inside my balaclava, my mouth tried to smile.

The first road sign I had passed, just outside Kirkenes, was a finger-post pointing south. It took a while to decode it. The letters were Cyrillic, and the tightened drawstrings of my outer headwear had narrowed the world to a tiny, fleece-framed slot. Murmansk. I didn't know much about the place, but it had the right kind of deep-frozen, John le Carré ring to it. What an ideal prompt for quest-launching contemplations: the curdled dream of a socialist utopia and the umpteen millions who suffered in consequence; the threat of nuclear annihilation that had blighted the first half of my life; the general vibe up here in the twitchy ears of the Russian bear's looming shadow, at a time of East/West tension unparalleled in the post-Curtain era. It wasn't even snowing at that point, but even so, and with no more than a single hill and 2km under my daft wheels, I'd been too shattered and shell shocked for any such insightful context. Now, with twilight stealing in across a desolate winterscape and the temperature into double digits below, my brain was running on empty, bypassed by a crude, numb instinct for survival.

Onwards I inched and slithered, squinting through shotgun volleys of windborne ice at the grim, grey Barents Sea, the stunted birch skeletons waist-deep in billowed white, and my multifunction Garmin GPS, its terrible data barely legible beneath the slushy smears of my screen-clearing efforts with a weary, thrice-gloved hand. In five wretched hours I had covered 36km; the old man reckoned Näätämö lay at least 20 further off.

At the hotel in Kirkenes I had mixed two litres of steaming hot water with energy powder and tipped them into my CamelBak fluid-pouch; I took a weary slug from the mouthpiece tube and found it plugged fast with ice. I lowered my right arm back towards its oven-glove handlebar mitt, and in doing so confronted a strange rigidity in the elbow. Dimly I grasped that frozen sweat had plaster-casted my anorak sleeves at a right-angled crook. Colossal frosted bollocks to the social history and geo-politics of the Iron Curtain age. I had my own cold war to fight.

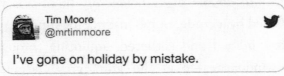

Tim Moore
@mrtimmoore

I've gone on holiday by mistake.

2. FINNISH LAPLAND

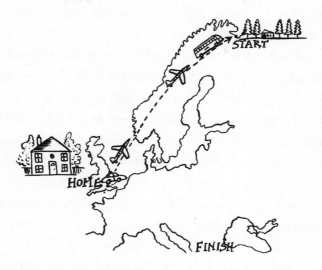

Two hours on I was laid bonelessly out on a bed, delivering slack-jawed, reindeer-mince belches at a ceiling splattered with last summer's mosquitoes. All the furniture had been crowded up against the under-window radiator and festooned with dank wool and polyester. Crowning the bed posts: my wretched last line of under-sock defence, a pair of inside-out supermarket plastic bags releasing their repulsive moisture in sour wafts.

Accepting that I might never be able to think straight again, I gave it one last shot. What had this day taught me? That five hours on an exercise bike – and a single lap of Kew Green on the bike now thawing out in the hall – was inadequate preparation even by my own abysmal historic standards. That I was going to see an awful lot of Finland, and in the slowest of snowbound slow motion: over 1,650km remained, and my average speed stood currently at 8.2kmh. That I would not be swept through this nation on a wave of public enthusiasm. Largely because there was no public: Näätämö stood atop the province of Inari, a region half the size of Holland that was home to 6,783 people – 4,500 of whom lived in two towns. Nor, extrapolating from my motelkeeper, would there be much enthusiasm.

A little old lady with maroon-dyed hair, she had reacted to my rather high-profile arrival at her reception desk by holding up a single hand, her gaze fixed dourly on a soap opera and its subtitled parade of dot-topped vowels. I shuddered and dripped for a full two minutes until an advert break allowed her to welcome the Rajamotelli Näätämö's newest guest – and, as I swiftly established, its only one. I've seen enough interviews with racing drivers to know that Finns operate a very limited range of facial expressions, but was nonetheless impressed by her stony indifference to my bike, pooling gritty meltwater across her lino, and especially to my face – a memorable study, as my bedroom mirror soon revealed, in partially defrosted mucus.

The day's final lessons had unfolded in short order. A heaving plate of lingonberry-smothered Rudolfburger and chips taught me that though I might starve to death between Finland's far-flung hamlets, within them I would be generously refuelled. The land-lady's habit of blankly repeating an approximation of what I had just said to her (Towels? *Toe-else*. Food? *Foat*. Bicycle here? *Bissa clear*) suggested communication would not be straightforward in the weeks ahead. Beyond 'reindeer', our only shared word was 'sauna' – both nouns uttered by her with some vehemence to announce a non-choice option. The second my fork chinked down onto an emptied plate, I was all but frogmarched along two dim corridors and into a volcanic wardrobe. Then, alarmingly, all but frogmarched out as I slumped there pink and nude and vacant: after much pointing at her watch and a brandished list of the motel desk's operating hours, I learned the hard way that I should have put my watch forward by an hour when crossing in from Norway.

Every time exhaustion lured me towards coma-grade slumber, the adrenaline of bewilderment and disorientation yanked me sharply back out. What the actual frozen crap was going on? In the thirty-eight hours since creeping from the matrimonial bed at dawn I had dragged my MIFA into and out of a minicab and a long-distance coach, through three airports and the doors of two hotels. I had put on so many clothes that I could barely walk, see or hear, then saddled up this tiny bike and ridden it for seven hours through deep snow and the occasional blizzard, at the speed of a dying tramp. My digits pulsed in cook-chill distress, and my toothpaste was still frozen solid.

And so to the day's toughest lesson. A remedial class, really, in which a frosted dunce learns that well-established trends in climatology are more valuable than his own half-arsed predictive dabblings. While planning my itinerary, I discovered that Northern Finland had experienced a comparatively balmy winter the year before, and was now enjoying an even milder one. I was thus incited to pooh-pooh the worriers who urged me not to set off until at least May, or to do the ride the other way up if I really couldn't wait that long – starting at the Iron Curtain Trail's Black Sea end with a view to reaching the Arctic Circle in high summer. (This latter option was never on the cards: as a slave to the 'idiot's gravity' of the map, I just couldn't begin to imagine heading from south to north.)

Every time I consulted the colour-coded online forecast for Lapland, all I saw was a sea of the very palest blue, with occasional islands of yellow. On my wife's birthday in mid-December it had been 1.9 degrees Celsius in the Näätämö area, and by the second week of February, winter seemed all but over. Yes, there would still be snow. Of course there would, and I wanted some – it

Tim Moore
@mrtimmoore

My washbag was in this front carrier. Just tried to brush bits of reindeer burger from my gob with frozen toothpaste.

was as deeply ingrained in my mental image of the Iron Curtain as coiled razor wire, border guards with peaked hats the size of cart-wheels, and a young Michael Caine being bundled into the boot of a Wartburg. But on 16 March, three days before my departure, the Näätämö mercury topped 8 degrees. So much for all those self-styled voices of reason, many of them thickly Finnish, who had warned me that the Lapland winter generally peaked in March, when the snow would be at its deepest.

My phone screen faded to black on the bedside table, thoughtfully concealing an online local weather map awash with negative teenage numbers. Winter had come back in from the cold. Why was this happening? It all seemed so unfair, and yet so very richly deserved.

*

BREAKFAST IS SELF. YOU EAT AS YOU WAKE.

If the printed welcome on the deserted dining hall's door failed to sharpen my appetite, then the view from its window would make that fourth bowl of cornflake muesli a challenge. Beyond the streaky double glazing, shimmering under a hard blue sky, lay a silent, white wilderness of the most terrible beauty, a very still, very lifeless still life. A garden bench just outside was buried up to the top inch of its backrest, encircled by conifers weighed down with chubby dollops of icing. Further, past Näätämö's desolate scatter of snow-wigged concrete barns, a monochrome nuclear winter tolled out in every direction: barren white slopes speared with dead black trees, the introduction to a huge and hostile nothingness.

The stretch south of Näätämö offered a choice I had wrestled with for weeks. Either a safe but scant 33km to the next settlement, Sevettijärvi, or the full-fat statement of intent set out by an

88km ride to a rentable lakeside hut much further south. This late-onset winter made the decision for me: no way on God's frozen earth could I manage 88km in these conditions. So an hour later, a fleece-faced, hi-vis klutz slalomed blithely past Näätämö's petrol-station grocery, knees-out on a kid's bike, off into the 20-mile void.

'Sevetin Baari?'

'Yes.'

'You are open?'

A searching look – what's that other word again, the not-yes one?

It was midday. Three hours of lonely but increasingly competent trans-Arctic pedalling had delivered me across a pin-sharp winter wonderland to the tiny, forest-nestled village of Sevettijärvi, and the bar-hotel-restaurant that welcomed the cold and weary from a catch-ment area the size of Yorkshire. The morning's achievements had hotwired my flatlining Arctic mojo, but this latest faltering discourse with an elderly Finnish landlady was heading ominously off-piste.

'No food?'

'Yes.'

'Yes, you have food, or . . . yes, you have no food.'

A small nod – that one, option B.

A tantalising coil of heat swirled through the door she was sticking her head through. This wooden-walled, steep-roofed oasis was self-evidently Sevettijärvi's one-stop shop, the only show in town: a parade of snow-covered receptacles around the front proved that locals congregated here to collect mail, buy bulk food and consume alcohol with crate-piling abandon. The surge of relief and achievement that had propelled me recklessly down the pine-lined Cresta Run that linked the bar to the road was swamped by a rising tide of panic. It was ten below and falling.

'Is there any other place to eat and sleep in Sevettijärvi?'

'Ah . . .'

'It's just that if there isn't, I might kind of die.'

The slightly constipated look that had annexed her compact features intensified, then abruptly burst. 'Camping – three-five metre!' Alarmed by her own ejaculation, she jabbed a finger north-east through the white woods and slammed the door.

Humming reedily, I heaved the bike off through a winding, path-shaped gap in the trees. At times the snow was thigh-deep, but at least there weren't any wrong turnings to take. For days there never would be. Finally, after the thick end of one-five kilo-metre, I found myself before a shabby farmhouse encircled by off-season camping chalets, each topped with a plump cushion of snow. Never has a cyclist been so glad to hear a dog bark.

The porch was home to a teetering pile of empty beer cans; after some cautious knocking, the door behind it opened. A tousled old chap in a tracksuit and hiking socks welcomed me forth into a bachelor's kitchen, its sink piled high with soiled crockery, the smell of blandly functional solo catering heavy in the air.

My host spoke English, enough for me to negotiate the purchase of a plate of lumpy mashed potato, smothered in stewed hunks of an antlered animal with festive associations. For twenty euros this hardly seemed an unmissable bargain, but I wasn't about to haggle with the nearest calorific competition three hours back down the frozen road. 'Only reindeer and salt,' he declared solemnly as he placed his steaming handiwork on the liver-spotted Formica before me. 'Very natural. You take one beer, yes?'

'I really couldn't.'

My refusal left him crestfallen. I suppose he just wanted to deny sole responsibility for that stack of shame in the porch, to roll his eyes and jab a thumb at it when he welcomed summer's first camper: 'Honestly, those English cyclists.'

A radio in some adjoining room pipped out the hour. I checked my watch: 2 p.m.

'Come my friend, *one beer*.'

My apologetic head-shake was followed by a semi-explanatory slurp from the CamelBak, laid on the table beside me. He surveyed this apparatus with rheumy disappointment. 'So, maybe I take one beer.' In a single practised movement he withdrew a can from a tracksuit pocket, popped the top and tilted it into his stubble. My firm intention to ask this fellow for an overnight bed seemed suddenly flawed, and a moment later I was fairly scooting back down the path I had cleared through the snow on the way up. I am here to report, just, that the liberated glee smeared across my features at this point was not there six hours later.

How do you adapt an old Communist shopping bicycle for a 10,000km expedition? The answer is simpler than you might think:

you cast a spell that turns it into a proper bike. While practising this, though, it won't hurt to seek advice from qualified experts.

My heart was already set on a MIFA 900 when I tracked down a German internet forum devoted to GDR two-wheelers, and posted up an outline of my intended mission plus a request for helpful input. The responses were universally discouraging.

'Why such an old MIFA? This little bike is very heavy, much more than it looks like.'

'The MIFA bike was really to ride only in a camping site, from the caravan to the small store for beer and bread. No further!'

'The core problem might be the weakness of the frame. Please avoid, it will become a horror-trip!'

Most damningly pertinent was the experience of a 900 enthusiast with a passion for long-distance touring. 'I had this idea too, for a Greek holiday, but I give up after biking 50km in five hours with the little MIFA.' (On the first day of my ride, it would take me two hours longer to cover 56km.)

I persevered. German eBay had offered up a tantalising trove of MIFAs, amongst them several 904s with double carriers and the less suicidal front brake. I had also discovered the frankly astonishing existence of nail-studded 20-inch snow tyres – a product surely of no interest to any small-wheel cyclist in their right mind. Before the manufacturer came to its senses and burned them all, I bought a pair.

Foolhardy as they clearly thought it, my determination seemed to impress the GDR bike fans. Helpful suggestions, however reluctantly couched, began to pepper their prophecies of doom.

'You must change origin gear ratio, very slow for the plain and unusable for the mountains.'

'The MIFA maybe OK with a strengthened, stiff hinge.'

'In DDR era, to make good the MIFA our dad or uncle weld the hinge and sometimes also add a strut.'

'If you want really to do it, you have my unrestricted respect for this performance! But I think you will still find disappointment in the brake.'

I considered all this, asked more questions and eventually decided on a compromise that preserved core authenticity while offering at least a fighting chance of making it to the Black Sea, and before my children forgot what I looked like. West German shopping bikes of MIFA vintage, I learned, had generally come with a two-speed rear hub – the marvel of Sixties engineering that was the Fichtel & Sachs Torpedo Duomatic, a self-contained, cable-free device allowing urban potterers to change from low gear to high and back with a backwards flick of the pedals. The lower ratio was intended to tackle nothing more than a gentle rise in the high street, but 100 per cent more gears was not to be sniffed at, and I found it predictably easy to convince myself that it wouldn't be cheating. If anything, this East/West, cross-Curtain vintage hybrid would surely make the bike even more appropriate for the task in hand. Unrestricted respect!

The plan seemed simple: I would take the back wheel off an old 20-inch West German shopper and whack it on a MIFA 904. However, I made rather a meal of the associated logistics, in a manner that ended with my old BMW spinning gaily around on a hail-bound autobahn, before coming to a sudden and uncomfortable halt against the concrete central reservation. A fortnight later the irreparable wreckage was repatriated to a salvage yard in Dover, where a big man with a crowbar helped me prise open the buckled boot. Inside lay the gold, Fichtel & Sachs-equipped, 1970s West German shopper I had bought from a Russian man in Bonn, an hour before the dark sky tipped icy marbles all over the A1 near Wuppertal. I brought it back to London in the hold of a National Express coach. A few evenings later, a Polish van driver arrived at my door with the white MIFA 904 I had been en route to pick up in Leipzig.

'Is not big,' he said, holding out the documents for my signature. 'But is heavy.'

Both attributes were apparent as I wheeled it into the garden for inspection. Before confronting the gold bike in Bonn, I had stubbornly failed to grasp the defining tininess of a bike with 20-inch wheels. For this I blame the Raleigh Twenty upon which I came of cycling age, a family runabout commandeered in order to master gravel skid-stops. As a nine-year-old with the saddle right down and the bars chin high, it had always seemed a beast of a bike. Dwarfed beneath our carousel washing-line, the MIFA looked a dismal, shrunken runt.

It was, if nothing else, original: the fat plastic saddle, the gaffer-taped dynamo and even the chubby, cracked tyres all bore their factory GDR stampings. Some previous owner had applied a decal that graced the frame's down tube with the possibly ironic legend 'Nice Ride', in cursive script. More importantly, this same tube was unencumbered by a folding hinge. Quite how such a screaming absence escaped me in the eBay photos remains a mystery, but I wasn't about to complain. The hinge had been flagged up by the MIFA collectors as an accident waiting to happen, and which now wouldn't.

In due course, once supplied with photos, these collectors would express some excitement about my two-wheeled curiosity. I just know you will too. With its caliper front brake and dual luggage carriers it was a MIFA 904 in all but name, a previously unrecorded non-folding model. A stamp under the bottom bracket dated it to the second quarter of 1990 – a forgotten child of the GDR endgame, knocked out in that strange hiatus between the Wall coming down in November 1989 and reunification eleven months later. 'Fold-bikes were a trendy thing in the 1970s, but completely out in 1990,' postulated one of my online German friends. 'Maybe MIFA figured that a 900 without a hinge could be more attractive for the new

West market.' If they did, then just like the Trabant production managers who launched a VW-powered model in the same ambitious spirit of this time, they were badly wrong.

With barely a month left until we flew off to the Arctic together, I set about readying this blameless old campsite runabout for the brutal ride of its life. I removed the dynamo and hit up the gold shopper for its Duomatic rear wheel, bell and kickstand. (This other bike, as a point of interest, was what you might call an extreme folder – when I unscrewed the central bolt the thing fell into two entirely separate halves.) The ferociously pointy-toothed snow tyres had almost eaten their way out of the cardboard box they'd been delivered in, and fitting them required the motorcycle gauntlets I had last worn twenty-five years before, while encouraging a vast and furious cat into his travel basket. Shod in these rotary maces, my MIFA exuded an improbable whiff of aggression, the sort of thing Mad Max's auntie might have ridden to the bingo.

My devotion to authenticity had never been entirely slavish, and as departure loomed the backsliding gathered pace. Could I reasonably be expected to straddle a vinyl breezeblock for 10,000km? To curl my fingers around bar grips of harshly ridged Bakelite over the same eternity, while pushing round tiny, twin-spindled rubber pedals with enormous Arctic boots? Addressing these issues and a few others was bad news for the bikes I'd be leaving behind in the shed. I took the saddle off my 1914 Giro bike, and mounted it on the chassis plundered from my eldest daughter's basket-fronted ladies' model. My daily ride – a thief-repellent eBay clunker – donated handlebar grips and flat pedals, and my mothballed Tour de France bike bequeathed its panniers. With a sigh and a dip of the shoulders, I then trudged shamefully forth to the darkened outer limits of acceptable compromise.

Even without a folding hinge, my MIFA's single-spar open frame had shrieked its pliable vulnerability to all who saw it. Rather than the double-braced diamond established as the time-honoured bicycle standard, here was a two-sided triangle. With its twin carriers laden with luggage and a grown ninny in the saddle, there seemed little reasonable prospect of such a design covering the full and bumpy length of Europe without profound structural mishap. There wasn't enough tubing, and what there was had been forged and assembled by Communists. Because try as I might, there was no forgetting my unhappy introduction to East German bicycles: the ten-speed GDR-built racer that was my sixteenth birthday present, a brand-new machine that died of old age before I could vote.

At any rate, the frame clearly needed some sort of brace. After a fiesta of scattergun Googling I found that scaffolding handrails came in tubes of appropriate diameter, sold with clamps that together might make a bolt-on crossbar. Just in case this scheme wasn't as excellent as it seemed, I did a search for 'amateur frame-builder' and emailed the first name that came up for a second opinion. 'My instinct on the scaffold poles is that they aren't a good idea, but I could be wrong,' replied Stephen Hilton, before politely explaining in elaborate detail why he definitely wasn't. Stephen's easy way with the language of fillet brazing and mitres marked him out as an unusually capable amateur. His subsequent actions marked him out as an unusually wonderful man. Within a week, he had taken my frame away to his domestic workshop in Chorley, fitted a bespoke bolt-on top-tube and delivered it back to my door. 'Just in time,' he said as my eyes filled with tears of grateful wonder. 'The front and back tubes were already way out of parallel.' Despite my repeated efforts, this noble paragon of self-taught frame-builders would not accept a penny for all that brazing, mitring and crawling up and down the M6. It's the least I can do to order you – yes, you – to buy one of his frames.

Alas, it is almost time to bring this enthralling tale of salvage, plunder and mechanical give-and-take to a close. But one chapter remains before the Dr Frankenstein of expeditionary shopping bicycles brings his ungodly creation to life, and it begins with our spirited protagonist flicking the Vs at a Thompson bottom bracket.

Soon after my MIFA arrived I noted that its between-the-pedals engine-room was home to that eponymous cottered horror, the same stupid, clonking mess that did its un-level best to destroy my 1914 Giro ride. Having bent down to insult this engineering travesty, I battered the hateful thing clean out of the frame with a club hammer. A cotterless replacement arrived in due course from Germany, and Peter from our pub-quiz team came round to help me coax it into place. Pooling our resources – his dextrous inventiveness, my crate full of century-old bike bits – we also fashioned a bracket to connect the arm of the rear-wheel coaster brake to the bike frame, and another to brace the wobbly rear luggage carrier.

The great unknown was the Duomatic hub, which to judge from the state of the 1970s bike it came off hadn't seen much action in decades. An online search unearthed an exploded diagram – more precisely a shattering detonation of microscopic ironmongery – which persuaded us to leave it be. To atone we slathered most of the bike in engine oil, then tightened everything up really, really hard, wishing we'd done these things the other way round.

'Any better?' asked Peter, when I returned from a five-minute test ride.

'Night and day,' I said, hauling my leg over Stephen Hilton's crossbar. This sounded preferable to full disclosure: with my departure three days off, that was the first time I'd ridden the thing.

3. THE WINTER WAR

'Please, anything. Bread? I am on a bicycle. There are no shops. Please.'

Two days in, and already pleading for my life. This lakeside hut renter was proving a reluctant Samaritan on the phone; I had just interrupted her assertion that the eighty-five-euro overnight tariff did not entitle guests to bedding, towels or sustenance of any sort. The hut was still more than 20km away, the daylight frail and frigid, and the next place to buy food was the town she was speaking from, a further 60km up the road. All I could be grateful for was that even here – way out in the frozen, lonely sticks – Finland's deep association with mobile telephony had endowed me a three-bar signal.

A pained sigh crackled from the speaker, at length followed by words. 'Some people stay also with you. I talk and maybe they give you food.'

 Tim Moore
@mrtimmoore

Lovely day except for the minus 14ness. And
the 11 hours to do 88km.

To the cyclist, snow is like sand. If you've ever ridden a bike on the
beach, you will have an idea of the consequent impact on speed
and ease of progress. Every kilometre was an attrition of gasps and
slithers, one more battle in this hopeless campaign to conquer a
hostile infinity. I gazed through that fleece-framed slit across iced
lakes and forests, my snood-muffled huffing the only sound in a
cryogenic realm of white silence. I saw my first reindeer, a mournful
taupe column shuffling through the snow with antlers downcast,
on their lonely trek to a farmer's casserole. Once every hour or so
a car barrelled waywardly past, piloted by a blank-faced man in a
docker's hat with a fag between his lips. To preserve my bond with
humanity I duly saluted each and every one, though with my
many-gloved hands wedged fast in my pogies (as I'm afraid those
oven-mitt handlebar covers are known), all I could manage by way

of greeting was a wink. Until we hit minus 13, and my eyelashes started freezing together.

Before setting off, I had researched the risks and rewards of riding a bicycle in extremely cold weather, as described by a plucky brotherhood of online 'ice bike' enthusiasts. The upsides seemed both vague and few, no more than a handful of rhetorical questions that begged for unkind answers: 'Need a place to reflect and unwind?' 'Want to push yourself right to the limit?' 'How does your own private road through an Arctic wilderness sound?' Not really; no; absolutely bloody terrifying.

The downsides, though, presented an endless litany of danger and distress. In the brutal days ahead I dwelt regularly on the scariest. Most centred on the human brain and body's suicidally whimsical reactions to extreme cold. When Captain Oates succumbed to frostbite on that sorry runners-up trudge back from the South Pole, he slept with his feet outside the tent: the agony as they thawed inside was literally unbearable. Take a bow, circulation and nervous systems – some lovely interplay there. (What a tragedy to reflect that if Oates had only been able to pull a pair of plastic carrier bags on under his socks, he could have starved to death with everyone else thirteen days later.)

Then there's the moronic package of death-welcomers we call hypothermia. In response to intense but sub-lethal cold, our brain essentially gets drunk – both quickly and extremely – and starts making giggly prank calls to every gullible body part. The hands that were frozen a moment ago suddenly feel pleasantly warm. Your eyes decide the map makes more sense upside-down, and a report comes in from your ears that a rescue helicopter is touching down just behind that hill. Before you know it your legs are striding enthusiastically off the path and up through a dense and snow-bound forest, and making good speed with those clumsy boots discarded. Soon your fingers are so burningly hot that you offer your gloves to the centaur at your side, who gobbles them whole and vomits up the paisley Travelodge that will somehow evade the hikers who chance upon your clenched remains four years later.

To fight off this insidious malaise, I had learned that one must first conquer the enemy within: sweat. If perspiration accumulates inside multiple layers and does not (bleargh) 'wick away', in very cold conditions it is likely to freeze. This is much to the detriment of your all-important core temperature, and when it happens, you already have one bare foot in the grave. Since the frozen-sleeves anorak incident I had been on paranoid alert against sweat and its causes, a vigil that began even before I set out in the morning. Fully clad in all my many layers, at room temperature I would begin to froth up like a salted slug within two minutes. The answer was to breakfast in thermal vest and long johns – sorry, landladies – before pulling on the rest in a sort of controlled frenzy, then waddling swishily out into the Arctic like a big fat love doll.

That was the easy bit. Once the body hit normal operating temperature out on the road, any vaguely concerted effort would slam down every lever in my sweat factory. I'd survived a frosted-elbow scare while labouring up a gentle hillside before lunch, but the challenge now ahead was an open invite to heavy perspiration – concerted effort, and lots of it, was unavoidable if I fancied reaching that hut by nightfall. And that was before I factored in the circular conundrum presented by another capricious failing of psycho-physiology: if there's one thing guaranteed to make you sweat like a pig, it's the knowledge that doing so might kill you.

It was way past six now, and the sun's long goodbye was gilding the alabaster wilderness in a manner that would have doubtless looked wonderful through a heated windscreen. I lowered my glassy gaze to the Garmin screen, and watched the temperature flash down to minus14.2°C. A pitiful sniff froze my nostril hairs with a space-dust crinkle. Somewhere inside their six-layer cocoon of rubber, merino wool and polythene my toes died, a farewell klaxon-scream of agony fading into wooden numbness. Far more terrible, though, was the message that soon emerged from within my pogies: the thrice-gloved fingers that had been clawed rigid round the bars all afternoon now felt fluidly, lazily aglow, drawling for release from their four-walled thermal prison. Frozen shitlords! Here they came, the opiate delusions of hypothermia, luring me off to a peaceful, stupid death. The very thought squeezed my sweat glands like ripe citrus; both armpits prickled and a rivulet wriggled its way down the back of my neck. No! I arched my back to blot this bastard harbinger against an inner layer, and in doing so made a discovery that sent a steamy shriek of terror across the Arctic wastes. My anorak – the whole thing, sleeves, torso, collar and all – had frozen solid from the inside, an exoskeleton of iced sweat that I could have taken off and stood up in the snow beside me. Then befriended and gone off with hand in stiffened cuff, over the snowy hills to find that helicopter.

Withdrawal, confusion, sleepiness, irrationality . . . My mind riffled desperately through the stages of hypothermic conscious-ness that preceded 'apparent death' in an online chart I'd found, hoping to recall which one bore the dread footnote: 'by this stage you may already be too far gone to recognise the problem'. It didn't help that sleepy, irrational confusion had been my default state for forty-eight hours. Then came the suspicion that the very act of hosting this inner monologue proved I was already too far gone to recognise the problem. How much further? With a dying groan I looked down at the Garmin and met a blank screen – the battery had gone. Hysteria welled in my guts. Did I have 5k left? Ten? The

celestial dimmer-switch was on the twist from dusk to dark, and I
hadn't seen a car for at least two hours. When the road now curved
uphill I succumbed to full-blown panic, pedalling so hard that my
studded rear wheel begin to fishtail wildly through the snow and
its underlay of polished ice. Sweat fairly sluiced down me,
defrosting my eyelashes and stinging the mad red orbs behind
them. Calm the fuck down! With a supreme effort I steadied my
breathing, slithered to a halt and got off to push. This was better.
Slow and steady, easy does it, we're not at home to Mr Apparent
Death. Bit slippy in these boots, mind, but . . . *sweeesh* . . . just one
foot in front of . . . *sweeeeeeesh* . . . the other, and I'll soon be
*sweeeeeeeeeesh-thwosh-*FLOMP.

I sat and watched the stricken MIFA slide gently back down
the hill, exhaled remnants of body heat wisping out through my
crusted fleece-hole. 'The first rule of Arctic Bike Club is: you do
not join Arctic Bike Club.' My epitaph dwindled to a croak. 'Rules
end.' Then I turned my head and there, winking through the trees
and the frosted gloaming, was a cluster of lights.

So unfolded the longest, hardest days of my entire life. The mornings
began with a bleary, fearful peek through many layers of bedroom
glass, scanning the sullen sky, the thermometer nailed to the window
frame outside, and beneath it the wobbly, last-gasp slalom my wheels
had traced through the snow the night before. Twelve hours later I
would stumble into a hotel reception, or a log cabin, or a reindeer
farm, or a decommissioned bank, and stand there, shuddering and
melting, while my refrigerated, under-nourished brain struggled to
process thoughts into speech.

Winter duly fought on to the last man, and even as I crawled
ever southwards that little red column of alcohol held its ground
in the thermometer's horrid depths. By mid-morning my feet

would be gripped by a perverse torment that seared their soles like a red-hot ice-axe. The price of a single afternoon on full-defrost in the blazing Arctic sun was a burned and blistered balaclava face-slot, a fast-track to the full Fiennes. It would be weeks before I saw grass, tarmac or water that wasn't coming out of a tap.

The morning after my brush with exposure, the temperature hit minus 22°C, so extravagantly bracing that a haze of ice hung in the air, and every inhalation punched the back of my throat like a death-eater's fist. 'But our cold here is a sort of dry cold,' said one of the woolly-jumpered snowmobiling chums whose weekend holiday hut I had almost died outside.

Nice try, I thought, fumbling a spoonful of their reindeer soup between my chattering teeth. Your cold here is a sort of fucking cold.

It was bitter; it was lonesome. After that grocery near my Näätämö motel, I endured a barren 170km – two full and terrible days – before the next commercial establishment of any sort asserted itself from the tundra. Overbearing desolation is what northern Finland does best, and I would routinely have entire afternoons to myself, watching the illimitable, primordial scenery fail to evolve and wondering if the regional authorities had intro-duced human hibernation.

Even the major national route I crept along for two days was a ghost road. So far-flung were the towns that my eyes would dampen as I approached that black-on-yellow skyline sign, and imminent reacquaintance with those wonderful places I dimly recalled, where people lived and did stuff. Ah, a petrol station, a bobble-hatted family in the café inside squirting condiments all over a shoebox of chips, a man filling up his snowmobile with 95 unleaded. The sound of silence at last punctured by chainsaws and barking; a roster of smells beyond pine resin or wood smoke.

It would be some time before I noticed that these towns weren't terribly appealing, their iced streets broad but empty, drably lined with low-rise regional headquarters and other slush-bordered studies in post-war concrete. Even when I did notice, I didn't care.

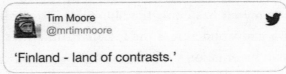

Tim Moore
@mrtimmoore

'Finland - land of contrasts.'

Between these rare urban oases yawned bleak refrigerations of forest and frozen water. I would gaze at the depthless horizons of spruce-girdled white lakes and think, then say, then bellow: *FINLAND, LAND OF CONTRASTS*. The woods started creeping me out, so dark and primitive, the big-bad-wolf backdrop for a million scary stories since the dawn of time. 'Few are the forests like Finland's, with four-point-four hectares per Finn!' Trilling out self-composed jingles seemed a good way of keeping my spirits up. Instead, they always sounded like someone's final utterance in a slasher film.

Crawling onwards I succumbed to an unlikely trio of tribulations: exhaustion, terror and boredom. The snowed-in wastelands had first emitted the stark and awful majesty of a fairy-tale curse, but their stern beauty palled. And so my gaze inevitably dropped down to the Garmin screen, with its dispiriting record of glacial stasis.

Polar shopper cycling is a cruel mistress, with a taste for drawn-out Tantric sadism. Each day seemed to last a week, a Sisyphean torment of slithering sloth. How I struggled to recalibrate my entire concept of acceptable progress. On the flat, 14kmh was a balls-out, breakneck blast; the tiniest incline dragged me down to low single digits and empathy with Captain Scott's men, hauling their own sledges up ice-shelves after their ponies froze to death. The Garmin's odometer clicked up kilometre-tenths with such dismal reluctance that I repeatedly thought it had stopped recording. Some of these 100-metre chapters went on for ever, but I stared them out to the bitter end, like Gollum watching Ceefax. I can still remember 267.3. And 324.9, that was another. Maybe you had to be there. Just be very glad you weren't.

And the snow kept coming, now flicking me painfully in the eyeballs, now drifting atop my pogies and front carrier, now smothering out the whole wide world. It wasn't going anywhere either. For a reminder that Finland's snow lay deepest in March all I had to do was take a single step away from the carriageway, and watch the waist-high accumulations come up to meet me. I was thus a prisoner of the road, compelled to conduct all my out-of-saddle business in the lonely bus stops that broadened it every few miles. Warmth was painfully stamped into feet, supermarket burgers fumbled from mitten to mouth, discoloured holes left steaming.

Two or three times a day a demonic cacophony announced the approach of an Arctic Machine – an infernal, implacable snow-plough with that legend writ large across its fearsome blade. I learned the hard way that this was the cue to hurl the bike into the roadside drifts and crouch behind its panniers, face to the forest and arms round head. As the grating roar climaxed, a bow-wave of snow and compacted ice nuggets would crash over me, followed by the gritted tornado that every large vehicle trailed behind them up here. In truth, I rather enjoyed these painful and terrifying cannonades, simply because they gave me something to do that wasn't pedalling very slowly into a blizzard or pissing all over my mittens at a bus stop.

The natives I encountered in these difficult days embraced

every national stereotype, which is to say both of them. This is a country whose self-referential comedic lexicon is focused on lugubrious alcoholism, with an entire joke genre devoted to the knockabout adventures of two men marooned in a lonely cottage with a case of vodka. In my favourite, Kimi ransacks the tool shed after the last bottle is drained, and comes back with a jerrycan of antifreeze.

'We could drink this,' he tells his friend, 'but we'll probably go blind.'

Mika looks slowly around the cottage and out of the window, then says, 'I think we've seen enough.'

Every village mini-market I went into was home to a stubbled, booze-breathed Mika like the chap who had cooked me reindeer stew, shambling furtively about in the cider aisle (anything stronger than 5 per cent demands a visit to that triumph of feel-good branding, the state-run 'Alko' store). The woolly-jumpered snow-mobiler who told me about Lapland's 'dry cold' did so during single-handed combat with a three-litre wine-box. (In eloquent – but shameful – testimony to my diminished state, it was a week before I even remembered the half-litre of Norwegian duty-free vodka buried in my panniers. And another week until I perfected the Dirty Rudolf: two parts vodka, one part Hi5 citric energy powder.)

Like the winter that defines their homeland, Finns can come across as bleak and chilly. I never heard a raised voice, or a cheer, or a roar of laughter; to borrow from Dorothy Parker, they run the gamut of human emotions from A to B. It would be a mistake, though, to interpret this dour dispassion as heartlessness or disdain. I made this mistake again and again. I made it when the snowmobilers greeted my near-death stagger across their cottage threshold by asking me to take off my boots, as they'd just swept the floor. I made it when a UPS driver listened to my blathering, blizzard-muffled request for directions, then said: 'An airplane has crashed in the Alps. Everybody is dead. *Everybody*.' And I made it when an elderly hotelier explained where her restaurant was by pointing first at the petrol-station grocery over the road, and then at a microwave in the corridor.

The last time I made it was just after my first puncture, mysteriously suffered on a thick bed of snow in the standard middle of nowhere. As I battled the rear tyre off, bare fingers raw and shrieking, an ancient Audi rumbled up from the bleached horizon and slowed to a noisy halt. The window squeaked down and a mournful wail of blues guitar burst out, followed by a ginger-bearded face. 'I think you are not from Finland,' declared its owner in the default toneless blare, and I told him he thought right. He flicked the stereo off and impassively surveyed my predicament. 'A bicycle is a bad idea. *That* bicycle is a very bad idea.' Then he nodded, turned Blind Kimi up to maximum volume and shouted his farewell: 'If you need help, you will ask.'

Enlightenment dawned as I watched the Audi wobble and slither away. There was no malice or misanthropy in his words, just naked truth, baldly delivered. Finns were people of few words, understated to the point of bluntness. I would never meet a Finnish bullshitter. Dauntless, hard-core journeys were part of everyday winter life up here, so mine wasn't about to impress anyone. And it wasn't as if I *needed* to do this at all, certainly not at this time of year and on this sort of bike. If I'd chosen to make it harder for myself, then that was my own silly fault. Redbeard had simply called it like it was. His was a land of harsh sincerity, where spades were spades, and daft little bikes were daft little bikes. Where you got help if you asked for it, but otherwise didn't. Where bad ideas went to die.

My progress was punctuated with reminders of my idea's many-headed badness. Some taunting memento of kinder seasons, an upturned kayak on a frozen lakeshore or a field of snow-smothered holiday caravans. Being overtaken by a cross-country skier. An old lady dragging home her weekly shop on a sledge. My arrival, after ploughing south for days and days, at the EU's most northerly tourist destination – the full-on ski resort of Saariselkä (of course I stayed at Santa's Hotel, and of course – look away now, kids – I ate reindeer pizza there). The evening afterwards I phoned home, and learned from my son that I was still seven degrees north of Anchorage, Alaska.

Every morning was the start of a new expedition, off into an unpeopled void with nothing but blind faith and three bowls of guest-house porridge to sustain me to the next staging post. More than once I wheezed wretchedly into the only settlement I'd be passing through all day to find its solitary shop or café closed. On one such occasion, pressing my desperate face up at a locked glass door in the village of Tanhua, I spotted a tiny crone inside stacking shelves. Emboldened by hunger into a land beyond decorum I successfully gained her attention with uncouth yells and a tattoo of knocking. Then promptly lost it with my follow-up mime, a primal caricature of ravening, hand-to-mouth consumption. Her eyes widened, her head slowly shook and to my horror she shrank cravenly away down a dim aisle.

As her retreat unfolded I caught my reflection in the glass. The man before me was not an obvious object of sympathy. A persistent headwind had inflated the top of my gimp-mask snood into a Klansman's cone. Scoured and reddened by regular facefuls of iced grit, my eyes burned out through the balaclava slot beneath. Set off with a baggy, hi-vis tabard, this was a look that said: Terrorist steward. Poor old dear. But it was 43km to Mrs Santa's Cabin in

Savukoski and I wouldn't be doing that on the permafrosted Snickers wedged somewhere in my anorak.

'Oi. OI!'

The glass bowed and sang like a saw beneath each furious blow of my mittens, which along with an intemperate accompaniment of vocal decibels may explain why I wasn't aware that a police van had arrived until one of its occupants tapped me on the shoulder. A consolation occurred as I turned to face the young female officer: however this pans out, I'll probably get fed.

'There is a problem, yes, no?'

I explained my predicament and after a curt nod she strode wordlessly to the shop's door, which opened before she had a chance to knock. By the time she re-emerged I had begun to ponder the attractions of a custodial resolution, which for a breach-of-the-peace conviction might secure me a week of catered warmth. It was not to be. 'You will buy her food, use her kitchen and drink her coffee.' I gave the officer my rather awkward thanks, then looked past her inscrutable face at the shopkeeper's very scrutable one, crinkled into a wan attempt at welcome through the open door. If you need help, I thought, you will ask. And then I thought: Don't whatever you do try this in Russia.

For long days the route had led me away from the border I had set out to follow – no Arctic waste is wastier than north-east Lapland, and no inhabitants meant no roads. But after some sustained eastwards veering, EV13 was now bumping hard up to Russia: I had, at last, picked up the scent of the bear, and with it a faint whiff of Curtain. At Saariselkä the gift shops had been full of Cyrillic keyrings, and the night afterwards I turned the telly on in my fish-shop-café chalet (yes, really) to be greeted by a dead-eyed Vlad-matic newsreader, reciting approved information above a tickertape clotted with back-to-front Rs. Placing my dinner before me, the café owner explained that wealthy Russian visitors had transformed the tourist industry up here over recent years. The dispiriting principal lure: non-counterfeit luxury goods. 'They tell me in Russia everything can be fake, even shoe and whisky.' But then the rouble had collapsed, and almost overnight the flood dwindled to a trickle. 'In this situation I lose ten thousand euros in every month.' He sighed, taking away a plate very lightly smeared in residual reindeer stew. It would be two days before I encountered my first Russians, a couple in a spanking-new Range Rover. Their faces gave them away before their number plates: expressions of aghast disbelief that shared nothing with the native motorist's studiously deadpan reaction to my presence. *What the actual fuckski?*

It was later suggested to me that Finland's brooding and reserved national character is a legacy of their traumatic wartime interactions with the bear over the border. As the suggester had by that stage repeatedly saved my life, I am happy to agree. The 1,000km balance of my ride down Finland would take me right through the strung-out slaughterhouse that was the Winter War of 1939–40, the coldest of cold wars. Many times a day I stood humbled before a modest memorial stone or cartwheeled artillery piece on some lonely white road, imagining the snow stained pink beneath my feet, and the peaceful forests echoing with violent death. When the world's largest military power took on one of the smallest there could only be one outcome. Before reaching it, however, the scarily redoubtable Finns would mete out some of the most one-sided defeats in military history, accounting for 250,000 Russian soldiers in the bloody process.

The Finns are a definitive breed apart, their extraordinary language sharing nothing with the otherwise closely related Nordic tongues;

its speakers are thought to have originated in north-western Siberia before settling in Scandinavia's least hospitable corner. Survival has always been a harsh and marginal affair up here. A third of the Finnish population died in a famine more recent and more merciless than that caused by the failure of Ireland's potato crop. Even today, 90 per cent of the nation is classed as a rural wilderness.

As its regional rivals developed and prospered, Finland remained mired in rustic poverty; it is remarkable to consider that this archetypal first-world technocracy was fundamentally medieval until a couple of generations back. Male life expectancy languished in the low forties well into the last century, and times were so hard in the Twenties that when the first border posts went up along the boundary with the fledgling Soviet state, the Finnish guards' principal task was to stop their countrymen fleeing to Russia in search of a better life. A rural tradition of talismanic sorcery that lingered well into the Thirties was mercifully distilled into the creation of the Moomins. In 1950, half of all Finns worked in farming and forestry, and right up to the Sixties, native woodsmen used horses to pull logs and slept in crude forest dormitories, the bunks fitted with screens to prevent inhalation of a neighbour's tubercular sputum. They were lumberjacks, but they weren't OK.

You can read about the impoverished deprivation in guidebooks, or, if you find yourself in a warm supermarket with a core temperature to restore, on multilingual product labelling. The Finns, I found, have native words for only the humblest human needs – water, milk, nuts, corn. Everything else, from vinegar to sugar, from ham to pornography, is borrowed from Swedish. (There may not have been any pornography in the supermarkets.)

But extremely resistible as this dirt-poor wilderness was in most respects, Finland's strategic importance as a back-door land bridge from Europe to Russia made it a valued and much-swapped pawn in the Baltic zone's imperial struggles. For the thick end of a millennium it was never more than an outpost of the Swedish, Danish or Russian empires; 'Finland' didn't exist in name until the eighteenth century, and the Finnish language was recognised only in 1893. Independence was finally secured in 1917, but the nation only had twenty-two years to enjoy it before the Russians rolled in. Stalin's dumbfoundingly cynical non-aggression pact with Hitler had freed him to swing the Red Army sledgehammer right at Finland's nuts, intent on securing a generous buffer zone against the Nazi invasion everyone knew would come: Leningrad – St Petersburg as was – lay no more than a grenade's throw from the Finnish border.

Stalin was assured that the Finns would hold out for no more than a fortnight, and by generals who were well placed to judge. Before 1917 Finland had been a Russian satellite for over one hundred years, and much of its military equipment still dated from that era: the bulk of the nation's artillery, modest as it was, had last seen action in the 1905 Russo-Japanese War. The Russian top brass knew they could fire more shells in any given day than the Finns possessed in total. They knew that the Finns had a mere dozen fighter planes capable of keeping pace with even their most lethargic bombers. As their troops massed along the cold border, they knew that the hapless enemy was outnumbered forty-two to one. Excitingly for me, but probably less so for them, the Finnish army had been obliged to supplement its single operational tank with several 'bicycle battalions', mobilised to repel the largest armoured assault the world had ever seen. On the mismatch scale, this was Goliath taking on David's nan.

The Winter War began on 30 November 1939, when a Russian air-raid killed 200 Helsinki residents. In the days ahead 425,000 troops surged over the Finnish border in ten places that spanned almost its full length – an invading force nearly three times larger than the one that crossed the Channel on D-Day. But many Red Army soldiers didn't even make it out of the motherland. The winter of 1939–40 was shaping up as the harshest in a hundred years, and the Russians lost a tenth of their troops to frostbite before they crossed the border.

Read an account of the Winter War and you will spend a great deal of time shaking your head in disbelief. Ride through its bloodiest theatres on a shopping bike in deep snow and those head-shakes will come with a side-order of heavy, mist-breathed sighs. How terrible to imagine the massed ranks of the Red Army trudging numbly through these forests in soleless felt boots and cotton tunics. How easy to forgive them for building the suicidally conspicuous bonfires they huddled around at night, great stacks of blazing trunks that drew Finnish sharpshooters from afar. And how very cruel to picture the Russians shuddering into a vacated enemy command post to find that even on the frontline, every Finn could expect a hot meal and a sauna. When one frozen and ravenous Russian battalion overran a Finnish field kitchen they were powerless to resist the cauldrons of sausage stew still bubbling away; as they stuffed themselves by the warm stoves the cooks regrouped, returned and slaughtered 400 men.

As Stalingrad would later demonstrate, the Red Army's great forte was the iron-willed defence of the motherland. Attacking a harmless neighbour presented a more awkward motivational challenge. Many Russian soldiers didn't even know the name of the country they were invading, let alone why they were doing so. One especially pathetic POW told his captors he'd been dragged off the streets of Murmansk by a military commissar while buying his wife a pair of shoes, and sent directly to the front after an hour's training. When the Finns emptied his pack they found the shoes still neatly wrapped at the bottom.

Stalin's boundless paranoia had despatched three-quarters of the Red Army's officers to the gulag or the firing squad, endowing his invasion force with a leadership sorely lacking in experience, and understandably fearful of showing initiative or questioning even the most flagrantly catastrophic orders. Of those there were plenty. A typical Russian advance sent hundreds – sometimes thousands – of men marching in tight formation across a yawning frozen lake in broad daylight. Presented with this khaki-on-white turkey shoot, the Finnish machine-gunners on the opposite shore could hardly believe their luck. Soon the wholesale butchery so sickened them that many were evacuated with post-traumatic stress. Each attack was a pocket Somme that left the ice strewn with corpses; in one representative engagement, 4,000 Russians failed to take a position held by thirty-two Finns, suffering more than 400 fatal casualties in the process.

The Finns had a rubbish hand but played it brilliantly. Short on men and abysmally equipped, they atoned with pragmatism, imagination, cold-cured winter resistance and a fierce determination to defend their nation and its new-found, hard-won independence. Cunning volunteer officers – amongst them MPs, lawyers and the president of the State Liquor Board, Old Man Alko himself – fashioned and honed the nimble, freelance guerrilla techniques that are still regarded today as textbook tactics against a massively superior force. White capes and skis allowed Finns to slide right up to their enemy unseen and unheard. The Molotov cocktail was a Finnish Winter War invention, named in mocking honour of the Soviet foreign minister who drew up the pact with Hitler. More than half a million were mass-produced by Alko, each bottle bundled with two storm matches. The Molotov's pimped-up apotheosis was a blend of petrol, kerosene, tar and potassium chloride, ignited on impact by an ampoule of sulphuric acid tied round the neck. This glass bastard could take out a tank, though getting close enough to do so was rather a big ask. The even more challenging alternative was a 'satchel bomb', lobbed directly under an oncoming T-34, ideally after a well-built colleague had wedged a log in its tracks to slow it down. Such tactics explain why the mortality rate in anti-tank combat units hovered around 70 per cent.

The Finnish campaign was littered with acts of indomitable valour. The corporal who commandeered a carthorse and rode it bareback along the Russian front line, towing a cannon that he would unhitch and fire at tanks from point-blank range. The lieutenant who took on a pair of T-34s with his pistol, unsettling the crews so successfully that they swung around and retreated. The old woman who whitewashed and scrubbed her cottage overnight, after being told by a Finnish officer that he would regrettably be returning in the morning to burn it down as part of a scorched-earth retreat. 'When you give a gift to your country,' she explained in a note left for his perusal on the kitchen table, 'you want it to look nice.' On the floor sat a can of petrol and a neat stack of kindling. (The Finns' fanatically efficient rearguard torching of any structure that might have sheltered Russians explains the post-war concrete dreariness that defines every single town in this part of the world.)

Stalin's two-week war was soon a bloody two-monther, with ten Red Army troops dying for every Finn. Near Suomussalmi, ski troopers surrounded an entire Soviet division as it plodded up the road: the ensuing siege reduced the Russians to eating their horses, and would cost them 40,000 lives to the Finns 1,000. The mercury dropped below minus 40°C, adding new chapters of frosted woe to an already weighty catalogue of incompetence. Russian guns seized up in the cold; the Finns freed theirs with alcohol and glycerine. Russian medications froze; the Finns taped ampoules of morphine to their armpits. A trainload of skis belatedly arrived but the Russians didn't know how to use them; a troupe of volunteers went off to practise in the woods and never returned. Spooked and confused by invisible snipers and silent ambushes, neighbouring Russian divisions would regularly engage each other, sometimes exchanging fire for hours at a time. When the Red Army took to crawling forward across the ice behind armour-plated shields, the Finns simply crept around to the side and shot them all in the bottoms. It was now so cold that fallen comrades froze to brick in an hour, providing useful but rather demoralising cover.

Yet all the while, both sides understood that despite their derring-do and murderous ingenuity, the Finns were merely delaying an inevitable. By the third month they were down to Dad's Army reservists fighting with captured weapons, and Stalin ordered a regroup that naturally began with many generals being lined up against the wall (one was executed for 'allowing fifty-five field kitchens to fall into enemy hands'). Duly inspired, the Red Army finally broke the Finns with a concentrated assault of unparalleled ferocity, hitting their southern borderlands with 600,000 troops, the heaviest artillery bombardment since Verdun, and history's first carpet-bombing. 'May the hand wither that is forced to sign such a document as this,' said Finland's president, before applying his pen to the surrender treaty. A stroke three months later obliged.

The Russians' scarring Winter War humiliations would stand them in good stead fifteen months later. By the time the Panzers rolled in, the Red Army had already learned every painful lesson. Their abysmal performance against a rag-tag force of caped skiers also encouraged Hitler to overplay his hand, assured that the Nazi war machine would crush them in short order. One may reasonably posit that the plucky Finns thus indirectly defeated the Nazis – especially if one overlooks the awkward regional endgame, which from 1944 onwards saw Finland fighting alongside Hitler's troops as full allies.

But the grim bottom line underscoring the Red Army's Finnish campaign and all their subsequent costly, blood-soaked victories was this: kill me, kill him, kill every soldier you see and keep killing, but understand that you will never kill us all. Short on acts of individual bravery, the Russian invasion of Finland was unsettlingly characterised by dead-eyed, almost apathetic mass sacrifice, the plodding, dutiful acceptance of casualties on a horrendous scale. This was Soviet collectivism reduced to its grisly essence: sheer weight of expendable human numbers was the ugly, blunt weapon that eventually undid the Finns and would also see off the Nazis at Stalingrad. The Finnish commander in chief, General Mannerheim, referred to 'a fatalism incomprehensible to Europeans'.

Perhaps the general was familiar with what must rank as one of the most appalling spectacles in the history of human conflict, described here by William R. Trotter in his definitive work, *The Winter War*: 'In one sector of the Summa battlefield, repeated attacks were delivered straight across a massive Finnish minefield by men who used their own bodies to clear the mines: they linked arms, formed close-order rows, and marched stoically into the mines, singing party war songs and continuing to advance with the same steady, suicidal rhythm even as the mines began to explode, ripping holes in their ranks and showering the marchers with feet, legs, and intestines.'

I'd brought Trotter's book along for the ride, but for days had been too exhausted to open it. With Russians now so near at hand, I wish I'd kept it closed. They really didn't sound like people a cyclist ought to be sharing a busy road with.

Tim Moore
@mrtimmoore

Went past the Winter War Museum this morning. It's only open in summer.

4. NORTHERN OSTROBOTHNIA

'You probably won't die,' said my wife the night before I left, 'but I do worry that you might go mad.'

This gladsome valediction recurred as the deserted infinity rolled on, and hypothermia's cold, dead hand on my shoulder evolved from stimulating novelty to ever-present bore. The ruminative pace of my progress would have been acceptable if there'd been something to ruminate about, something that wasn't trees, snow or silence. Maybe once every other hour I'd see a fox or a farm or a red squirrel or a road sign. With so little data coming in from my eyes and ears, my emptied head would slowly fill with a dribbled slurry of gloom and delusion. Home seemed a year and a million miles away. I tried and failed to imagine the kinder months of my journey ahead, a future in which nature enhanced life, instead of making it a total misery, then doing its level best to bring it to a tragic, lonely end.

Things that weren't there began to loom up in the snowy

distance: a wolf on its hind legs, a burning police car. I took to narrating voiceovers from some tarmac-based sequel to Michael Portillo's *Great Railway Journeys*: 'Finnish National Route 4 has been called Europe's loneliest road, threading its way through an Arctic wilderness of wood and water. As I travel along it I'll be meeting some of the extraordinary characters who call this bleak but fascinating place home, and hoping to somehow once more avoid the violent public shoeing I so richly deserve.'

After that, traditional Lapp aphorisms:

'If weight of snow bends trees down flat, leave the bike at home, you twat.'

'The remedy when frostbite's looming: petrol, matches and a Moomin.'

Tim Moore
@mrtimmoore

'When weight of snow bends trees down flat, leave the bike at home you twat.' (trad. Finnish)

'Frisbee, ear wax, Richard Gere – a wandering mind means death is near.'

With the roads enduringly flat I could at least handle the physical challenge, no worse at this stage than riding all day on an exercise bike, in a meat fridge. And I was getting to grips with the conditions, learning that the road's iced peripheries offered superior traction for spiked tyres, and sticking my leg out speedway-style on the sharper corners. How glad I was for those tiny wheels, which seemed the perfect fit for my handling skills, and meant I didn't have far to fall when they let me down.

Indeed, the little MIFA seemed to be coping commendably in general. Yes, the back wheel had developed a fairly major wobble, but as it only kicked in above 15kmh this was rarely a problem. The chain guard and rear mudguard bracket kept rattling loose until I remembered Pub Quiz Peter's going-away gift, a zip-lock bag of locking nuts. The saddle slipped a bit, the original rubber luggage straps were starting to split, and as my German friends had promised, I was finding disappointment with the brake. But despite all this, and the MIFA's inherent long-distance, foul-weather impracticality, I could think of no other bike I'd rather have been riding.

Such at least was my heartfelt belief at the time. Writing those words now in all their deluded wrongness, I fear I may have succumbed to what psychiatrists call Helsinki Syndrome, so named after a bank siege where the captors shot themselves and everyone else froze to death.

The man in the Cossack hat flagged me down as I floundered towards him, jumping out of a VW Golf to wave through the flake-flecked twilight. I could only guess how many hours had passed since I'd last seen a car, though I vividly recalled the circumstances:

with her approach silenced by the heaviest snowfall yet, I shrieked and flailed and fell in response to the elderly driver's close-quarters horn toot. Indeed, I had spent much of the day kissing snow or the iced gravel that underpinned it, on a circuitous trail that wound through my journey's first sustained undulations. Crossing a frozen lake the track had completely disappeared, leaving me to pick a line through uprooted orange marker poles scattered distantly across the ice.

To minimise my falls and their severity I eventually hit upon the canny ruse of going even more slowly than usual. Even so my shins and ankles burned from regular violent introductions to pedal edges on their way to ground. Keeping an overladen shopping bike upright in pannier-deep snow had if anything been even tougher on my arms, now palsied and useless from shoulder to wrist with the effort of bullying the bars straight whenever the front wheel started to go. On the helpless, slithery descents, the back one kept coming round to meet me. 'That which does not kill us makes us stronger,' said a small voice in my head. 'Though as a rule it also scares the piss out of us and really hurts,' replied a bigger one.

I had little useful idea of my whereabouts, except that I was now in Northern Ostrobothnia, which had an even colder and lonelier ring to it than Lapland, and sounded very much like some-where you would be banished to with no hope of return. At some point I grasped that my idea of where I might overnight in this frigid outback was even less useful. Jabbing at my phone with clumsy, numb digits, I made the first of what would be many emer-gency calls to Raija Ruusunen.

'I'm going to put you in touch with our contact in Finland,' the European Cycling Federation's Ed Lancaster had written many months before, in an email littered with polite suggestions that I consider setting off at a less ridiculous time of year. Thus was I introduced to Raija, whose stoic and noble reply accepted my schedule, and its implicit consequences for both of us: I had made my stupid mind up, and she would therefore be getting me out of a succession of fine messes. 'Cycling in Finland in March is winter cycling, it's still snow almost all over the country here near the eastern border. There will be no people or traffic, the lack of places to eat and sleep is a huge challenge. This is really a wilderness biking tour. I give my personal phone number (open 24/7) and help you, if you are in trouble or need something.' (Perhaps sensing the need for a positive spin, her PS threw me a feel-good lifeline: 'There is research on well-being and forests, it says that even fifteen minutes in a forest gives you positive effects. In this case after 1,700km in Finland you will be very well.')

I would never understand Raija's miraculous modus operandi, nor in all honesty did I ever try to. It seemed appropriate simply to accept that a guardian angel should work in mysterious ways. Feeding into a frost-withered grapevine, this cyclo-evangelical university lecturer from Joensuu – a city I never went near and which at this stage lay 400km to the south – was somehow able at the shortest notice to persuade far-flung strangers to set off into the Arctic emptiness and drag an unknown English shopping cyclist from death's frozen door.

My Cossack-hatted saviour rather uneasily absorbed my snood-filtered babble of gratitude, then beckoned me to follow him to a clapboard cottage set back from the road through a rank of conifers. As a rustic Finn he proved a man of few words, none of them English. I will leave you to imagine his attempt to imitate the act of ice swimming, and my own response when I realised this was a serious invitation relating to a shore-side hole in the small lake just below us. The only time his features broke into life – I'm fairly sure this applies to every Finn of middle years and above – was when he threw open a door in the cottage basement, and an almost visible wall of heat fell out on top of us.

The sauna is an invention cobbled together from Finland's most abundant natural resources: wood, water and vowels. To call it a popular national tradition would be like calling respiration a hobby. There are more saunas than cars in Finland, three million for a populace less than twice that. Sitting in a stupidly hot cupboard really is way up the hierarchy of Finnish needs – above sexual reproduction to judge from the sleeping layout in the off-season holiday cabins I'd been routinely staying in, which. typically featured four single beds per room. In one of them, a two-storey building that slept ten, the only internal door was the one that kept heat in the sauna.

On the sweaty red face of it, Finland's enduring sauna obsession seems an embarrassing indictment of a failure to follow their fellow north Europeans up the Goldilocks learning curve: outdoors in the snow – too cold; indoors in a pine-lined crematorium – too hot; stretched out on a sofa in a centrally heated home – just right. But rather admirably, they don't even bother trying to justify or articulate their addiction to broiled claustrophobia. To a Finn there is simply no problem that cannot be solved by another sauna, especially if that problem is wondering what to build next to your sauna. When the winebox-draining, woolly-jumpered snowmobiler told me that his new summerhouse was home to no fewer than three saunas, and I asked why, he shot me a look of puzzled affront: *it just is.*

I fired up saunas in Finland every day bar two, but it took a while to appreciate them as more than handy defrosting suites for clothing, feet and toiletries. After a week or two I learned to savour the sauna as a sort of blazing-hot chill-out zone: a wooden womb in which to gestate the day's events, and with more fondness than their deep-frozen horror generally deserved. But the sauna that Cossack Hat had now left me alone in was off the scale, an overdose of mind-messing centigrade so fiercely volcanic that within a minute my hair – ow! – was too hot to touch. Reflexively, I scooped up a ladle of water from the usual wooden pail and tipped it onto the magma briquettes. In the super-heated circumstances this was in itself an indicator of irrational thought; when the cartoon hiss of igneous steam thus explosively released hit my head I very nearly keeled face first into the furnace. Instead of spooling through them at my mental leisure, the day's events now rushed unbidden through my broiled mind with nauseous, blurry haste, beginning with the porridge and herring breakfast buffet. That ruined farmhouse with the stoved-in, snowed-up roof, a line of dinosaur-sized elk prints tramping into the woods, the old man fishing through a hole in the ice who got up and walked away when he saw the camera . . . everything seemed foggy and unreal, like a fast-forward, soft-focus episode from someone else's previous life. I rose too fast to my feet and almost swooned, then swayed drunkenly to the door, escaping just before rivulets of molten memory dribbled out of my nose.

This mildly hallucinogenic experience was to prove a handy primer for the hours ahead, and the days that followed them. Events and encounters seemed tinged with surreal improbability even as they unfolded, and I can only now be sure they occurred in real life courtesy of hard photographic evidence. Tip another ladle on the sauna, pour yourself a Dirty Rudolf and kick back as I leaf through this compelling album.

DSC02967. Cossack Hat has picked me up from my cottage, and deposited me at a lonely wooden farmhouse. I am pictured inside, where the unseen residents – a mother and her adult son – have recently watched their surprise guest consume five bowls of salmon soup. Snow has drifted halfway up the window behind me. On the wall is a photograph of the son's paternal grandfather as a pre-teenage Winter War reservist. Inveigling themselves into frame atop the big brick hearth to my left are a group of memorable photo-bombers: two stuffed birds, a rather lugubrious wolverine, and a very pointy-mouthed skull with a Post-it note stuck to its jaw, reading: WOLF. The mother has just explained, largely through the medium of splendid mime, that her husband shot this animal and she skinned it: like the wolverine, it had been caught with its teeth in their antlered business assets. In a while, I shall be impelled to watch the English version of an educational DVD on a TV just out of sight, which will begin thus: 'The reindeer is an animal with long legs and four toes.' And after that, I will go out to feed bell-necked, stick-headed jostlers with the son, who will be wearing a jerkin his mother fashioned from the wolf's pelt. And I will still be wearing the very particular outfit that envelops me in this scene: a red-felt, four-horned Lapp hat, and the capacious hide of a pale-coated reindeer.

DSC02973. This less immediately captivating image shows a crudely skinned side of smoked trout on a background of melamine-faced chipboard. It is the following afternoon and I am in the staff kitchen of a recently decommissioned bank at Juntusranta, 38 very snowy kilometres from the Hossan reindeer farm. The trout looked a lot better when a fisherman handed it over after letting me into the bank. Since then I have hacked the oily pink flesh off with a bread knife and eaten it all. I have also been into the bank's basement and enjoyed the wood-fired staff sauna. In a while I shall make my bed in the manager's strip-lit office, before a night's sleep interrupted by a bleary trip to the loo, which will almost end with me locking myself in the facility featured in DSC02975: a James Bond-grade security vault.

DSC02991. Continuing a clearly fixated theme, this still life depicts the interior of a well-provisioned refrigerator. Its door and shelves are crowded with toothsome calories and refreshments: meatballs, sardines, a variety of yoghurts, tomatoes, cheese, ham, fruit juices, chocolate milk and two large bottles of beer with snarling bears on their labels. A pair of companion images portrays a groaning fruit basket garnished with Snickers bars, and a kitchen work surface piled with the full spectrum of bakery products and a range of preserves. I have progressed a day and 57km south through a filthy and frictionless world of slush, a world that has left its cold, brown mark on man and machine. The house I am in stands marooned between Suomussalmi, scene of Finland's greatest military triumph, and the Winter War museum, which of course is only open in summer. And I have this house – kitchen, sauna and all – entirely to myself, having let myself in with a key left in the mailbox. The landlady lives 25km away but has at some earlier point driven over to deposit this key, make up a bed, crank on the heating and assemble the three-scene cornucopia just described. I have not met her and never will, but know all this through a telephone conversation conducted in the bank that morning. 'I cannot take any payment because I am sponsoring you,' she told me then. 'We are all sponsoring you, because you are on a bicycle, and because it is winter, and because you are mad.'

What humbling, remarkable days these were, being passed from stranger to welcoming stranger through the Ostrobothnian wilderness, suckling deep on the refrigerated milk of human kindness at every stage. And never once footing the bill: my various hosts shunned every offer of payment with such vigour that I always paused before wedging a twenty-euro note under the kettle as I left, wary of causing offence. They didn't even like me thanking them. For some time I wondered what on earth Raija must have said to unleash such weapons-grade hospitality: that I was the easily displeased vanguard of a mighty legion of shopping cyclists whose custom would bring great prosperity to their struggling settlements, or an escaped Ostrobothnian freedom fighter, or the wolverine's ruthless nemesis. My last landlady's explanation had offered a more accurate insight, and Raija later gave me her full take on it: 'When you live in a difficult region and find a bad situation, you must depend 100 per cent on other people. They didn't *want* to help you, they *needed* to. Now they feel happy and more safe, because they can believe that someone will be there to help them when they need it.'

One good turn and all that. Arctic karma. As much as it troubled me to know that I would never be there to reciprocate when these wonderful people needed help, the way Raija told it I basically did them all a massive favour. Don't mention it.

March was over, and though the conditions didn't exactly scream April, Finland had begun to shed its winter coat. Streaks of bare tarmac appeared, along with the odd patch of brown soil and zebra-stripe of liquid lake. I took off one of my four hats and the middle pair of gloves. For the first time I began to examine the map over breakfast with something close to anticipation rather than neat dread; I'd crossed the Arctic Circle and the miles were getting easier by the day. A shopkeeper asked if I was heading south or north, a choice that hadn't sensibly existed hitherto. No longer did I stab listlessly at the camera wondering if this would be the last picture I'd ever take, and imagine it being projected on to a courtroom wall so that the coroner and my loved ones could deduce what I'd been trying to tell them with a close-up of a snow-sculpted cock and balls.

But progress, as I somehow felt it might, came at a price. I was fairly caning it along some evergreen corridor, head down and

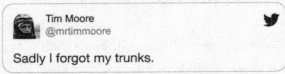

Tim Moore
@mrtimmoore

Sadly I forgot my trunks.

knees out in hot pursuit of the magic 1,000km mark, when the left-hand pedal began to miss a beat at the top of each revolution. This soon swelled into a quarter-turn missing link, and, very shortly after it did, the whole crank fell off and hit the road with a slushy chink. I propped the bike on its stand, retrieved the crank and frowned at the square hole at its non-pedal business end. It was much less square than it should have been. Than it had been when Pub Quiz Peter and I threaded it on to the bottom-bracket spindle thing. I pictured this moment and saw the two of us chortling at the handwritten instructions enclosed by the German vendor, a man who signed himself Thomas. 'You must mount this crankset with 35–40Nm. I Wish You Success.' Ha ha! 35–40 *what*-nows? Wish away, German Thomas! And so I reached the very shallow bottom of this mechanical mystery.

In these numbing conditions, every alfresco spanner session was a fumbled, sometimes tearful frustration, like trying to make an Airfix kit in boxing gloves. I reattached the crank as best I could, which meant it fell off again half a mile up the road. An hour later I pushed my stricken MIFA up the snowy approach to a farm-house with a smoking chimney. I had often wondered how on earth a Finnish farmer occupied himself in winter, those long months with nothing to do but sit by the stove in his socks adding vowels to stuff. The door opened and I shortly found out: he sits by the stove in his socks with a gigantic tool kit in his lap, awaiting the knock of a distressed cyclist. If you need help, you will ask.

How splendidly capable these backwoods Finns were, I thought, pedalling smoothly away from the farmstead ten minutes later. Perhaps it was just natural selection in an unforgiving environment that didn't suffer fools gladly: all the hopeless idiots had long since frozen to death or been eaten. I had already come to a related conclusion in regards to the astonishing proficiency of Finland's surviving drivers, who would shoot slickly past at intemperate speed on surfaces you could barely stand up on. My nightly chapters of *The Winter War* had outlined the Finnish male's multi-competent tenacity, and now I was having it coloured in before my eyes. And in the very finest detail, because in the hours ahead the crank repeatedly worked itself loose anew, requiring the attention of two further farmers, both bearing an air of silent focus and a hefty metal box full of hard-core man stuff. Their task was not made easier by my own remedial efforts when the crank fell off between farms. Have you ever played Rock, Log, Bike? The rules are pretty simple: rock beats bike, log smacks bike.

The snow was coming down again by the time I pushed the MIFA into a hibernating holiday village beside a frozen lake. Raija had worked her magic once more, persuading the elderly owners to open up a chalet for me, and advising the husband of my ongoing mechanical plight. I hoisted the bike onto my chalet's bleak veranda and he went to work, at length separating the essential components. He held the crank up to the porch light and together we stared at a very round hole that could never again be home to a very square peg. He nodded gravely, then said: 'Smoke sauna, seven o'clock.'

My eyes were still red when I woke up the next morning. And only partly on account of the smoke sauna, a rasping, soot-lined dragon's lung from which I had staggered forth mired in smutted body fluids. An hour later, with my laundry strung up and a belly full of broken biscuits, I had opted to unwind before bed with a fireside Dirty Rudolf: the meaty old wood burner was laid with logs and ready to go. It was a decision that once acted upon very promptly filled my pine chalet with choking billows and aggressive electronic beeping. When the old man barged in through the front door I knew our bluff friendship was over. For one thing I had disgraced myself, indeed brought the entire male gender into disrepute, by unaccountably failing to notice the hefty chimney-blocking iron paddle that he now yanked free from its slot in the flue. For another I was still struggling into a wet pair of pants.

With a bill to settle and a broken bike, sneaking away at dawn was regrettably not an option. Instead, I now walked to his garage whiffing of shame and cinders, fairly certain that the boiler-suited man standing with him outside it had come to help thrash some common sense into me. Once again I had underestimated the kindness of Finnish strangers, and, I strongly suspect, Raija's ability to wring it out from afar. Harri was an amateur mechanic with strong arms and a patient eye, who married crank to bracket with forty minutes of careful filing and reckless brute force. 'Is OK now for some few kilometre,' he said, lighting a celebratory cigarette. He took a long drag, then allowed the tiniest flicker of amusement to pass across his oily features. 'You are maybe too hot with trousers?'

It was 50km to the next town, on a road Harri assured me lay impassably smothered in overnight snow. A bike fixer does not a weatherman make: I made it to Kuhmo in under five hours, and walked into its solitary hotel no more than lightly buttered in slush. My room was a microcosm of Finnish towns in general, and this one in particular: clean, bland and cheerless. I would be savouring these attributes. I don't make a habit of weeping on the phone to anyone who isn't a vet, but of late my calls home had been routinely blighted by blubbering self-pity and other unedifying expressions of the loneliness of the long-distance shopping cyclist. My wife might forgivably have barked at me to snap out of it. Instead, she and my son were coming out to Kuhmo to keep me company for a few days, bringing along nappies, my favourite blanket and some new life-insurance documents that apparently needed an urgent signature. An enforced day of rest preceded my support crew's arrival, and I would largely spend it watching a bulldozed mound of skanky, late-season snow retreat very slowly across the hotel car park, and being glad I didn't call Kuhmo home.

'I saw your bicycle. It is not what I expected.'

The hotel receptionist's morning greeting was a variation on the English phrase I most regularly heard in Finland, stripped of the usual reference to my MIFA's modest dimensions. I hated not being able to reciprocate, to coax out even a single intelligible word in the native tongue. But what a twisted tongue it was. As he waved his hand over a map full of blue numbers and tumbling white asterisks, the TV weatherman always sounded like some kid messing about in a language he'd just made up. Even words that generally had some common cross-border ground in most European dictionaries – things like days of the week and months of the year – were over the hills and far away in Finnish. April: *huhtikuu*. Friday: *perjantai*. I abandoned all hope of getting even the loosest grip on the language when the German owner of the Tankavaara gold-mining theme resort (that's right) told me that Finns decline their nouns in twenty very different ways, and have a single word that means 'I wonder if I should run around aimlessly'. (Much as *juoksentelisinkohan* sounded like the desperate product of an especially long Finnish winter, it also seemed like a thought I would inevitably wish to articulate in some endless forest or other, so I had him write it down for me on one of his business cards, along with the words for 'thank you' and 'bicycle'.)

After breakfast I went to a supermarket over the road to nose about the wrinkled fresh produce, then enjoyed a quick tour of Kuhmo's wide-set, four-square civic and commercial structures. It seemed awfully quiet for what I had just realised was the Easter holiday weekend. I found out where everyone was a few hours later, while treating the MIFA to a 1,000km service in a shrinking square of low-voltage sun outside my hotel's slabbed façade. A steady stream of locals old and young passed by as I oiled and tweaked, heading into the hotel's basement bar. In dribs and drabs they periodically emerged, blinking and much less steady, to mill glassily about and smoke. A leather-coated man of about thirty came and sat down on the steps next to me, lit up at the sixth attempt and then toppled slowly over onto his side. He enjoyed the balance of his cigarette in this position, and was crawling back to the door by feel when I went back indoors to read. I looked at my watch: 2.17 p.m.

I still had eight hours to kill, and shot a few in the face immersed in the tale of the White Death. The Winter War sniper awarded this sobriquet was a 5ft 3in outdoorsman by the name of Simo Häyhä, who without any military training single-handedly accounted for 542 Russians in a hundred short and sunless days. Häyhä was a handy shot – most of his victims were gunned down at a range of 400 yards or more – but an absolute maestro of stealth. He used simple iron sights on his rifle to avoid the tell-tale reflections of telescopic glass, teamed his white cape with an eerie white mask, and spent hours tied high in trees or crouched behind drifts, stuffing snow in his mouth to avoid betraying himself with steamy exhalations.

The Red Army were so spooked by Häyhä that he became the regular target of bespoke artillery strikes. In the last week of the war, a Russian marksman finally got him in the jaw with an explosive bullet; with half his face blown off, Häyhä calmly picked up his rifle, steadied himself, and shot the Russian dead. After a slow and difficult recovery, the White Death lived on to the age of ninety-six, frustrating breathless interviewers to the end with the sheer force of his Finnishness. Those who made a pilgrimage to visit the deadliest sniper in history could expect the same one-word answer to all queries about the origin and honing of his skills, and their lethal application: *juoksentelisinkohan*. (Actually it was 'practice'.)

My support crew arrived late, but I was so delighted to see them I didn't mind, not even when they greeted me in the car park with a stream of woe about tackling Finland in an underpowered rental vehicle. That morning I had spent some time in front of the mirror, trying to see myself through the eyes of long-absent loved ones. This was time well spent, as it prepared me for the concern and mild revulsion that annexed their expressions when we went inside and they beheld me in the light. The blistered, ruddy face with its flash-fried, snow-burned balaclava slot. Clothes hanging loose on a shrunken torso. Fingers so feebly arthritic I couldn't close them around the handle of my wife's suitcase. And coiling forth from my once-tight trousers, now held up with a luggage-strap belt, a nose-wrinkling odour that I no longer even noticed: from force of habit, I had that morning unnecessarily smeared my loins in Savlon.

5. CENTRAL AND SOUTHERN FINLAND

With the sun out and my panniers in the support vehicle, I rode on through a different Finland, a world of carefree speed and achievement. The slush was in full retreat from the road, running down the gutters in gritty brown rivers, and shrinking into damp Rorschach blots on the surface. After two weeks of under-wheel creak and crunch, my ears attuned to the novel thrum of spiked tyre on tarmac. Lorries delivered my first facefuls of dust. Dabs of life and colour enlivened winter's dead palette: a tentative leaf bud, a blue bottle, the occasional big red barn, Scandinavia's architectural gift to the Midwest. In fact, I was now routinely reminded of rural America: the big-country emptiness, the shabby farmsteads strewn with rusted pick-ups, the steel guitar twangs that leaked out of most passing vehicles. Even the bleak and sleepy towns, now that I thought of it, had a *Fargo* feel to them.

Off the road, admittedly, Finland wasn't very different at all: it was still well below zero in the shade, and the countryside lay under a thick white blanket. But at least there were people out in it now, getting their Nordic skis out for one last time before spring, or despoiling the restive calm with harsh and buzzy snowmobiles. At least once a day I would pass an old guy in an earflap hat, standing by his mailbox with a snow shovel and giving me the look I was to see so often in the months to come, a gaze of curious disparagement that said: What a stupid thing to be doing. Like rounding the Isle of Wight by pedalo, or running a marathon in a suit of armour, it was already plain that the epic scale of my undertaking would always be undermined by its inherent foolishness.

In mid-morning my support crew would pass by with a deranged volley of toots, or without one if my sober and focused son was at the wheel (in fairness, this wasn't just his introduction to driving on the wrong side of the road: since passing his test the month before, he had yet to drive on the right one). Shortly afterwards I would ingest several pre-packaged supermarket burgers in a bus shelter, and very nearly enjoy doing so now that lunch was just a meal, rather than a death-forestalling imperative fumbled desperately into my chattering maw with numb claws. Many flat and easy kilometres later I would arrive at our overnight stop to find the two of them warming up the sauna or lighting the fire, and on one memorable occasion speeding across the ice on a dogsled.

My wife had brought out a replacement crank, supplied on request by my friends Matthew and Jim after Harri had given his repair job a very limited guarantee. By a small miracle, when the crank did go one late afternoon I was coasting up to the rural guest house we had arranged to meet at. The proprietor politely took over the replacement process after tolerating my unschooled veranda batterings for as long as he could bear to, then went back in to prepare us a meal of Michelin-grade complexity. Jarkko was his name, and I am happy to rank him as the second most impressive human I have ever met, just behind the Vietnam Special Forces veteran with whom I re-enacted the summer of 1775 in a Kentucky forest. Jarkko spoke fluent English, and used it to articulate his informative and entertaining views on history and literature. He was a wine connoisseur, an omniscient naturalist and a marine engineer who owned the largest socket set I have ever laid eyes on. That said Jarkko also arranged for us to stay at the Howling Wolf Inn.

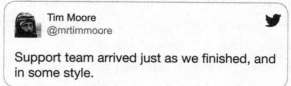

Tim Moore
@mrtimmoore

Support team arrived just as we finished, and in some style.

Survey route 5223 on Google Street View, as I just did, and you will find yourself gazing down a smooth, winding sylvan corridor, flanked with the Finnish autumn's rouged and gilded splendour. This is not the 5223 I remember. I arrived at its lonely commencement already a depleted figure, indeed an almost unrecognisable one. Earlier in the afternoon, much earlier, I had passed a triangular warning sign: the word '*Kelirikko*' below a giant exclamation mark. For a jolly five minutes I speculated on its meaning. Unexploded Molotovs? Moomin cull? Perhaps people had stopped wondering if they should run about aimlessly, and were now doing it all over the road. A less jolly sixth minute introduced me to what I would later learn to be the seasonal thaw, and its dramatic impact on unmade roads. Wikipedia offers a pithy encapsulation of the related challenge: 'The only practicable vehicles during the *kelirikko* are hovercraft, hydrocopters or aircraft such as helicopters.' So began my one-man, two-wheeled, three-hour tribute to the German retreat from Stalingrad.

The support crew had passed as I floundered up a hill of half-set cement, two slithers forward, one slide back, stopping to offer words of succour and three Snickers bars. My son phoned a couple of hours later just as I was pushing the MIFA on to 5223.

'Sorry, this Howling Wolf place is a bit further down here than we all thought.'

'A bit?'

'Quite a lot. Also the road is unbelievable, way worse than that other one. We lost a hubcap.'

I could hear my wife saying something in an urgent tone.

'Oh yeah, the woman here told us to watch out for bears. Literally, she wasn't joking. "Bad bears," she said. And there's a couple of . . . *ccccggggghhhh . . . mmk.*'

A terminatory beep was followed by silence. I checked the screen: for the first and only time in Finland I had strayed beyond signal coverage.

It wasn't my first warning. The reindeer farmers said they'd seen two bears the previous summer, and the fisherman who put me up in the bank had a sideline organising bear-spotting tours: 'We have very many brown bears in the forest, 300kg adults and babies.' He told me they wandered over from Russia 'because there is nothing there to eat, not for animal, not for people'.

In case you hadn't noticed I'm a frightful weed, but somehow these worrisome revelations hadn't troubled me – not even when the fisherman added that a jogger had come to a very messy end in the woods a few years before. I have a feeling I was just too scared too care, my fear gland already saturated with hypothermia and starvation and incapable of soaking up any more perceived danger. But my family's uplifting presence had squeezed out this mental sponge, allowing it to absorb the impressive metaphorical bulk of a 300kg omnivore emerging from hibernation with an empty stomach and a bad temper.

Thickly spread with muddy slush and hemmed in by deep snow and dark trees, the desolate 5223 made an extremely convincing backdrop for murderous predators and doomed bids to escape them. The road was unrideable; the forest impassable. I began to feel like a Red Army conscript in 1939, a hobbling, shivery sitting duck tracked by unseen enemies entirely at home in these conditions, biding their time for the perfect moment to strike. I checked my phone and again stared wanly at that zero-bar void. Had my son been trying to communicate some additional warning at the end of our truncated call? A couple of what? Apart from bears, was there anything else – anything at all – that a vulnerable pedestrian might possibly expect to be threatened by on the lonely approach to the Howling Wolf Inn?

The night before, Jarkko had outlined the definitively Finnish concept of *sisu*, raising it in relation to his country's extraordinary wartime conduct. 'It isn't easy to find a word in English,' he'd said. '*Sisu* is courage, determination . . . maybe like your stiff upper lip, but with fighting spirit.' The way he told it, *sisu* seemed another product of Darwinian selection – survival of the hardest. Anyone who lacked this quality up here either buggered off after one winter, died of whimpering haplessness or went the full Captain Oates.

Sisu was the Winter War sergeant who'd been shot through the chest, telling his commanding officer he was ready to get back to the front as it was 'so much easier to breathe with two holes in my lungs'. *Sisu* was also, it seemed, a fifty-year-old man trying to ride a shopping bike for 10,000km down the Iron Curtain. 'Of course! You made a decision and you stick with it, even though it was a bad decision and everything is going wrong. This is absolute *sisu!*'

I decided this was a compliment, and had fancied myself tapping deep into rich and syrupy reserves of neat *sisu* during the *kelirikko* ordeal. Yes, I would struggle on, through thick and thicker, cold and colder, defy the odds until they defied me, and still be found with a grim smile on my frozen face. Is that a stiff upper lip, Mr Moore, or have you been dead for three days?

That was then. Now I felt the last watery dregs of Sisu Zero drain from my core, dribbling it into the slush behind me like the pathetic slug I was. After all those weeks of deep-frozen silence the woods around were fitfully alive with percussive, deep-bass *thwomps* – the sound of some thaw-loosened wodge of snow falling heavily to earth from a lofty branch. So at least I told myself, in between a roster of high-pitched internal reassurances. What if I didn't meet 'bad bears'? Perhaps a good one might help with directions and offer to share his kill with the weary traveller. Surely wolves didn't eat people outside folk literature, and even then they only ate really small people. And come on, not even the most ravenous bear would trouble himself with emaciated human flesh wrapped in hi-visibility nylon. God, no. No no no. No. Chocolate and wounded animals – that was the preferred ursine menu related to me by a Yellowstone Park ranger some years before. Chocolate: you know, the sweet brown stuff, as for instance found in the three Snickers bars currently packed about my person. My person: you know, that hunched stumbler currently perfecting his impression of a wounded animal.

The light began to die; the wind picked up. Tall trunks swayed, and so creaked. I felt entirely estranged from the world of men. *FLUMP!* Another arboreal avalanche sent my right hand diving into the anorak pocket, primed to hurl out Snickers like a Chinook helicopter distracting an incoming attack with a cloud of chaff. My features slowly solidified into Ron Weasley's idiot gurn of terror. Around this time I realised that every craven, squelchy lurch was taking me closer to the already very close Russian border, start line for the annual post-winter Hungry Bear Dash and notional barrier to the world's largest population of wolves. Something I hoped was *kelirikko* began to pool inside my boots.

After an hour I began to fear that I may have somehow missed the Howling Wolf; after another I knew I had, and was numbly resigned to posthumous identification by dental records. In between I remembered the anti-bear pepper sprays on sale in every Yellowstone Park gift shop, and then the bottle of Tabasco recently purchased to extend the pre-packaged supermarket burger's palling appeal. I was still toting it pathetically at the forest when a loud but not entirely convincing wolf howled out from the distant gloom.

'You took your time,' said my son when I dropped the MIFA at his feet. 'Mum's in the sauna with a couple of gold miners.'

'When I hear what you try to do I laugh until the tears are coming down my face. But later you send me the picture of your bike.'

'And then it stopped being funny?'

'No, then I thought I would really die from laughing!'

Not the fate of many a Finn, I fancied, but then Raija Ruusunen was a very singular woman. Having gone the extra mile for me on so many figurative occasions – most recently by sourcing the lakeside cabin whose fire we were all now sitting around – she had this time done so literally. It had taken Raija two hours to drive here, simply in order to deliver the bicycle – her own pride and joy – that would allow my son to ride along with me for a few days. A life-threatening guffaw at my expense seemed a small price to pay, though our books were almost balanced by the snorts of disparagement emitted as she flicked through my Garmin screens. 'Your average speed is 11.5 kilometres per hour! It's unbelievable! On my tours I make 25, and with many bags of camping equipment!' Having as yet never even momentarily attained that speed, I thought this rather harsh. Was it my fault that I didn't have a proper bike, and was a few years older than Raija, and had chosen not to emulate her daily habit of going to the gym at 5 a.m. to perform 250 squat thrusts? (Yes; no; yes.)

Raija listened to my travails on the road to the Howling Wolf Inn with polite interest. She had lived for many years in a farmhouse deep in the predator-rich woods, her sole neighbour an unimprovably Finnish character with whom she exchanged words about four times a year. 'Once I met him outside and he asked who was my new friend. I didn't understand, and he says, "Last month I look from my window and you are walking to your door, and directly behind you there is walking a bear."'

Round here, she said, I was more likely to meet a wolf: 'They have 40,000 in Russia.' As a lecturer in tourism, Raija nurtured a keen interest in the rouble-spilling oligarchs who crossed the border; as a Finn, she felt very uneasy about accepting their custom. The Winter War had traumatised two generations of her countrymen – Raija seemed certain that her elders' cold detachment was a consequence of formative exposure to carnage and deprivation. Indeed, she sometimes wondered if the Russian invasion and its aftermath had permanently rewired the national DNA, shaping that clichéd character of insularity and hard drinking. 'I don't like that we must now rely on people who made this happen.'

The recent collapse of its currency might have put a brake on the trade, but Russia's influence was still pronounced in these parts: the mugs we drank from were decorated with crude cartoons captioned in Cyrillic, and Raija seemed embarrassed to confess that the cabin was owned by a Russian, and largely rented to his countrymen. 'We maybe get the bad type here, the ones who go to our supermarkets and think the queue is just for little people, who put money in your face and expect you do everything for them.'

Jarkko had said much the same: he didn't like Russians, and the Winter War artillery piece at the end of his drive was hardly a welcome mat. 'We don't offer what they want,' he said, and what they wanted was high-end shopping. Perhaps by force of rural austerity, the reindeer farmers enjoyed a more symbiotic and less hostile cross-border relationship: they nipped over a few times a year for cheap booze and petrol, and to recruit a very different sort of Russian to help out with their summer berry harvest. But the 6,000 Russian troops recently transferred to the Finnish borderlands had gone down like a very leaden balloon. 'Putin bad man,' the farmers told me.

When the wartime tide turned against Hitler, Finland was hardly alone in backing the wrongest of wrong horses. Yet of all the Russia-hating regional nations who pinned their colours to the swastika – Romania, Hungary, Bulgaria and by default the Nazi-occupied Baltic states – only Finland emerged from the post-war shakedown as a free country. They lost a fat slice of territory to the east of the border I was riding down, and a big lump near Leningrad, but stayed on the right side of the curtain – largely because Stalin was still spooked by their *sisu*. 'Everybody respects a nation with a good army,' he said in 1948. 'I raise a toast to the Finns.'

That respect knew few bounds and crossed many borders. By way of illustration let us consider the remarkable story of Lauri Törni, who joined the Finnish army at the age of nineteen, just before the Soviet invasion. In a campaign crowded with heroes, Törni displayed such exemplary valour and imagination fighting behind enemy lines that his eight battlefield decorations included the nation's highest military honour, the Mannerheim Cross. After Russia finally brought his country to heel in 1944, Törni was swiftly recruited by a German-backed resistance movement, which saw him taking Soviets on in an SS uniform. This earned him first an Iron Cross, and then, with the war over, a six-year sentence for treason. After the Finnish president pardoned Törni in 1949, he fled to America; as soon as its government awarded him citizenship, he enrolled in the US army. A nation who had put an ex-Nazi in charge of its space programme was predictably relaxed about certain blots on the CV of such a rare military talent. The man who now called himself Larry Thorne was quickly transferred to the Special Forces, with a combat-proven speciality in survival techniques and guerrilla tactics. In his mid forties, Captain Thorne returned from a first tour of Vietnam with two Purple Hearts and a Bronze Star medal, but he didn't return from his second until 2003, after a Finnish–US team found his remains in the remote wreckage of a helicopter. Whatever else we can take away from Lauri Törni's fabled exploits in the armies of three nations, it is clear that here was an extremely brave man who really didn't like Communists.

Few Finns did by 1945, but in the interests of preserving their national independence they buried their inner Törni: sharing a 1,700km border with a stroppy nuclear behemoth meant playing an extremely careful hand. Throughout the Soviet era Finland maintained a precarious neutrality, staying out of NATO and dutifully participating in every rubbish Eastern Bloc knock-off, from the Friendship Games to the Intervision Song Contest. Finnish film censors banned *The Manchurian Candidate* and several others for their anti-Soviet sentiments. Critical books were removed from public libraries, and the mass media never had a bad word to say about its looming neighbour. The nadir of 'Finlandisation' – coined as shorthand for any painfully lopsided relationship between adjacent nations – came in 1961, when the Finnish government was dissolved and reformed in a coalition of Khrushchev's choosing. The Finns even bought Trabants, and more Ladas per capita than anywhere else in the West.

'The Russian state always has its nose in our business, in its own people's business,' said Raija as I walked her out to her car. 'It is like this in Russia for many centuries. So Russian people don't like to get involved in problems of other people, because they are scared that the state will make it their problem also.'

She plipped the car open and turned to me. 'In Russia, you knock on a door but nobody will open it. You fall down and nobody will help you to get up.'

I was beginning to understand why she was telling me this, and wished I didn't.

'I have worries for you in Russia, if you will have problems like you have had here.'

With that I watched my guardian angel fly away through the black-skied, white-floored woods.

Side by side on the cabin decking, Raija's bike and my little MIFA made a much more obvious father and son than the bona fide duo walking out towards them. Other than the mountain bike I'd seen being ridden to school a week before – by a heavily insulated child who weaved away as I manically dinged my bell in fraternal welcome – Raija's was the first rival machine I'd seen since setting off. How vast it looked, yet how svelte. It was only a matter of time before my short, fat MIFA found itself mercilessly Finlandised. All those gears, all that alloy . . .

'Don't even think about it,' said my son, hoisting a ski-trousered leg over Raija's crossbar and scooting exuberantly off into the morning sleet.

My plan for the days ahead was straightforward and ever so slightly reprehensible: I would tootle behind in my son's twenty-one-yeared, twenty-four-geared slipstream, towed along as he punched a father-shaped hole through the cold air. To facilitate Project Bastard, I had outlined a system of communication: one ding of my bell meant slow down, two was an order to raise the pace. It was a single-ding morning. Again and again I had to tinkle him back to heel as he slid impetuously ahead through a punishing stretch of *kelirikko*, then powered on when the road flattened and cleared. Only now were the entry-level physics of small-wheeled inefficiency laid out before my stupid eyes: to keep pace with my son meant turning the little MIFA's pedals three times to his two.

We were hugging the Russian border's treeless death-strip when the first scabs of sleet flicked us, and more especially him, in the face. The scenery was soon swallowed by a thin, wet blizzard, smearing out what would have been my first sight of a watchtower. I only noticed I'd reeled my son in when my front spikes bit harshly against the lip of his rear mudguard. Ding-ding! He jerked to attention then instantly sagged, like one of Pavlov's dogs who'd wised up. His head dropped further and his speed fell away. His front wheel began to wobble through the slush; when the wind eased I heard low, despondent moans. It was like following myself on day one. I didn't trouble my bell again.

'Burgers, just the way you like them,' he muttered an hour later, tossing me a pair of plastic pouches. 'Cold and raw.'

We were squeezed together in an enclosed wooden bus shelter the size of an outhouse, with a heart-shaped window in the door.

'They're not raw,' I said, unsheathing one defensively. To be honest they might easily have been, but by now I'd eaten far too many to care.

Since his arrival my son had expressed amazement and no little revulsion at the stuff I shoved in every pocket before riding off each morning, nurturing a genuine belief that diet was the most awful aspect of my ordeal. He'd now found out the hard way that it wasn't, but with Project Bastard shelved this was no time for *schadenfreude*. Before we left the cabin I had lovingly bagged my boy up, pulling supermarket carriers over his undersocks in a tender rite of Arctic passage. I had lent him my mittens – a Kevlar-coated ex-German army pair – plus a hat and a pair of long johns to supplement all the turquoise skiwear he'd borrowed off our neighbours. He was well layered, young and fit. But wet snow had blotted its way in through his hiking boots and the tops of his carrier bags, and his knees, unaccustomed to this surfeit of rotation, were aflame.

I broke my son four hours later. The sleet had cleared but a heartless cold wind screamed in our faces, frost-welding wet wool around my fingers and his toes and pushing us almost to a standstill. Labouring past the sign that welcomed us to Tohmajärvi, our destination, I looked back and saw a small turquoise figure in the very far distance, off his bike and pushing. I waited and we walked together in silence through the decrepit hinterland of a dying lumber town, all empty marshalling yards and boarded-up hardman bars. After all those drably functional settlements, this was my first Finnish craphole.

The support crew was reunited at a creepy and peculiar motel built for Russians who'd stopped coming. 'Check out the clocks,' whispered my wife when we shuffled rigidly into its reception to meet her. There were two on the wall behind; both told the wrong

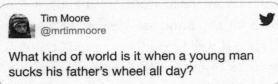

Tim Moore
@mrtimmoore

What kind of world is it when a young man sucks his father's wheel all day?

time, but the wronger was labelled Москва. The desk beneath them was manned by a pair of laconic young wasters with bleached hair.

'This town is finished, my friends,' said one by way of introduction. 'Last year they close even the police station.'

'Maybe police decide we're so good we don't need them no more,' added his colleague with a mirthless smile.

'Yeah, maybe. But they make sure to close the Alko store before they go.'

The motel only had apartments: ours was huge, new and shambolically austere, like a looted show-home. The curtain rails were all falling down and the kitchenette drawer was home to one bent fork and a meat thermometer. Marooned in a corner of the cavernous living area stood a sort of glass-fronted pine Tardis. I peered into this curiosity and read aloud from a label stuck above its integrated bench: 'Infrared sauna. Do not use with alcohol.

Please no animals.' My son, who had yet to speak and was still very fully dressed, pushed me aside, opened the door and cranked all the dials up. Then he shut the door and sat down, blank faced in the deep red glow, until his boots began to steam.

I fully expected to ride alone the next day, so was surprised – and indeed rather proud – when my son's approach to the breakfast table came accompanied by a tell-tale underfoot crumple: he was bagged up and ready for more. With clear roads and clear skies it would be a different story, at least until the last few chapters. We ate lunch by one of the many heaps of conifer trunks awaiting collection along the road; my son fell fast asleep with half a sandwich in his gloved hand. I roused him, then spent the balance of the afternoon watching my first born reprise every ugly phase of my ride's early days, from damp-eyed distress to full-blown madness.

When Raija said I would find the endless Finnish forests mentally invigorating, she probably didn't imagine me shattering the wilderness with bellowed 'Geordie Beyoncé' numbers and animal noises. My son's preferred lunatic mantra was spawned during a very Moore family discussion on the feasibility of living off the deposits from discarded beverage containers (ever the contrarians, Finns only chuck stuff out of the window if it's worth something – there were never any crisp bags or fag packets crumpled into the roadside drifts, just a regular parade of cans and plastic bottles with a displayed refund value of between ten and forty cents). The pan-Scandinavian words for 'deposit' gleaned from the forensic phase of this study would tear forth from my son's throat all through the lonely late afternoon, in reflexive riposte to inclines, headwinds, a proffered Snickers bar or my wheedling efforts to coax him back into the saddle when he dismounted and dropped his bike into the roadside slush. In Finland, no one can hear you scream 'PANTTI-PANT!'

We met my wife at a lakeside retirement hotel with a captured T-34 on the lawn. Some of our elderly fellow residents were playing bingo in the dining hall; others tottered gamely down to a shore-edge ice hole in their swimsuits. It seemed an awfully long time since I'd slept somewhere normal. As normal my son slept for an awfully long time: he went to bed at nine, reappeared eleven hours later and announced that his knees had gone and he'd had enough. I didn't try to talk him round. A hundred miles in two days seemed the humane limit in these conditions.

It was my support crew's last full day and Russia loomed. After dismembering Raija's bike and wedging it into their hire car I set about pedalling these twin woes clean out of my soul. The world is never a blur on a MIFA 900, but I did my best to smear it a little that day, speeding through my first cultivated landscapes and the ever-closer, ever-larger towns of southern Finland. On snowless roads my spiked tyres let forth the rising drone of a Tube train;

elbows in and head down on a straight descent between green fields, I finally bested the speed that Raija averaged all day on her bike.

Finland had welcomed me with a cold, hard slap, but was seeing me off with a warm wave. Chevrons of high-flying geese crossed a cloudless sky. Lakes had fully thawed to a deeply becoming midnight blue, most of them speckled with green islands, and most of those gaily bestrewn with clapboard holiday homes, each sprouting a flagpole trailing a streamer in the blue-and-white national colours. Butterflies wafted clumsily about the road; I shared my bus-shelter burgers with the first ants of spring.

It was Saturday, and the towns were alive with the weekend trappings of civilisation in its slow-paced, clean-living Scandinavian essence. Unisex footballers on garish AstroTurf. A woman vacuuming her front drive. Tippy-tappy Nordic pole walkers patrolling the suburban pavements. I rode on my first cycle paths, broad and sleek, and on them encountered my first adult cyclists. Nearly all were standard-issue middle-aged men in Lycra, and not one returned my comradely half-waves and lifts of the chin. A glance in a shop window ensured I didn't take it personally: what a painstakingly thorough twannet I looked in my bulging snood and flappy reflective tabard, the under-anorak CamelBak tenting out my profile like a participant in some Help4Hunchbacks charity ride. A hi-vis ogre bent over a tiny bicycle. 'You know what I think every time I watch you ride away?' my wife had asked me at breakfast. 'That a kid reckons there's something wrong with his bike, and has just asked his dad to take it for a test-ride round the block.'

When at last a fellow cyclist did acknowledge me, side by side at a red light, it was to ask where my helmet was. I showed him: clipped to the top of the rear rack, ready for Russia. I'd never even tried squeezing it on over my four hats, and explained why: 'Thing is, it's really, really cold in Finland, but you only have about twelve cars. It's a question of relative risk.'

'A helmet here is the law,' he said, a little stoutly, tugging his chin-strap tight as the lights changed. 'Also, my brother has three cars.'

Last and largest of the towns was Imatra, home to the first old buildings I'd seen in Finland, and the only handsome ones. I met my family at the art nouveau Castle Hotel for a farewell festival of starched linen, silver-lidded breakfast buffets, generous tipping and all the other stuff that wouldn't be part of life once I was left to my grubby own devices.

The next morning I changed my tyres on the hotel's stately fore-court as the support crew packed up, bullying off the spiked set and pushing on the standard smoothies my wife had come out with. This had always been the plan, as it was to send her home with a holdall full of mittens, boots and skiwear; but after no more than two full days of clear tarmac and positive centigrade, both strategies now seemed a little hasty.

As I waved the family off, lower lip slightly a-wobble, an Asiatic hotel guest came out and sparked up his first cigarette of the day.

'Where they go?' he asked, tilting his head at my departing support vehicle.

'Home.'

My condensed breath mixed with his exhaled billows in the clear, cold air.

'Where you go?'

'Hell.'

6. RUSSIA

'So you are two more come to see death of socialism.'

Flicking through the excellent journal my wife kept during our distant odyssey through Scandinavia and Eastern Europe, I see we were thus welcomed by a border guard of the Union of Soviet Socialist Republics on 18 August 1990. I say excellent, though from a personal perspective this document is more a tireless litany of shame, and Nostradamus-grade lifestyle prescience. After three weeks under canvas, our first night in a campsite chalet, eating prawns from a cardboard box in the dark, is pithily billed as 'Nazi Tim's special treat'.

In Denmark, when our supply of cheap German tins is exhausted: 'Food becoming bone of contention – T's yoghurt and lentil surprise had me in open revolt.'

In Sweden: 'Mosquitoes unbelievable – T hysterical.'

In Norway: 'T came out of supermarket with bacon and mince stuffed down trousers. Had also refused to buy proper map. After furious row we got lost. Karma.'

Finland was despatched in five days, and not many more words:

'Drove for eleven hours straight, nothing to see but trees.'

'Swedes warned us Finns all drunk and mad, but towns totally dead.'

Our USSR visa was running down and after 2,253 miles in Scandinavia – as I say, it's quite a journal – endless wood and water had begun to lose its appeal.

We arrived at the Soviet border rather traumatised, having spent the previous two nights in the company of a very distant relative of hers, who even in death still reigns supreme as the rudest man I have ever shared a tiny Baltic island with. His catchphrase, delivered when turning over all my cards during a candlelit game of Hearts, or raising the lid of the waterless centrifugal toilet after my panicked emergence, or inspecting the remains of the glass timer that unaccountably fell off his sauna's wall when I opened the door: 'Why did you do this? I am baffled by your stupidity.'

The border guards worked as a team. While the one with more stripes and a bigger hat spooled out a lugubrious inner monologue, his junior colleague carefully disembowelled our decomposing Saab, and laid its copious and unlovely contents on the sunny asphalt like the world's worst car-boot sale. 'Gorbachev no good, everything here bad. I have dream of London, Piccadilly, tower of Nelson.' He only brightened when his subordinate discovered the cache of Western unobtainables we had brought along for the purposes of bribe and barter. 'He took a blank VHS tape and let his mate grab two packets of Marlboro,' records my wife. 'Then they waved us through: "Welcome in Soviet Union and good journey."'

In the generous interim I had never once returned to Russia. How apposite to now find myself riding across the very same slice of crap-scattered no man's land, towards the very same border post on the Helsinki-to-St Petersburg E18, with the very same blend of terror and exhilaration percolating in my guts. Then, as now, it felt like going behind enemy lines. After all these snow-blind, head-down weeks with nary a peek of my objective, I was at last crossing the Iron Curtain, or at least a residual slice of its pelmet.

It was Sunday and the queues were short. At the first dim booth a stern woman with magenta hair and jarringly vivid make-up – in a bluer suit she could have been David Bowie performing 'Life on Mars' – snatched my passport and the weighty sheaf of visa documents. As she scanned them a look of incredulous outrage contorted her features, as if I'd tried to palm her off with a couple of used scratch-cards and a TV licence application filled out in the name of Vladimir Poo-Poo Poo-Tin. It was three months since I'd endured a ghastly afternoon before a variety of such expressions at the Russian Visa Office in London, faces that wordlessly demanded to know exactly who I thought I was, coming in here with this correct vast sum of cash and all these exhaustively completed forms explaining (this is absolutely true) why I had left my previous two jobs, and listing the names of every country I had visited during the past ten years, along with the exact dates of each visit. The cheek-clawing absurdity of it all is that while pulling those faces, they're not actually paying your documents the slightest genuine attention: nobody at the visa office challenged the invented hotels I had put down as my overnight stops for each day in Russia, and nor did they here at the border.

'Timoteya! Timoteya!'

Sour Bowie had passed my papers to a colleague at the next window down, a very much jollier young man peering cheerfully out from under one of those rearing bin-lid peaks that accessorise Russian military caps to such entertaining effect.

'So, Mister Timoteya – you come from Lon-don on *velociped*?'

'Gind og,' I said. I'd managed to pull the snood on over my helmet, but it was a tight fit. I unclicked the strap.

'Kind of. I started in Norway.'

'It is good, you are English gentleman!' He beamed winningly, very pleased with himself and at least slightly impressed by me. Then he stamped my papers with a quick-fire flourish – *pah-donk-ker-chunk-ba-thunk*! – and raised the barrier.

In August 1990, the Soviet Union was falling apart at the seams; the next year it would be completely unstitched. The Russia we drove into seemed unsettlingly rudderless: our border welcome had vacillated between the hidebound authoritarianism of old and that anarchic every-man-for-himself vibe which always seems to set in at the end of an empire. Nowhere would epitomise this unravelling of law and order more memorably than the E18 from the Finnish border to St Petersburg.

We had heard a vague report of bandits lured to this road by the magic combo of a new influx of Western tourists and the sudden evaporation of police. Nonetheless, my wife implored me to stop when, barely a mile into Russia, we drove up to a man waving dementedly next to a Lada with the bonnet up. I'm a pretty bad Samaritan at the best of times, but had started to slow down when my wife looked up the road and saw another Lada with the bonnet up, with another man flapping his arms beside it. I floored it and in the next five minutes or so sped past a further half-dozen raised bonnets, and a rather more imaginative would-be mugger rolling theatrically about in the road clutching his knee. After swerving around him I looked in the mirror: he was on his feet and toting a huge spanner, a study in thwarted rage.

Twenty-five years on, Bandit Alley was broad and freshly re-tarmacked. I suspected this might be a classic bit of borderland window dressing, and correctly so: within a couple of hours I was engaged in the pothole slalom that would characterise my under-wheel experience until I returned to the European Union. Other-wise the cross-border culture shock was astonishingly stark – one of our continent's great frontier mood-shifts, right up there with Italy–Switzerland. That spick, span asphalt was densely bordered with the full spectrum of litter, winking CD shards and discarded sanitary-ware poking through the last grubby outcrops of winter. I traced a careful path between plastic bottles filled with what British street-cleaners have gamely euphemised as 'driver Tizer'. After 1,700km of odourless, aseptic Finland my nostrils were befouled by a rolling miasma of unregulated neglect and decay: sulphur and solvents, fermenting rubbish, burning plastic, poo and wee.

It stank like some crushingly over-populated third-world slum-land, yet there was absolutely nothing around – just a hefty, pan-flat slice of reclaimed Finland razed to the ground and left vacant as a Cold War buffer zone. And though I wasn't attacked by people pretending they had broken down, I endured several near-death encounters with people pretending they could drive. Average speeds were close to terminal velocity and every blind corner was the cue for urgent overtaking. I can't speak from experience, but you'd imagine that peeing into a half-litre Coke bottle while on the move must present a potentially lethal conflict of focus for any lorry driver who values his trousers, particularly if, like most Russians, he's simultaneously on the phone. At any rate most vehicles were piloted in a consistently wayward manner. In consequence of all this, the roadside litter festival was regularly interrupted by elaborate accident death-shrines, granite crosses inlaid with photographs of smiling young men, and decorated with plastic flowers and dented reliquaries, sometimes a glassless wing mirror or a singed hubcap, once the stoved-in door of a black Lada. Even at this very early stage I found myself dwelling unhappily on the extremely low value that so many Russians seem to place on their own lives and everyone else's, the die-and-let-die fatalism that stained Finland's snow red in the winter of 1939–40.

Vyborg delivered my first encounter with urban Russia, and looking back the city showcased everything that lay in wait – fear, filth, incompetence and colourful family fun – all in one ramshackle package. On the way in, crossing a high bridge over some Baltic inlet – the first sea I'd set eyes on since day one – I peered down and beheld a sprawling yard of mothballed military vehicles – hundreds, perhaps thousands, of radar trucks, tankers and ambulances in dusted khaki ranks behind a watchtowered wall. I photographed it, then almost instantly rode up to a police checkpoint and wished I hadn't. (I needn't have worried: the sole occupant was happily engrossed in a roadside dog-end harvest.) The outskirts were a shocking mess of dumped cars and bleary winos, and the thirteenth-century Swedish castle that presided stoutly over old Vyborg looked down on cancerous stucco and gap-toothed cobbles. Old men in battered camping chairs dangled rods into a poisoned creek bordered by derelict factories and a forest of rusty cranes. I passed an ancient wall that must have recently collapsed, its rubble imaginatively recycled to fill the many van-sized craters in the road beneath.

Then, without warning, I juddered down a hill to find myself in a square overlooked by immaculate Baroque structures and alive with happy noise and balloons: a well-attended children's carnival was in full swing, performers in garish traditional costume belting out electro folk tunes to a jiggling crowd of candyfloss kids and piggyback dads. 'This really is not Finland,' I can just be heard saying above the amplified balalaikas on a short video souvenir recorded here. Until the war, of course, it was. The communal merriment seemed as bewilderingly unFinnish as the squalid hardship.

Surgically stripped of the former, Sovetskiy was half as bewildering but twice as horrid. The day was almost done when I bumped and clattered into this eponymously old-school town, and found its populace diligently engaged in an experiment to define the precise point at which civic unfriendliness tipped into open hostility. Stray dogs gazed sullenly from a roadside strewn with old furniture and carpets. Truculent men with extremely short hair shambled by, dragging lengths of scrap wood. Sovetskiy's junior miserablists fixed me with *Children of the Corn* stares from their pushchairs and playgrounds. Even the ubiquitous 'stack-a-prole' five-floor prefab tenements didn't seem to like what they saw, firing out scar-faced confrontational glowers like the weather-beaten tramps they were. Russians don't like outsiders. They don't like insiders much either. When *Who Wants to Be a Millionaire* was first broadcast here, the producers swiftly binned the ask-the-audience round: instead of being offered assistance, contestants were deliberately misled.

My experience of the Russian service industry, distant as it was, stood me in good stead for my reception at the Hotel Chaika. The woman at the desk tracked my progress towards her with the thin-lipped, cold-eyed disdain of that nurse who has Jack Nicholson lobotomised in *One Flew Over the Cuckoo's Nest*. 'Oh, marvellous,' said her face. 'A guest. With a bicycle. A really stupid bicycle.' Her revenge came in the usual form, or the usual forms: three in all, of archaic design, balefully handed to me for laborious completion.

Not a word was exchanged, until I attempted to chain the MIFA to a fire extinguisher across the lobby.

I couldn't begin to imagine how Sovetskiy had lured visitors in sufficient number to merit the existence of this low-rise hotel. In truth, it probably never had. The institutional strip-lit corridors had an air of long-term disuse, silent as Chernobyl and about as welcoming. I was borne haphazardly upwards in a big tin yo-yo masquerading as a lift. My landing remained home to a battered sentry-post armchair reserved for one of those gimlet-eyed female 'floor commandants' I remembered from my 1990 visit, though she was now long gone and no one had watered the pot plants since. Was the hotel built during or after what I would learn to call the 'socialistic era'? It was very hard to tell in a country where everything, from concrete to people, seemed to age in treble time.

Behind my door many redolent sensations awaited rediscovery: sheets that would part with a ripping crackle of static, a towel which kissed the flesh like a bearded welder and above all a great wave of wilting, fetid heat. In Russia you are never, ever cold indoors. You are nearly always hungry, though. In the murky basement restaurant I spent an increasingly light-headed half-hour procuring a menu, around twenty-nine minutes more than it should have taken with two waitresses and just one other occupied table. As the staff scratched their ears and gazed through my invisible form, Raija's warnings tolled fuzzily through me: Russians just don't want to get involved, even when it's their job to.

The ordering process forged a template for the bulk of my subsequent meals in Russia. The menu I opened that night and every other was entirely in Cyrillic: an alphabet that meant little to me, spelling a language that meant nothing. After a pained examination of several pages of inverted mathematical symbols, I decoded words that looked a bit like 'cutlet' and 'salad', another that at least shared some letters with the Italian for tomato, and *pivo*, which any Londoner who has had his house redecorated in the last decade will know means beer across most of Eastern Europe. I attracted the waitress with a nautical flare then jabbed at appropriate areas of the menu; in a spirit of adventurous whimsy I also let my finger alight on an entirely mysterious 'lucky dip' selection. In due course, and displaying all the bonhomie of a dead Finn, she came back with a tomato salad, three extruded kebab things, half a litre of lager and a separate plate with two hardboiled eggs rolling about on it. One was bright pink, one was lime green, both were stone cold. In an act of curious reflex, the moment she turned her back I whisked these psychedelic appetite suppressants straight into my anorak pocket.

I'm not sure if it's widely acknowledged, but Russians like a drink. During our 1990 trip we learned the hard way that the carafe placed unbidden on every restaurant table the minute you sat down at it was brimming with a fluid that merely looked like water. That hard way unfolded at a hotel in Vitebsk, now in Belarus, where we consequently made quick and very dear friends with two young Aeroflot pilots on the next table. If I'd been writing our journal, that would have been the full account of a three-carafe evening. As it was, my wife was somehow able to recall and transcribe many of the night's wonderfully bipartisan toasts:

'Propaganda of all nations!'

'Victory in sport!'

'Struggle for peace!'

'Women of the world!'

(I regret to confess that her final observation in this entry reads: 'T did Lambada with Hondurans'.)

The next morning, cursed with hangovers so vast and oppressive it felt like having a couple of carsick bouncers in the Saab with us, we were compelled by our state-ordained itinerary to drive several hundred kilometres to Minsk; the Aeroflot pilots left at dawn to fly many more real passengers much further.

This episode came back to me as I watched my fellow restaurant guests, a table of four well-dressed middle-aged men, work their way through an entirely liquid Sunday dinner. It seemed almost a grim duty, bottle after bottle of vodka despatched in near silence. In fairness, drinking yourself to death isn't much fun, which might be why Martini don't major on it in their adverts. Here are the related thoughts of Sir Richard Peto, Professor of Medical Statistics and Epidemiology at the University of Oxford: 'Russians clearly drink a lot, but it's this pattern of getting really smashed on vodka and then continuing to drink that is dangerous. They drink in a destructive way.' Indeed they do. When Russia last published a detailed analysis of its national disease, it counted forty million officially recognised alcoholics in a population of 270 million. A quarter of Russian men die before reaching fifty-five, compared with 7 per cent of those in the UK. At sixty-four years, a Russian male's life expectancy is lower than his Indian counterpart. Whether through violence, accident, suicide or the roster of related medical hazards, two out of three Russian men die drunk. I'd like to say this is why I called it a night after one beer, but in reality I couldn't face ordering another.

A few days before leaving, I'd shown my neighbour Chris where I was off to this time, assisted by the European Cycling Federation's pocket-sized map of its entire continental network. He inspected this modest document with interest, then asked a question that betrayed many years' familiarity with my standards of preparation and professionalism: 'Are you, um, taking any other maps?' Oh, Chris! I'd laughed then, but it seemed rather less hilarious now.

The Garmin's navigation screen had gone blank the minute I left Finland, and my EV13 route guide – a three-volume, ring-bound anthology patchily translated from the German original – assumed that a sensibly fun-focused cyclist would hop on a ferry from Helsinki to Estonia, skipping out Russia entirely. In consequence I wasn't just off the beaten track, but effectively off the map. For the next few days I would pedal uneasily away from every cross-roads praying I'd chosen right. More than once, now that it was routinely visible, I took my bearings from the sun.

Passing a rural bus depot I learned two hard lessons: Russian guard dogs are not chained, and they cannot be outrun on a MIFA

900. I failed to make my escape to a chorus of harsh laughter from the lunchtime drivers milling about outside the gates, but lost no more than a glove in the process. I would miss it, though. Nipping through the trees for a peek at the mist-smeared Baltic, I found its desolate foreshore heaped with fractured slabs of washed-up pack ice, like polystyrene crazy paving.

I had failed to coax roubles from every cashpoint in Sovetskiy, and kept failing as I inched towards St Petersburg. No doubt all those fathomless Cyrillic on-screen pronouncements were informing me how much I had just transferred to the personal account of a Mr V. V. Putin. The least appealing consequence was a bus-shelter feast of those pink and green Chaika eggs, their slate-grey innards crushed into a pillaged breakfast roll. Everyone had urged me not to drink tap water – the St Petersburg region has a long-standing reputation for hot and cold running dysentery – but with no cash I had no choice.

Looking back I must already have been infected with a very Russian malaise: fatalistic nonchalance. Why fret about a runny tummy when every passing vehicle might give me a flatty heady? The driving was stubbornly rash and heedless, with overtakers overtaking each other three abreast, and blind undertaking that desecrated my hallowed strip of crumbly verge. Russians have an innate ability to look right through you – irksome in a restaurant, murderous on a bike. My hi-vis tabard might have been a no-vis stealth suit fashioned from potholed tarmac. Lorries as ever were the worst; many of them requisitioned military leviathans whose thunderous approach always sounded like the last noise I would ever hear. There's a fine line between the stoic acceptance of mortality and a full-on death-wish – a line that Russian road workers seem to have painted right over my skull and back.

Sitting wide-eyed through all those YouTube Russian dashboard-camera compilations over the years had previously seemed a colossal and unsavoury waste of my time. What a sensible, indeed life-saving investment those hours were now proving. As well as equipping me to second-guess every manoeuvring insanity, my empirical research was also a potent discouragement from ever taking issue with the power-sliding, elbow-clipping maniacs: the video evidence showed that such confrontations generally ended in an appalling display of one-sided violence, sometimes involving firearms.

I willed Russia to smile on me; instead, it sneered. Half of it at least. The head-scarfed babushkas and pram-pushing young mums merely gazed listlessly as I creaked and juddered out of the mangy pines and into their forlorn collation of corrugated hovels, but there was always a gauntlet of derisive male moochers to run. This was my introduction to the default appearance and bearing of twenty-first-century Russian man: stocky, close-cropped, pincered fag twixt thumb and forefinger, patrolling his patch with an extravagantly cocksure rolling gait. Every hamlet and town was thick with these under-employed swaggerers, each one a ludicrous parody of hard-man gangster entitlement. I hastily convinced myself that their posturing posed no immediate personal danger, but was rather the poignant, even pathetic embodiment of a nation's nostalgic desperation to be taken seriously as a macho superpower. This, I thought, was why Putin does all that topless hunting, and why Russians vote for him as a result, rather than cringing themselves to death.

Occasionally I would trundle by some neglected celebration of the Soviet heyday, a scabrous concrete space rocket soaring forth from the roadside weeds, or a washed-out mural depicting square-jawed comrades of all stripes bearing test tubes and pickaxes into the heroic future down the side of a derelict warehouse. You couldn't pass this stuff and not feel at least a faint urge to tilt your chin up and gaze flintily at the horizon, the ghostly strains of that rousing anthem playing through your head.

Universal healthcare, housing and education; equal rights for women; full employment and billion-degree central heating for all: these were the front-line Soviet achievements, and rightly heralded. Albeit brutally, they pushed through an agrarian and industrial revolution that dragged a country largely composed of illiterate serfs five centuries forward in a single generation. They did more than anyone – much more – to save the world from Nazism. Yes, the USSR can't have been much fun when you needed a bag of sugar, or fancied seeing the world, or developed a fondness for democracy, but at the height of its powers it must have stirred half a billion souls.

What a glorious collective past; what a miserably divided present. For I had by now been exposed to the shocking polarisation of

modern Russia, the horn-blaring, out-of-my-way Audis and factory-fresh BMWs, the shiny fat pipelines laid dismissively across humble farmsteads, the new-build, tin-pot-oligarch executive compounds that bookended even the most decrepit villages, their Tesco Extra turrets poking up above wire-topped perimeter walls. On my second night I somehow wound up in a country-club resort with complimentary bath robes and paunchy, punchable guests who smoked cigars in the sauna. How had it all gone so wrong?

I began to forgive Russia at the pewter feet of a colossal hammer-handed labourer, standing vigil over a lonely lay-by. A hero worker, I guessed, some disciple of the stupendously industrious Alexei Stakhanov, a coal miner who lent his fabled name to a national drive for quota-battering productivity. All the sour-faced hostility, I now mused, was perhaps just a hangover from that intoxicating age when Russia was the Soviet heartland, torchbearer of the common man's ideological struggle against those Western fat-cats and their running-dogs. How miraculous, how bold and brave, to beat the imperialists into space, to match them warhead for warhead and medal for medal.

And as this epiphany unfolded, I looked up at the big metal Communist beside me and felt a spark fizz across to the smaller one between my legs. Oooh! I turned the MIFA back to the potholes and mayhem, but from now on it would be a little different. The Soviet anthem blared waywardly within and my propaganda newsreel alter ego was born: please to welcome Comrade Timoteya, Stakhanovite hero cyclist, on glorious mission to celebrate majesty and large scale of Soviet Union, to admire mighty border defences against rapacity of capitalism and lackey who snivel, to live proud dream of friendship and cooperation in socialist brotherhood. Struggle for peace! Victory in sport! Small bicycle of world unite!

It wasn't always easy to strike a convincing pioneer pose astride a shopping bike, but I did my best, and the internal commentaries proved durably invigorating. Comrade Timoteya make toast to 112 kilometre in single day: new record of shopping-class *velociped*! Comrade Timoteya kick unchain running-dog in face! Comrade Timoteya defy 'hour of rush' in number-two Soviet metropolis!

St Petersburg was as unnerving as I feared it would be, an insane Grand National of jockeying, twelve-laned boulevards. Things got so out of hand when these funnelled into the centre that a traffic cop nipped out of his little hut and waved a sympathetic stick at me: Don't be daft, son, just get yourself on the pavement. I obeyed for a while but the going was just too slow. More than that, after a thousand miles of snowbound silence it was seriously unnerving to find myself enmeshed in such a jostling cacophony: St Petersburg is Europe's third largest city, delivering more faces every minute than I'd seen since leaving home. I remembered Raija's account of a visit to Tokyo, and her horror-struck ordeal at a subway station that processed the equivalent of half the Finnish population every day.

With no map I followed the coast as best I could, weaving between trams full of listless faces, up and down soul-clenching flyovers, past factory chimneys cheek by smutty jowl with gilded Orthodox domes. I didn't catch even a glimpse of the Hermitage or all the showpiece sights I'd seen when it was Leningrad, and my wife and I jumped museum queues with dollar bills and ballpoint pens. Comrade Timoteya didn't need to know about that. In any case, he was preoccupied with the afternoon's Five Hour Plan, which required an inland diversion away from the extensive restricted zone around the Sosnovy Bor civil and military nuclear area, then delivered him through freezing sleet, mad traffic and the odd flooded culvert to an unreconstructed Commie hellhole.

I arrived at Gostilitsy hollowed and frigid, one-gloved, filthy, my nerves shot by the ever-closer attentions of buses and lorries on a road that grew busier as it narrowed. After a van grazed my off-side pannier I had in desperation heaved the MIFA down an overgrown embankment to what looked like a parallel footpath. The adventure in establishing it was not left bike and man encrusted with vegetation, slush and the grimly malodorous contents of an under-road drainage channel.

My little rechargeable lights had been on most of the day, and were diminished to a sickly glow as I creaked into the first town I'd passed in hours and my last chance of a bed. How hopeless that seemed as I stumbled through Gostilitsy's burned-out cars and skeletal tenements, then into a ghostly central plaza furtively patrolled by head-down youths in hoodies and those more senior barrel-chested swaggerers. At its dingiest periphery stood a plinth-mounted bust of Lenin, the first I'd seen of Vlad the Elder since entering Russia. 'Comrade Timoteya pay homage to father of revolution,' I bleated internally. Perhaps if I rubbed that bald brass head he'd grant me a wish, and against his better judgement an Ibis Budget would shoot up through the weed-fractured paving. Every actor and prop from Raija's tales of woe seemed to be lurking around this stage: people who wouldn't help, doors that wouldn't open. Then I pushed my MIFA round a corner past a battered old grocery, and encountered quite the opposite.

'Oat-yell?'

A tall man in overalls was leaning against one of those wire-topped sheet-metal gates that screened off every executive compound. Before I could answer his hailing cry he yanked it ajar with an unlubricated shriek, exposing a brand-new barn of a building. Its ochre façade was decorated with words I would presently be reading on a beautifully handwritten A4 sheet.

'Hello, my name is Tatiana, many welcome to Mini Motel Gostilitsy.'

I read; I beamed and nodded; I followed the receptionist's finger to the next item on the calligraphic list in her hand.

'I hope you can enjoy your stay.'

Further beams and nods accompanied the finger on its downwards progress.

'Will you like dinner?

'The breakfast is from 07.00 serviced.'

'With our pleasure your Fichtel & Sachs Duomatic hub will be dismantle and renovate.'

Maintaining her amiable silence, Tatiana cheerily held out a room key and put the list in a drawer. What a touching document this was, even without that fictitious last entry. And what a miraculous discovery, this oasis of comfort and gentility. Tatiana was a new kind of Russian: the biddable, welcoming opposite of staff who had conducted all my previous interactions with pantomime ill-will, as if fulfilling a deeply resented community-service order. Was this just the face of can-do capitalism? If so I wanted to lick that face for ever. It didn't yet trouble me that I was now one of the bastard haves, in here with the water coolers and the tropical fish tanks, fenced off from the grubby have-nots in an ugly desecration of Comrade Timoteya's mission. Of more immediate concern was my graceless, unkempt appearance: clothing studded with furzes, burrs and frosted St Petersburg swamp mud; trainers – now the only shoes I possessed of any sort – expelling a squelch of accumulated brown water with every horrid step beneath the foyer's gold chandeliers. Having repeatedly been thus manhandled, the

MIFA aptly looked to have been dragged backwards through a hedge, and was now tied up out of sight in a stairwell.

Tatiana was still smiling, but whoever drew up that charming list must surely have had a very different sort of Anglophone guest in mind. I couldn't help wondering if I was the first foreigner they'd ever welcomed, new as this place clearly was and so distantly off the beaten track. As I walked into my palatially proportioned suite, with its heavy-soil laundry facility/spa tub and sweeping over-wire views of impoverished dereliction, I imagined someone slipping a handwritten addendum under the door: *Please, why you are such disappointing mess?*

Dinner was eaten alone in an extremely gold room decorated with fabric bouquets, wooden elephants and airbrushed couples in evening dress locked in erotic embrace. The ordering process was memorably conducted by Tatiana, who dictated the Russian menu into a translation app on her phone. With the halting, tone-less authority of a digitised train announcer, this device then offered me suggestions it was very difficult to listen to politely.

'Meat Beach Gardens.'

'Children's Alexander.'

'Tea Pork with JW Boils.'

'The Sultan Episode.'

Tatiana's enthusiasm for this technology did not ease the ordeal; battling my features into respectability, I looked up at her open, expectant face and falteringly ordered support beef with titles of mushroom. She smiled and scribbled, then spoke once more into her phone.

'What is not a drink?' it mused in response.

'*Pivo*,' I said.

With a flustered look she shook her head and a free hand, then held the phone to my mouth promptly.

101

'*Pivo*,' I told it.

The device said something in Russian that seemed to disappoint her. She pressed the screen a number of times then showed me its suggestions, translated back to English:

'You knew. Pencil case. Peugeot.'

We tried again.

'Beer,' I said.

'Bill,' offered the phone. Then: 'Pace of the warp.'

'Heineken!' I blurted, launching into a strident roll-call of ales that began with Champions League-grade ubiquities and went very sharply downwards, 'Amstel, Budweiser . . . Skol . . . Carling Black La—'

'Ah, *piva*.'

Unaccountably, my support beef and its accompanying refreshments were delivered by a young man who spoke better English than anyone else I met in Russia.

'Your bicycle, it is different,' he said by way of introduction. Let me guess: was it the colour? 'I think it is not easy to do many kilometres on such so-small bicycle.' I concurred. Viktor was a font of wistful observation, the son of an Uzbek English teacher who had come to Russia two years before and said he would always feel like a foreigner. 'Gostilitsy is not wonderful,' he said superfluously, placing before me ten dice-sized cubes of dry meat and their meagre fungal garnish. 'Important in last war, but now not important. I like to work in St Petersburg, maybe as translator or in shop.' I began and finished my meal in the course of this brief address; when I asked Viktor to see the menu again, the cloven hoof popped out: 'It is too late, kitchen closed!'

In September 1941, Gostilitsy's defenders heroically withstood the Nazis' hitherto relentless advance on Leningrad, forming a bridgehead that somehow held firm until Hitler was pushed back two and a half years later – a last line of defence that helped foil the Führer's well-developed plan to wipe a huge, proud city right off the map.

With its grim legends of rat pies and bark-eating, the Siege of Leningrad was well known to me. Or so I had thought. In fact, my grasp of this slow-motion atrocity didn't come close to an appreciation of its horror. Cannibalism became so common that the authorities had to amend the criminal code with two new articles for 'special category banditry': those who ate corpses (and were generally imprisoned), and those who killed people for food (and were shot). At the height of the siege ten cannibals were arrested every day, three-quarters for the non-capital offence; by the end of 1942, 2,105 cannibals had been charged, and the siege still had a year to run. In one six-month period, 1,216 citizens were murdered for their ration cards.

The individual accounts are unbearable. 'I watched my father and mother die,' one man remembered. 'I knew perfectly well they were starving, but I wanted their bread more than I wanted them to stay alive. And they knew that about me too. That's what I remember about the siege: that feeling that you wanted your parents to die because you wanted their bread.' When it was over Leningrad had suffered the greatest loss of life any city has ever endured in war or peace: 1.5 million citizens died, mostly through starvation. There have been moves to classify this human tragedy as an act of genocide.

Though extensive, my incomprehension of Russian menus was in truth not quite all-encompassing: every dish, indeed every ingredient in every dish, was always followed by brackets containing its requisite weight in grams. I might never know what went into a Children's Alexander, but I could tell you it had 180g of one thing and 15g of another. It was the same now at breakfast, when Viktor laid before me the specified 20g of porridge, prepared with 100g of milk. The common denominator, as exemplified by my support beef's desiccated tininess and the finger-bowl of cooked oats now congealing before me, was unabundance – what those of us in the long-distance shopping-bike game call 'not nearly enough food'. If, as I did now, you ordered bread, you received, as I would shortly, a single small slice. I had previously ascribed this phenomenon to lingering socialist parsimony, or some pilot project to starve foreign cyclists to death. Now, though, I wondered if these carefully weighed, tiny meals might be a legacy of traumatic shortage and hunger: more than four million Russians died of malnourishment between 1941 and 1944, adding to a pre-war toll perhaps twice that across the Soviet Union, courtesy of famines inflicted by Stalin's ruthless imposition of collectivised agriculture. It was an extremely sobering thought, and one that meant Comrade Timo-teya pedalled away from Gostilitsy's grocery with many high-calorie capitalist confections concealed about his person.

If Finland had hosted the hardest weeks of my life, then Russia was home to the longest days. The last was a *War and Peace* job, 120km of all-weather, multi-surface tribulation. Through sleet-slitted eyes, I watched careworn figures drag themselves to village bus stops for their ride to work, bent into the malevolent headwind that would be trying to push me back into Russia all day. It was back below zero and each one of these bundled-up strugglers seemed to embody the blunt old maxim that might as well be Russia's national motto: life is shit, and then you die. Then it was out across a scorched bleak-ness of derelict farmland, the broken hulks of cream-brick Stalinist mega-barns marooned in burned hogweed and gorse. Try as I might, it was hard to imagine these draped in the agricultural propaganda banners I had read about that morning in my habitual breakfast companion, Anne Applebaum's authoritatively withering *Iron Curtain – The Crushing of Eastern Europe*:

Colorado beetles are smaller than atomic bombs, but they are also a weapon of US imperialism against our peace-loving workers!

Every artificially inseminated pig is a blow to the face of the imperialist warmongers!

The surface declined to a state more pothole than road; as the sleet cleared I could see cars bumping mazily about ahead, gingerly picking their way through hostile, cratered terrain like the Mars Rover. Speeds at least were way down. On such roads the native motorist's habitual pace would reduce a car to its component parts in minutes; a Russian car in seconds. The shambolic degradation of Ladas and Moskviches still in apparent daily use invited much unkind speculation on the rigour of a Russian MOT: I imagined an inspector slamming the driver's door, ready to sign off a pass if fewer than four things fell off in consequence.

None of this was doing the MIFA many favours. Quite how I avoided hourly punctures in my shards-of-Lada verge-zone remained a mystery, but with 2,000km up the bike was now trailing a reedy, pained shriek. Along with occasional terminal-sounding clonks from the hub area this demanded investigation, but it was now far too cold to muster the requisite dexterity. I swapped my one glove between hands every fifteen minutes, then every ten, and spent a fruitless and painful after-lunch session in a bus shelter attempting to swaddle my numb feet in gaffer tape. My virgin saddle sore had ripened to a nexus of the purest agony and my jaws ached from their battle with permafrosted Snickers. Like Hitler and Napoleon before me, my Russian campaign was being derailed by the durably awful conditions. Paging Comrade Timoteya! Comrade Timoteya to the saddle please!

My first race was the turning point. It was a straight fight between me and another elderly shopping cyclist, a docker-hatted old geezer who I reeled in as he laboured through the outskirts of a village. The wave of fraternity as I passed was clearly misconstrued: twenty minutes later, back out on the lonely plain, a dour rearward grunting announced his presence in my slipstream. I turned my head and met the blotchy, challenging face of Rocky's trainer: *You're gonna eat lightning, and you're gonna crap thunder!*

Instinctively I pushed down hard on the pedals, then reflected and eased off. His little front wheel and its green mudguard hoved alongside, then with a jaw-rippling effort he toiled past and took the wind in his hard old face. I watched him judder and weave away, thinking: Have your fun, Granddad. You're fighting battles, I'm waging a war. This ride of mine wasn't a sprint, but a yo-heave-ho marathon in the grand Soviet tradition. The indomitable knuckling-down to an impossibly vast task, the forbearance to endure the grimmest reversals and come back for more – that was how to beat Hitler, or cultivate the steppes, or ride 10,400km on a shopping bike. That morning I had for the first time surveyed my little map of EV13's entirety without the urge to burn it or hurt myself. My goal remained distant, and my daily increments towards it negligible. But progress had now been tangibly made, there in the marker-pen line I'd traced from the northern tip of Norway to the southern Baltic coast. Inspired, I put the hammer down, and took a regrettable trophy snap as I barrelled past the old man in the next village along.

When the sun came out and I passed my first sign for Estonia I could have cried. So I did, a bit. But Russia never goes down without a fight, and I duly spent the late afternoon wrestling my steed towards the stilted old border watchtowers lined up in the sunset. I hauled it over a teetering mountain of rubble and on to

an endless railway-side path interrupted by many more of the same. I dragged it up an overgrown embankment to avoid a dog ready to bark himself to death in defence of a car bonnet. Twice I lugged it across the rusty tracks. Finally and most memorably, I raised it over a large log that a stout old woman had levered across the path, with effortful deliberation and a pitchfork, when she spotted my distant approach from her lonely cottage threshold. With folded arms and a placid air she watched as I lowered the MIFA back to earth and remounted; I looked back a moment later and saw her forking the log back to its original station.

Then there were great queues of lorries, a slight contretemps with a guard's Alsatian and all the usual po-faced border rituals, borne this time with a very different sort of anticipation. In dusky light I wheeled the MIFA across a no man's land bridge beneath the meaty witch-hat towers of Hermann Castle, and with prickling eyes past that hallowed circle of gold stars on a blue background. My phone trilled; I kissed the screen that welcomed me to Estonia, where calls were charged at the standard EU rate. Class Traitor Timoteya seduce by empty promise of imperialism, sentence in absence to inseminate many pig and airbrush from all archive.

My mood of exultation blinded me to the fact that Narva, whose twilit streets I now gleefully patrolled, was dominated by stack-a-prole Soviet blocks and Cyrillic script. In this same heady, heedless spirit, I found a hotel, fairly bounded up the stairs and told the young receptionist how very, very happy I was to be out of Russia.

'That is good for you,' she said, handing me a key with a rigid smile, 'but bad for me.'

'Is it?'

'I am Russian. Here we are all Russian.'

7. ESTONIA AND LATVIA

The night before entering Russia I had lain in bed thinking of all the things I'd miss about Finland. It was an extensive list that covered most human needs: on the most starkly fundamental level I was exchanging a country where you could drink from the hot tap for one where you couldn't from the cold. The morning after leaving Russia I made an even longer list of what I wouldn't miss about it. My first Estonian meal had been a cornucopian rebuke to the era of 20-gram Alexanders, a weighty platter of bulbous sausage, cheese and fried bread, brought to me along with many frothing steins of ale by a game old dear in a *bierkeller* outfit. Everyone here might be Russian but I'd spoken English all night, and been smiled at in the right way. I'd slept under cotton sheets. My satnav maps were back, as were the euro and the Latin alphabet. So too bike paths, and not just any bike paths: weaving back from the restaurant I'd passed my very first Euro Velo sign (for EV10, which EV13 followed through most of the Baltics). Belatedly I realised I couldn't grant Russia the get-out clause that has allowed me to tolerate the failings of so many nations over the years: it hadn't even been especially cheap.

The unRussianness of my new world cheered me all morning as I whistled up the River Narva's broad brown estuary, flicking the Vs at Putinland, over there on the other side. All through the Cold War years, I'd thought of the Soviet empire as a single, one-nation entity: we called it the Eastern Bloc, though its component countries had never been in any way united prior to 1945, and effectively had nothing in common. How good it was to be reminded of their resurgent idiosyncrasies. Estonia's roads were smooth, and overtaking cars gently whooshed past at a respectful distance. A policeman drove by in a brand-new Skoda Octavia, a compelling contrast to the humiliating old Ladas and MASH-era jeeps foisted on his cross-border counterparts, which might as well be plastered in stickers reading: *Funnily enough, yes I am amenable to bribery.* If these people were ethnic Russians then they were house-trained: they didn't chuck bottles out of the window, shave their heads or let stupid, furious dogs run loose.

And yet so much of the backdrop was Russian, or at least Soviet: those prefab tenement blocks, the memorial T-34s and hero tractors on mossy plinths, the rundown Commie spa resorts out of town with their muddy, joyless pleasure gardens and bullying concrete hotels. I overtook an old chap on a bike weighed down with scavenged firewood, and saw a few more picking discreetly through bins. This was the EU, but not as I knew it.

Even the weather went Russian on me after I hit the cliffy Baltic coast and turned left. At once a stinging gale punched me in the face, pushing my snood hard against its ever bonier contours. Why was this still happening? Here we were in the second half of April, with forests full of birdsong and violets and fields flecked with sheep. Yet there I was, having ridden south for 2,000km, stopping at a seaside resort to buy more socks. I had a great idea for a book as I pulled them on in the lee of a wheelie bin: man rides bike through Finland and Russia, then puts bike in car and drives to Black Sea.

Buffeted gulls and geese shrieked their dismay, two flaps forward, one flap back over the tussocked bluffs and the mean grey sea below. I chuntered bitterly into my head coverings, letting the wind know in no uncertain terms what I thought of its behaviour, loud and often, and cursing that awful disconnect between what my eyes saw and my legs endured, the torture of cycling up a vast hill that wasn't there, of battling Mother Nature in an invisible rugby scrum. My eyes streamed and my snood hid a multitude of sins, principally the sin of drool and the sin of horribly snotting yourself.

At diminishing intervals I took shelter behind the old pillboxes and ruined barracks strung out all along the clifftops, warming hands in armpits and rusting the Iron Curtain's stumpy foundations with wayward sprinkles of rider Tizer. Nowhere on earth had a worse war than little Estonia, burned and bombed to bits by Nazis and Soviets, its menfolk conscripted by both armies in turn. Factor in Stalin's post-war massacres and deportations and the country lost 25 per cent of its population in the 1940s. Here and across the Baltics, Horrid Joe made up the numbers with a concerted programme of Russification, resettling a million ethnic Russians in a deliberate move to erode national identity. In 1945, just 4 per cent of Estonian residents called themselves Russian; by 1989, almost a third did. It was much the same in Latvia and Lithuania, and in the weeks ahead I would hear a lot of nervous mutters about Putin's sabre-rattling, and which of the Baltics

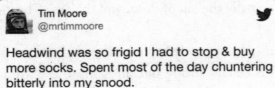

Tim Moore
@mrtimmoore

Headwind was so frigid I had to stop & buy more socks. Spent most of the day chuntering bitterly into my snood.

would be first on his to-do list once he'd ticked off Ukraine. Just occasionally an ethnic Russian would whisper that things were more complicated than they looked.

Our 1990 route had looped around the Baltic states: they were still in the Soviet Union, and therefore a royal pain in the arse to travel through. With so many resident Russians, it's perhaps not surprising that the drive for independence was a little slow off the mark here. Nor that this drive rumbled to life in Estonia, which had always been an outsider, a nation with a funny Finnishy language where most TV aerials were turned to Helsinki. The drawn-out Baltic uprising that saw off the Soviets is collectively known as the Singing Revolution, but they barely mustered a hum in Latvia and Lithuania: Estonia was the iron-throated crucible of this very particular pro-democracy rebellion. For four years, huge crowds – regularly containing a third of Estonia's entire population – would gather to bellow out banned national folk songs, a tide of anger and pride that swelled unstoppably. The Soviet Union had stubbornly clung on to the Baltics as all its other satellites defected to democracy, but after Yeltsin sat on that tank in Moscow and the hardliners' 1991 coup unravelled, the last outposts of empire were lost in days.

In Sillamäe, I pondered all this while stuffing rolls into my numb face behind a derelict office block. More of the same were mingled with Soviet tenements, all leading down to a line of giant chimneys along the seafront. The town's faintly entertaining name had attracted my attention during the breakfast route-survey; the history of Sillamäe was anything but. Built more or less from scratch by the Soviets in the 1940s and populated exclusively with shipped-in Russians, this was a closed town that appeared on no maps, known to the postal service by the code-name 'Moscow 400'. The reason: the plant beneath those chimneys produced over 100,000 tons of elementary uranium, refining it for use in the Soviet's first nuclear warhead and no less than 70,000 of its successors (how very hard it was to process that dumbfounding figure, along with the subsidiary revelation that at its peak in 1985, the Soviet nuclear arsenal comprised 39,197 weapons).

As I came to discover, the Soviets commandeered endless stretches of the Baltic coast for nefarious ends: though my compact map showed EV13 clinging to the beach, it actually spent most of its time skulking distantly behind the dunes, diverted around radar stations, nuclear waste dumps, naval bases and training camps. These were the legacies of the Soviet Union in its ruthless, paranoid pomp. The leaders who sent in the tanks to crush revolts in

Hungary in 1956 and Czechoslovakia twelve years later would never, I thought, have allowed 300,000 Estonians to trill away en masse in praise of nationhood and democracy. In reality that irresistible tide of pride and anger was eminently resistible. For tempting as it is to imagine the USSR being undone by humanity's irresistible urge for freedom, in truth it just lost its mojo and fell apart. With the bomb built, space conquered, its people housed and all the other big boxes ticked, the Soviets ran out of motivation and momentum. A general hardening of the arteries set in, literally so for the ageing old guard. The rise of Mikhail Gorbachev was in many ways just a fortunate accident – the politburo had no idea he would push through the reforms that got the revolutionary ball rolling. (Nor in truth did Gorby himself: as an ardent Leninist he believed that Communism simply needed re-energising, and was quietly aghast when his attempts to do so precipitated its collapse.) The two general secretaries who had followed Brezhnev were frail veterans who lasted barely a year each, and the Soviet top brass simply saw Gorbachev as a slightly more vigorous candidate who wasn't about to peg out. In a tweaked alternative universe, they might plausibly have plumped for the thrusting young KGB colonel Vladimir Putin. We can only speculate how the man who describes the USSR's break-up as 'the greatest geopolitical catastrophe of the twentieth century' would have handled the Singing Revolution, but I can't see him clapping along in the chorus.

And so Estonia meandered flatly onwards, up and down peninsulas, in and out of the lonesome pines, past truck-sized 'erratic boulders' strewn across the landscape by glacial retreat like abstract installations. I filled my gust-emptied husk with stew and beer at a hostel full of multinational wind-farm erectors, who conversed in English replete with casual profanity: 'In fucking Sweden, I can go out of any town and just drive super fucking fast, I'm fucking serious, dude.' I watched moonlight dapple the Baltic from my balcony in a converted Commie fish warehouse. I stood humbled before the Memorial to the Victims of Soviet Cruelty, and in sad disbelief at a visitor information board that hailed the regenerative input of Finnish 'alcohol tourists' ('*Purpose of visit: alcohol tourism*'). I poked uneasily about in derelict Red Army bases, their tiled floors littered with rolls of film and audio tape, hoping that the next dusty drawer I opened would reward me with the blueprints of a plan to invade the Isle of Wight, or an expertly doctored photographic depiction of Richard Nixon kissing a naked sailor. When the snow came back one horrid afternoon I bagged-up in a bus stop and bought two pairs of gardening gloves at a hardware store. I dug deep that day, and fell face-first into the frozen hole.

And at last, one windless, blue-skied morning, I rode EV13 as I'd ridden it in my pre-departure daydreams, freewheeling through sun-speckled pines on smooth and car-less tarmac, the view refreshed by glimpses of twinkly sea and fairy-tale woodland cabins. The moreish tang of fresh coffee and logs on a smouldering hearth, the chorus of chaffinch and woodpecker, the festive pop of my Browning automatic as another yapping farm dog was silenced for ever. All this and the brain-bending thought that for more than half of my life, and nearly all of my father's, the simple act of riding a bike through this densely forested coastal exclusion zone would have had me imprisoned and very possibly killed on sight.

How could a tiny country like Estonia host such a gigantic wooded wilderness? Though I had by now spent around 417 years cycling through what is properly known as the Eurasian boreal forest, the unending immensity of this dark world of spruce, pine and birch remained a lingering amazement. Stretching from

Norway to the eastern edge of Siberia, the EBF isn't just the largest forest on earth, but the largest terrestrial eco-region of any sort, our planet's default state on dry land: over two million generally chilly square kilometres of big, bad woods. Such is its global influence that in the brief summer growing season, the EBF singlehandedly elicits sharp opposing spikes in our planet's levels of carbon dioxide and oxygen.

Russia is home to the vast bulk of the forest, and in consequence to more trees than Canada and Brazil combined. Although being Russia, it's having a good go at wronging that right: of late, its swathe of the EBF has been shrinking by an area the size of Switzerland every year. On the plus side, there's no such thing as an ancient boreal forest: regular lightning-strike fires burn them down every few decades. Rare is the Russian tree that reaches 100 – so rare that Vladimir Putin sends each one a congratulatory telegram, printed on 101-year-old wood pulp and with a PS explaining that at current rates of deforestation there won't be any trees left in Russia by the time he celebrates his own 250th birthday with another facelift.

Tallinn, capital city and home to a third of all Estonians, felt like some overcrowded Brothers Grimm theme park. The old town's tilting cobbled alleys were thick with the first tourists I'd seen, gawping up at Rapunzel towers and Pied Piper gables, badgered by peasant-smocked gingerbread sellers and medieval innkeepers offering two meads for the price of one. I looked at the foreign guests waving their iPads about like camera-enabled tea-trays and thought: I am not as you are. But of course to them and the locals I tragically was, and then some – not just any old sightseer but a cyclo-tourist, and not just any old cyclo-tourist but a grade-A twat on a kid's bike. Such was the martyred fate of the trans-continental shopping cyclist. What rare joy I brought to all the rickshaw taxi-riders: look, a dafter bike than ours!

My hotel room was designed for some agoraphobic toddler-goblin, an illegally compact cell with a bench-wide bunk and a one-sock sink, its floor space dominated by a wastepaper bin I would trip over twice in the night. I winked through my window bars at the MIFA, chained to a copper drainpipe in the courtyard below, then went out to hit streets I'd last hit on my only previous visit to Estonia, twelve years before. Tallinn was then enduring a scourge that I had come to report on: in the early years of this century, no other city exerted a more powerful lure for the British stag party. My billet was a 'rock and beer' hotel by the ferry terminal: every morning I would be greeted by the massively enlarged faces of Metallica gurning down at me from the bedroom wall, along with the sickly whiff of complimentary breakfast lager seeping in under my door. 'We are not a place that will tell someone they have had enough to drink,' said the rather dead-eyed young manageress, before confessing that mattress protectors were on urgent order. I did most of the fieldwork before noon, when there was at least a chance of procuring a coherent sound bite from those young men in matching T-shirts, if not an especially considered one; as I dutifully filled my notebook with phrases such as 'pound-a-pint tottie fest', I found it hard to imagine cobbling them into an article fit for intelligent publication, and history would prove me right. All that said, it remains a matter of profound personal regret that I missed out on what must be the ultimate stag-tivity: in tones of blurry reverence, half a dozen Mancunians told me of the out-of-town field where for a modest fee they had drink-driven Ladas into each other, then shot up the wreckage with AK-47s.

Happily for Tallinn the stags seemed to have galloped messily away to pastures new, though I did see two men in pink wigs striking a predictable pose before the sign that identified a city-wall bastion as Kiek-in-de-Kok. A stint as a stag city seems to have been a tawdry rite of passage for most ex-Soviet capitals, some sort of lowest common denominator on the journey to an open market and free expression. On that 1990 trip my wife and I were aghast to see sweet old dears selling hard-core porn from trestle tables in the Budapest metro.

Today's less sordid but more durable blight on Tallinn is a cobble-clogging glut of historic-city-break weekenders and the likes of me. Avoiding the likes of me meant I ended up eating vegan tortilla wraps in a shisha bar full of bearded local hipsters. On the way back I passed a 10-foot slab of concrete mounted on a plinth, embedded with a plaque that was perhaps a Banksy-pattern spoof, or an indication that Estonia still had some way to go on that road to true freedom, or simply an indirect order to destroy a planet that has gone entirely to shit: *This piece of the Berlin Wall, originally located at the Potsdamer Platz, was donated by Sony Corporation.*

'Do you speak English?'

Every previous Estonian had reacted to this question with an offended snort: like, *der.* But the rotund, bespectacled pharmacist's wordless response was unblemished by patronised irritation, or even the pained head-jiggle that says 'only a little'. Instead, I met an open-faced study in blithe ignorance: 'I have absolutely no idea what any of that meant.'

The pharmacist's own language was of course no less a mystery to me, though its comedic impenetrability had provided an entertaining roadside alternative to watching the Baltic Sea being steadily reclaimed by low cloud and cold mist. Whenever my spirits flagged there was always a *Koogi Keskus* or a *Postipanki*

Puutookoda to raise them; I once wobbled right off the road in total hysterics beside a poster that yelled *MUUA KRUNT!* Entering the pharmacy my features had still betrayed their recent exposure to the bold magnificence of *LOOMA POOD* writ large over the shop next door, though that smile was now long gone. In defiance of my linguistic preconceptions and that four-square, short-cropped appearance through the window, the pharmacist was not a man and spoke no English. Neither revelation seemed likely to smooth an already awkward mission.

The previous afternoon I had been welcomed into her town by a billboard declaring that Smokie (*'Legendaarne hittsingel Living Next Door to Alice!'*) were due to play the Piiskopilinnuse Hoov in August. Haapsalu was a seaside town in a strangely fetching state of drawn-out decline, lined with once-grand holiday homes and bandstands that had been decorously shedding flakes of paint and slivers of elaborately carved wood since a brief tsarist heyday. My less decorous accommodation was an otherwise empty dormitory above a sports hall, and it was there, to an accompaniment of misty-mouthed grunts and roars from discus throwers in the outdoor training ground beneath, that I experienced the sudden flaring of an irritable rash in the inner saddle-sore department. Procuring temporary relief of its insufferable chief symptom was, as I soon established in a pizza restaurant up the road, an unacceptable public activity. Twelve hours later the need for remedial medication had progressed from urgent to imperative; I smiled helplessly, looked the pharmacist straight in the horn-rims and let my fingers do the talking.

While flaying myself alive in the night, it had occurred to me that my malaise must be no more than an intimate relative of athlete's foot, for which a remedy might be requested with minimal embarrassment. So it was that I now raised a shod foot to knee height, and before the pharmacist's curious gaze began to scratch it with an expression of orgasmic release.

'Ah – *postipanki hittsingel*,' she may have said when I was done, stooping down to the shelf behind her. As she did so, I suddenly recalled the aftermath of a wasp sting in my school years: holding a swollen finger up to the headmaster's secretary I had told her a bee was to blame, obscurely thinking it sounded more impressive. 'Acid for wasps, alkaline for bees,' she intoned sagely, as I wanly prepared to have injury added to injury. Thirty-six years was a long time to learn a lesson, but needs must. My loins were on the line here.

'Hang on!'

With the selected tube of ointment already in hand, she slowly turned her large head and gave me a prompting look.

'In fact, it's not so much the . . . well, you know, it's just kind of a bit further up.'

I flapped a vague hand across my torso and pelvis. Behind her glasses the pharmacist's eyes narrowed quizzically.

'Yes, so . . . still really super-itchy' – and here I reprised my scratching, subdued and repositioned to suggest a shy and incompetent guitar solo – 'but sort of here . . . ish.'

The round face before me was once more stripped of any trace of comprehension. I might have been teaching a cat how to make gravy.

In the end, of course, I simply did what my groin had been silently screaming at me to do all morning. No slack-jawed euphoria in this performance: I attended to myself in homage to a bitter zoo chimp upsetting his young visitors. The pharmacist's features sped through many evolutions, settling into a look of inward disappointment, as if she should have known all along it would come to this. Then with a tiny, brisk sigh she laid the tube already in her hand onto the counter and nodded at it. We looked down at it together, and while completing our transaction shared a silent moment over the futility of that regrettable finale.

'*Kiek in de kok*,' I mumbled, and went outside to cool my face.

The weathervane turned and I was hurried through Estonia with almost indecent haste, swept in and out of faded seaside resorts, past blurred signs for Krapi and Catwees, shooting by all those erratic boulders with nary the time to conjure my habitual translations of the incomprehensible plaques that often decorated them ('On 13 September 1725, Pastor Koogi Puutookoda discovered a blacksmith's boy in an obscene embrace with this "Shame Boulder", and forcibly betrothed the pair on the spot.' 'When this rock split apart in December 1898, farmworkers found the disgraced poet Keskus Hoovpood hiding inside. He threw his shoes at them and burst into flames.')

If a persistent headwind feels like some ancient curse, then a tailwind is a gift from God, a miracle, a blessing, cupping you in its hand and bearing you magically along almost above the road. Miles were delivered to me on a nice flat plate, and I found myself thinking what a wonderful base Estonia might make for a cycling holiday, especially if you didn't like cars or hills and were startled by scenic variety. It had taken me a month and a day, but I'd finally cracked this long-distance shopping bike lark: all you needed, it transpired, was a snowless flat road and a force-7 wind at your back.

Latvia, the first country on my route that I had never previously visited, was very much not Estonia. The language seemed inevitably more sensible, the landscape regrettably less prostrate, the civic mood less Scandinavian and more Soviet. The first town past the mothballed border huts was dominated by a towering Mother

Russia war memorial, and the now-familiar trappings of totalitarian infrastructure lay absolutely everywhere, rusted starburst-pattern gates guarding some tumbledown assemblage of dirty cream bricks, perhaps a barracks, perhaps a weighbridge.

Most compelling was the sudden coarseness and poverty. The road went to pieces and the shiftless, littering shamblers were back in force. Public expectoration became abruptly de rigueur, with throats and nostrils exuberantly voided at every bus stop and school gate. After sharing the road with Estonia's smattering of sleekly kitted weekend club cyclists, I was now in the regular company of shonky old men on shonky old bikes, most with the dishevelled, reluctant bearing of recidivist drink-drivers consigned to a life on two wheels. Only now did I realise that though plenty of Latvians and Lithuanians decamped to Britain to pick vegetables and dig holes, I'd never heard of an expat Estonian community. They clearly had enough well-paid work at home.

My encounter with the very first EV13 sign I had laid eyes on came freighted with portent and farce: moments after the historic commemorative selfie, its successor pointed me inland down a trail of ochre gravel that seemed an unlikely right way, but was only confirmed as the wrong one by the time it was too late to double back. Channelling my Finland-honed mastery of loose surfaces, I skittered up and down scabby hillsides and through neglected villages that didn't seem to have changed since the Russians left – the first time, in 1920. As befits the sort of man I now am – a boring old one – I have become a connoisseur of the firewood stack, an outdoor art which in southern Estonia reached such a grand peak of Tetris-master geometric perfection that I took several admiring photographs. I took another on this lonely Latvian trail: a ramshackle cottage dwarfed by a heap of whole trees, sawn off at the base of the trunk.

Limbaži sounded as if I had strayed off-track by as much as two continents. It looked at least as many decades out too. Of late I'd been reminding myself how wonderful all these abysmal 1960s tenements must have seemed to their first residents, just as those now-reviled post-war estates and tower blocks in Britain were initially inhabited by often tearfully grateful ex-slum dwellers. Known as *Khrushchyovka* in honour of the Russian leader under whose aegis they were erected, these five-floor prefab blocks became the Soviet empire's default home: 64,000 went up in Moscow alone. They weren't perfect. Three generations routinely shared two small rooms, the baths were four foot long and early examples featured a shower/toilet combo. The GDR architect required to adapt the blocks for native construction described the design (several decades later, when it was safe to do so) as 'barracks for the Grim Reaper'.

But then the *Khrushchyovka* were only intended as a stopgap housing solution. In 1961, General Secretary Khrushchev proclaimed that the global triumph of pure Communism would be achieved within twenty years, ensuring, amongst much else, wonderful new dream homes for all. Because history badly let him down, millions of crumbling, leaky *Khrushchyovka* survive in former Soviet nations to this day. Rising expectations did as much damage as shoddy materials and poor design: a centrally heated tenement flat with electricity and running water might have been very heaven for a rustic raised on earthen floors, but his children grew up in these places and instead of Khrushchev's promised upgrade, watched their temporary homes slowly fall apart. Limbaži was full of them, and many more cracked and grubby reminders of endgame Soviet stagnation. In accidental homage I spent the night in one.

'Construction of the Berlin Wall allowed the GDR to proceed with its development without further interference from the west.

It served its purpose well, and the transition from capitalism to socialism was soon complete.'

Twenty-five years since I closed it, *Eastern Europe on a Shoe-string* still packs a punch when opened at a random page. Back in the pre-internet age, you never went on holiday alone: for better or worse, there was always a guidebook for company. *Eastern Europe on a Shoestring* – the only behind-the-Curtain print-based hand-holder then available – became an unusually irksome travelling companion on that 1990 trip. Not so much for its yammering doctrinaire rhetoric, tiresome though it was to be told that the CIA were to blame for the brutal Soviet crackdown that followed

the 1956 Hungarian rebellion, or that Poland's Solidarity movement had been 'defeated by its own excesses'. No, extraordinarily
enough, given the flush-fit dovetail between the book's title and
my own budgetary mindset, what really got on our wicks was the
author's unstinting devotion to parsimony. His, though, was an
alien tight-waddery, one borne of slavish ideological compliance.
Time and again we would arrive after dark in some unhelpfully
forbidding socialist utopia, crack open Comrade Shoestring and in
the Saab's frail courtesy light read something like: 'Timoteyagrad is
home to a well-appointed new western-funded hotel, but I'm not
even revealing its name because you will naturally want to bed
down on a straw-scattered pallet at the Young Weaver's Co-
operative (shared buffet trough, compulsory re-education class on
Weds & Fri).'

Anyway, I thought of Comrade Shoestring as I wheeled the
MIFA down Limbaži Youth Hostel's undulating linoleum corridor.
A familiar odour hung so heavily in the air that I could almost literally put my finger on it – the evocative blend of old cabbage and
young feet that was Eau de Silverdale Primary (1971: a vintage
year). The sanitary facilities were an eye-opener, indeed a stomach-
emptier. A dog-eared warning about HIV and hepatitis B looked
down on a shattered row of sinks, and the shower – oh, the
shower – was a unisex, curtainless enclosure that might have last
been used to shave a furious bison. As a pre-ritual courtesy this
beast had first been allowed to visit the toilets, and to prepare
himself a light meal in the communal kitchen. The four-bed male
dormitory was imaginatively floored with a yielding crust of paint,
accumulated in layers over many decades, though as its solitary
occupant I would at least be anointing my intimate complaints
without an audience ('Hey, chapskis – have I missed a bit?'). The
startling austerity of the facilities throughout painted Latvia's

youth as a primitive race that shunned toilet paper and soap, drank out of saucepans and spent their evenings pushing bottle tops around a chess board.

Limbaži's only restaurant was the canteen in the supermarket opposite, which I gratefully discovered was licensed to serve over-age youth hostellers with a narcoleptic excess of strong ale. When in the small hours I woke up to offload some of it, I established that the dormitory radiators were stone cold, and that there was thus only one way to ensure that the virus-marinaded laundry strung over them would be even half dry by dawn. This way did not result in further sleep, though it did save me the bother of having to get dressed in the morning.

I had taken the manageress's frown of greeting the night before as her way of telling me I was too old for this place; in the cold, damp light of day I saw she'd been trying to say this place was too old for me. Wringing her hands uneasily she summoned my only two fellow guests, a pair of sombre young girls, to translate a retrospective welcome ('She say I hope you very enjoyed your stay and sorry for kitchen') and the bill, a sum I had to ask them to repeat: 'Is five euro and seventeen cents.' (As a postscript to this experience, after the Wall came down Comrade Shoestring appears to have abruptly devoted himself to island-hopping in the South Pacific.)

I once interviewed a Latvian luge champion, shortly before descending a section of the track at La Plagne under her instruction, and smashing my watch to bits in the terrifying process. Her existence forewarned me that I could expect Latvia to prove rather hillier than its predecessors. How extraordinary that with over a quarter of this monstrous ride under my wheels, I had yet to tackle an extended series of inclines and descents; how predictable that I should flounder in the face of novelty.

The uphills, in truth, were straightforward enough. Despite that record-breaking programme of under-preparation, my aged body was serving me remarkably well, with the saddle sore in retreat and my knees emerging from a bad patch that had admittedly endured for over a thousand kilometres. The protracted downhills, though, presented an alarming reminder that I had yet to master – in fact, yet to even employ – the press-back-on-the-pedals coaster brake, a now compulsory supplement to the lever-operated front-wheel slow-me-down. My only previous experience of this continental apparatus, both brief and distant, had seen me wobbling to a series of unsatisfactory halts against Amsterdam's street furniture and pedestrians; barrelling erratically coastwards down Latvia's dry-tarmac luge runs, the uncomfortable equivalent targets were oncoming traffic and the spittle-flecked jaws of farm dogs. The knack, which I discovered without ever effectively mastering, was to stand up in the saddle and plant one's full weight down on whichever pedal first approached the apex of its revolution. This procedure necessarily involved a delay while said pedal rotated to said position, which to my mind seemed a fairly fundamental drawback: 'Ooh, a sudden emergency! How terribly exciting. Don't go away, I'll be right with you.' As it was I only once came a cropper, and that was my fault for trying to take a ride-by snap of two storks having it off in a field.

I approached the Latvian capital Riga through its bracingly old-school commercial hinterland, a lone shopping cyclist dwarfed by shipyard cranes, stripy chimneys and the soaring, grimy flanks of oil tankers and bulk cargo vessels. It was like riding through the pages of some Soviet Ladybird book, *How it Works – Centralised Economic Planning* or *The Story of Marxist–Leninist Achievement*. Riga has a Russian mayor and a fifty-fifty ethnic split, and the city exuded a familiar redolence: shambolic traffic management;

sinister, shuttered-up concrete edifices with fractured forecourts and a lot of rusty aerials on the roof; clanking old trams and unshaven pensioners playing alfresco chess in the muddy central park. You know a city is in trouble when beggars hassle touring cyclists for change.

A number of bare plinths had evidently been relieved of colossal representations of Soviet heroes, but I was intrigued to find a lavishly mutton-chopped bust identified as one George Armitstead, who had improbably served as Riga's lord mayor from 1901 until his death eleven years later. That night I read up on the extraordinary tale of this Yorkshire jute merchant's son, who was educated in Zurich and Oxford, worked as a civil engineer in Russia and wound up almost single-handedly transforming Latvia's capital into one of the Baltic's greatest cities, indeed the second largest metropolis in Tsar Nicholas II's vast empire. In a single prodigious decade Armitstead built Riga's tram network, its sewage system, its Parisian-pattern boulevards, three hospitals, thirteen schools, museums, the national theatre, the city zoo and Europe's first garden suburb. The tsar was so impressed he fruitlessly beseeched George to become mayor of St Petersburg. What a very exciting part of the world this was back then, a copper-bottomed land of opportunity for seaside developers, merchants and ambitious English engineers. How bright the Baltic burned in its turn-of-the-century heyday, and how quickly it burned out. Nine years after Armitstead died in office, Latvia declared independence from Russia; a mere twenty years later it was on the bomb-cratered road back to occupation.

It seems the Russians just cannot keep away from their favourite Baltic state: that night I stopped at Jūrmala, a resort where all the old tsarist dachas were being restored by oligarchs on the hunt for nostalgia and a wealth-laundering foothold in the Eurozone. The hotel receptionist who revealed this also told me – or more accurately warned me – that the only open restaurant would be full of them. 'It's strange, they have really much money but they never smile.' Why is this so often the case? It certainly was at the beachside restaurant, a try-hard establishment with square black plates and sporting-trophy glassware, offset by a completely wonderful view of the serene Baltic sundown. All around me short, round men with tall, blonde wives gazed through each other and across the gilded sea with dead eyes, bound together in pampered disdain. The only guest with any rightful claim on misery was the cyclist gazing down the menu's right-hand column of numbers in mute horror. And even he cheered up after his second vase of lager.

Latvia's wandering coastline occupied me for longer than I had hoped. It was partly my own fault. The first serious navigational mishap of my trip pitched me onto a busy motorway; I laboriously reeled in a chugging JCB and was pulled along the slow lane for an hour in its hydro-carbon slipstream, not quite in the right direction. Every time I caught a glimpse of sea through a gap in the pine/dune continuum, I plunged gaily through the forest, eager to fulfil a mind's-eye dream of riding along the beach; every time my wheels soon sank immovably into the sand, and, less gaily, I trudged back to the road. Rattling into Roja, a gloomy former naval base, I made the forgivable mistake of smiling at a woman giving a small boy a lift on her handlebars: the next morning, after my night alone in the converted Soviet quartermaster's stores, a familiar face presented my breakfast pancakes with a fancy-that beam of happy surprise, and followed it with a ninety-minute rundown of her hopes, dreams and woes in accomplished but alarming English. Pleasing as it was to hear myself encapsulated as 'a happy and great sport person', the ensuing comparison obliged me to make my excuses: 'My husband is a closed person with no emotion, he does not like Sinead O'Connor or understand my sand sculptures.'

In the Soviet years she would have had even less fun explaining her artistic pastime. Roja stood at the foot of the Kolka Peninsula, an area so profoundly sensitive that border troops raked its many beaches every night, checking them at dawn for tell-tale disturbance. The entire promontory, all 900 pine-plastered square kilometres of it, was a military exclusion zone: the eponymous small town at its shark's-fin tip still bristled with observation towers and few-windowed buildings of military aspect, and when I stopped to take a few snaps, a couple of old chaps on a bench stared hard as if committing my face to memory. How difficult to rein in that instinct, drilled in over long decades, to rush across, push me to the ground and stamp my camera to bits.

It isn't hard to see what attracted the Soviet top brass to Kolka. The cape looked out over a yawning expanse of NATO waters, yet remained so remote that not a single road pierced its forested vastness. Not until the Russians built one in the 1950s, a secret trail so epically broad that a huge stretch of it doubled as a military landing strip. The aerials and watchtowers went up and the peninsula was effectively sealed off, to the considerable disadvantage of the Livonians – Latvia's founding fathers, an ethnic group that had been a major player in northern Baltic trade and fishing for hundreds of years. There was nothing Stalin enjoyed more than a spot of cultural repression, and his unusually thorough programme of deportation to the Gulag, enforced assimilation and restrictions on trade and movement had already squeezed the Livonian community into a clutch of settlements along the coasts of Cape Kolka. The exclusion zone all but finished the job: today there are just 182 registered descendants of the people whose knightly order supplanted the Teutonics, and once held sway across the whole Baltic region. Only thirty of them speak Livonian, a clearly splendid language whose alphabet boasts thirty-nine letters, of which more than a quarter are variants of A and O.

The lonesome road down from Kolka's tip was another plumb-line, pine-lined Baltic gust factory, its bitter blasts shoving treetops hither and thither. Though mostly hither: once again I hunkered down over the handlebars, knees akimbo, as a boorish, jostling head-gale taunted my all-round inability to cheat wind. Woooo-hooo, just look at you, with your stupid upright shopping bike and your windsock snood and your Dumbo pogies. WOOOO-HOOOO!

For hours there was nothing but trees and wind, not a house, not a hut, not a bench. I lunched straight on the tarmac, squatting down on a bridge over a peaty river, brown as Bovril. At the end of my element-defying cheese-roll construction project, a shiny new four-by-four pulled up and lowered its window. The driver wore a stern look and a fishing hat festooned with colourful trout flies. Chewing hard I rose to communicate; after failing in Latvian and German, he eventually passed judgement on my picnic in slow, deliberate English: 'What you do here is not so beautiful.' With that he hummed his window back up, though not quite fast enough: my lunatic guffaw redecorated his headwear with a wind-borne spray of spittled food.

The next vehicle trundled by ninety minutes later as I was doing something even less beautiful up against a derelict guardhouse. I didn't care, indeed I barely noticed. To the detriment of my foot-wear, my wide-eyed, open-mouthed focus was fixed on the ghostly structures I had spotted distantly clustered along the weed-pierced concrete road that led away from the guardhouse. I wheeled the MIFA towards them in a state of neat awe; it would be two hours before I wheeled it back out.

I shall always be grateful that throughout my blighted late-teenage years, four cans of Kestrel lager could be procured for 99p. The early 1980s was a time to blot out horrors in bulk: Norman Tebbit, Torvill

 Tim Moore
@mrtimmoore

Never thought I'd see the day again, but here it is: I AM EATING LUNCH WITH MY GLOVES OFF.

and Dean, the kids from *Fame* and the ever-present threat of Armageddon. How grim to have lived through an age when nineteen million of my countrymen watched *Blankety Blank*, and slightly more – 40 per cent of the adult population – were resigned to a thermonuclear war occurring within ten years. It is difficult to convince my children, who are now the age that I was then, just how deeply ingrained the fear of annihilation was in those days. In fairness, it's proven tricky to find an educational middle ground between the Sheffield-melting apocalypse so horrifically depicted in the BBC drama *Threads*, and that Frankie Goes to Hollywood video of Ronald Reagan and General Secretary Chernenko wrestling together.

I don't remember being distracted by the imminent possibility of all my skin sloughing off in fiery strips until I was fifteen, when the Russians invaded Afghanistan. Thereafter, almost every month saw the world vault some new stepping stone on the road to mutually assured destruction. The Americans elected a president who called the Soviet Union an evil empire. The former head of the KGB took up the Soviet reins and broke off negotiations on arms control. Nuclear deployments sidled ever closer to the Iron Curtain on either side, like some holocaust-tempting game of What's The Time, Mr Wolf? A trigger-happy Russian fighter pilot shot down a South Korean 747 with 269 passengers and crew aboard. Rocky Balboa punched a giant Communist unconscious. The Americans invaded Grenada. I acquired a second-hand Missile Command arcade machine, and spent several hundred hours failing to defend six cities against a relentless hail of incoming warheads, greeted every few minutes by the most haunting, shattering Game Over sequence in history: a stroboscopic, red-white detonation that faded into the screen-filling words THE END, projected atop the annihilated husk of a lost world. What a traumatic time to come of age. Like I say, I drank a lot of Kestrel.

And that, in a roundabout fashion, was why I walked up the empty, rubbled streets beyond the guardhouse carrying rather more baggage than the filthy old crap that filled my panniers. Because around me, soaring up from a mess of broken glass and shards of sanitary ware, stood an array of windowless white hulks that had for thirty-four years housed 2,000 Russian scientists and military-intelligence officials.

Latvians now call this place Irbene, but they didn't call it anything when the Soviets were here. Even the Russians referred to their off-map un-city only by its codename Zvezdochka, or Little Star. The locals weren't allowed in, and without rarely granted permission, the Russians weren't allowed out. Everything the staff and their families required lay within its heavily guarded 400-hectare perimeter: a kindergarten and school, a post office, shops and leisure facilities. Beyond the ruins that once housed all these, up and over a lofty dune that I now breathlessly crested, loomed the extraordinary object that Little Star was built to service: there, high above the Eurasian boreal treetops and tilting its giant rusty face at the heavens, stood the largest radio telescope in northern Europe.

My mood was perhaps a little histrionic. There were never any missiles at Little Star, a complex built for weapons-grade eaves-dropping. In fact, no one really knows precisely who or what Little Star spied on, beyond a general assumption that it tracked and decoded satellite signals, aircraft movements and telecommunications. The Russians certainly aren't about to throw any light on the matter: they didn't even admit to the base's existence until 1993, a year after Latvian independence. The following year, with Little Star still off-limits, KGB engineers painstakingly decommissioned the site. They stripped the staff buildings bare, packed up and removed all documentation, and demolished two smaller radio telescopes. The 32m whopper was seemingly just too huge to destroy — its turning mechanism alone weighs 60 tons. Instead, the engineers disabled it, pouring acid on the operating motors and cutting electrical cables.

All the same, this was my most potent encounter yet with the Cold War: a vast secret lair hidden away in a remote forest, where 2,000 spies and technicians diligently scoured the heavens for tell-tale transmissions that might, in some distantly vague or directly urgent fashion, incite the imminent destruction of humankind. What a terrible situation the world got itself into back then. And – my dominant reaction as I gazed up at the telescope gantry from the foot of its mighty concrete plinth – what a gigantic waste of everyone's time and money this whole business had been.

By 1980, the arms race was a marathon run at a full sprint. On an average day – one single day – the Russian military production line churned out a nuclear missile, a fighter jet, and eighty tanks or heavy guns (as a former assistant to the Soviet defence minister rather poignantly noted: 'We built so many weapons because they were one of the few things we could build well.'). It is generally estimated that by the Eighties, defence accounted for a dumbfounding 40 per cent of the Soviet Union's budget – vastly more than it had been in the approach to the Second World War. The Americans were not to be outdone: in his first presidential term, Reagan spent more on defence than the combined cost of the Korean and Vietnam wars.

Part of the reason my Cold War lectures always fail to reduce the children to petrified silence, damn them, is that anticlimactic ending: it comes across like some forty-five-year game of Risk where the last two players broodingly accumulate huge armies, before even they get bored and go to bed. But in truth, and largely in secret, we came close to full-blown nuclear war more than once in the Eighties. Had I known how close, I'd have started on the Kestrel at breakfast. Though Reagan's mindlessly provocative evil-empire rhetoric was just that, it convinced Yuri Andropov – his short-lived Soviet counterpart, and predecessor to the even shorter-lived Chernenko – that America genuinely intended an aggressive nuclear strike. If you want a calmly rational, long-term overview of risk, don't ask a terminally ill ex-head of the KGB.

When NATO launched a nine-day war-game exercise code-named Able Archer, Andropov and his hand-picked team of hardwired paranoiacs convinced themselves it was the cover for a surprise attack. After double agents relayed this conviction to their Western handlers, it was initially dismissed as posturing bluff; the CIA was reluctantly persuaded otherwise, and at the last minute the exercise was scaled down. Documents that surfaced after the Soviet Union's collapse have shown just how crucial this intervention was in averting unfathomable disaster: 'I don't think the Russians were crying wolf,' said the CIA's former director of intelligence. The KGB's ex-chief of foreign counter-intelligence later offered a chilling summary of Andropov's strategic mood at this time: 'The Americans are ready to attack, so we better attack first.'

That was in November 1983. Two months earlier, and weeks after that Korean 747 was shot down, a duty officer monitoring the Soviet's missile warning system at a base near Moscow received an automated alert: a satellite had detected the launch of five inter-continental ballistic missiles from a site in Montana. One can only imagine Lieutenant Colonel Stanislav Petrov's state of mind as he digested this information, but we all owe him a Kestrel. Rather than instantly transmit the warning up the chain of command as per his orders, Petrov checked the ground radar and other data for any further evidence of incoming missiles, and having found none opted to keep the news to himself. His bold twin assumptions: the Americans would surely have fired more than five warheads in a first-strike scenario, and in any case the alert was probably a false alarm generated by Russia's dependably undependable technology. (It was the latter, of course – a report would conclude that the satellite had been confused by 'a rare alignment of sunlight on high-altitude clouds'.)

Had Petrov adhered to protocol, it is widely agreed that Andropov's doddering, jittery finger would have jabbed The Button. As a reward for saving the world (and in particular saving Britain, which we now know would have been obliterated more entirely than any other nation), Petrov was later reprimanded for filing incomplete paperwork. He suffered a breakdown soon after and took early retirement.

Petrov's workplace would, I supposed, have been very like Little Star. With an air of sombre reflection that soon degenerated into the base glee of illicitly poking about in derelict secret stuff, I trundled back down the telescope's service road to inspect the staff apartment blocks. At the foot of the nearest I rested the MIFA against a black hole that had once been a door, then strode inside with the enthusiasm of a man unaware that Little Star's erstwhile caretaker had been brutally murdered by squatters the previous year.

Beneath the entrance stairwell, newsprint poked out from under a pile of masonry; after kicking it away I was presented with a mildewed sheaf of *Pravda*s, the official Soviet journal. All were dated 1992, and topped with a masthead that married a hammer and sickle with the bald and goateed father of the revolution. My withered grasp of Cyrillic offered up no more than a headline with something strident to say about Americanskis.

A crunchy carpet of glass and plaster led me into a small bare room, patchily wallpapered with magazine pages. Nearly all depicted young women in fur hats, thick jumpers and long coats, smiling politely in front of snow-sprinkled civilian machinery: a steam locomotive, a Moskvich saloon, a lorry full of logs. Lining paper or pin-up erotica? These images had all the sizzling pornographic charge of my mother's old sewing patterns.

I gazed around, and through the mean little window that overlooked the matching ruin opposite. Even allowing for the looted dishevelment, everything seemed so shoddy and dated. Until the 1960s, the Soviets had almost kept pace with Western economies – rationing in Czechoslovakia and even Romania ended long before it did in Britain – but that was as far as they got. All the trappings of life on display here – the bog-paper newsprint and its drab typography, the primly wrapped-up dolly-birds, the lumpen architecture and hectoring, humourless propaganda – belonged to a time before I was born.

All at once my thoughts on the Soviet Union and the Cold War crystallised, the not terribly profound and the bleeding obvious coalescing with a clearly audible *schloop*. Soviet rule in these countries was a ruthless foreign occupation: they sent millions to the Gulag, murdered millions more, imposed a totalitarian police state that suppressed all opposition, and fenced off vast areas like this for their own malevolent ends. I wondered why people – people like me – seem so tirelessly fascinated with those what-if ruminations on how things might have panned out had the Nazis won the war: very simply, it would have panned out just like this. Yet that was hardly the fault of the Russian in the street, so why had I generally feared and despised him? It could only be my formative conditioning: to the Kestrel-fuelled youth in me, the boy who curled up with his short-wave radio and listened to creepy propaganda jingles, Russians were still the baddies. That was clearly an unfair conflation, especially as the Soviet Union was no more. And though this base was a derelict ruin, I'd hardly be allowed to poke around in the many US equivalents that still operated right across the world, with superior leisure facilities and ruder pin-ups.

Here's the rather sinister postscript, though. When the Russians disabled Little Star's giant radio telescope, they didn't do a terribly thorough job. A team of largely amateur astronomers managed to get the thing up and running again within two years, repurposed for the greater civil good to track asteroids and so forth. Many observers have pointed out the many simple ways in which the Russians could have permanently crippled the device – for instance by smashing out one of the giant ball bearings it revolves on – and pooh-poohed the suggestion that it was too big to blow up. The astronomers who restored it found that the cables had been severed with precision and some artifice, a very mannered sabotage that begged to be undone. The implication was clear, and delivered in fluent Arnie-speak: we'll be back.

Pedalling down to the gatehouse with my mind largely blown, I approached an old red minibus full of familiar faces. A generic familiarity, soon confirmed by the number plates: these were the first British people I had met since leaving home. I excitedly flagged it down and treated the grey-haired driver to a stream of animated gabble, asking if they had come to see the big dish which I hoped they had as it was pretty bloody incredible as in fact this whole site was and really how amazing that we had met here of all places kind of behind enemy lines ha-ha and slightly silly as it may seem I had ridden this bike all the way from Norway like the very top of Norway and was . . . was going . . . um . . .

The driver hadn't even lowered the window. More than that, he was fixing me through it with a cold look that I now noted also adorned the half-dozen middle-aged faces behind. Well, I thought, feeling my ears redden, sod you lot then. I remounted, wounded and confused, and as I did so suddenly recalled seeing a very similar minibus at some point in the recent past. The precise moment of this encounter was pinpointed by a female voice that now asserted itself through a wound-down window.

'We're astronomers,' it announced stiffly. 'I believe we passed you on the way in.'

A more muffled but even colder voice chimed in from somewhere further inside the van. 'By the gatehouse. Charming.'

The balance of Latvia came tinged with melancholy and the ghosts of better days, or at least busier ones. Ventspils is apparently the largest port in the Baltics, yet its docks conveyed only the hollow bustle of a Legoland diorama, full of container ships and mile-long goods trains but very little evidence of individual human activity. So many former sources of Soviet mass employment, I realised, were now automated and mechanised. Others were simply vacated: Karosta once hummed with uniformed life and leaking radiation from its resident fleet of nuclear submarines, but when the base closed in 1994, 20,000 Russians went home and left a landscape full of roofless barracks and stumbling solvent enthusiasts. The bloke who sold me a pizza in the town up the road spoke excitedly of a regeneration plan, but I'm not sure what the prospects are for a place that translates as War Port. Nor indeed for a scheme to reinvent his own rather careworn home as a holiday resort: 'We call Liepaja "The city where the wind is born".'

Its history was aptly bleak. As one of the first cities captured by the Nazis after they turned on Stalin, Liepaja suffered a pioneering fate that would become grimly familiar as my journey continued, a horror story told in memorials dotted along the windswept dunes. When war broke out, just 1 per cent of Germany's population was Jewish; the vast majority of Jews who died in the Holocaust were East European. So keen was the SS to embark on its ideological mission that Liepaja's Jews were being rounded up and shot even as the battle for control of the city still raged. Later, when the massacres began in earnest, German officers travelled from afar to witness them; sometimes more than a hundred 'execution tourists' would attend, arriving early to secure the best view. On a single day in December 1941, more than 2,700 Liepaja Jews were frogmarched out to the dunes at Skede, and forced to strip naked in front of a kilometre-long trench. Listed on the execution-squad staff roster was a 'kicker', whose job was to thus transfer victims into the trench after they had been shot in the head.

It was hard to look anyone in the face after standing at these sites, even my own in the mirror: how dreadful to admit membership of a species that did such things to its own kind in living memory. Yet some Balts couldn't wait: anti-Semitism was so entrenched in certain areas that Jews were being massacred even before the Nazi invasion. By the end of 1943, Liepaja's pre-war Jewish population had been reduced from 5,700 to precisely three; of the 350,000 Jews who called the Baltics home in 1939, only 6 per cent would survive the war. No other Jewish community suffered more.

My ride had reached a new phase, though I couldn't sense what it was just yet. Looking back, I seemed to have got through Finland and Russia on a messy blend of bewildered shock, mortal terror and eye of tiger: just a man and his will to survive. But staring out these blowy Baltic ordeals of sand and pine required a more measured approach. With 3,200km on the clock I'd already travelled further under my own steam in one go than I ever had in my life, but the halfway point was still a fortnight off and the infinite coniferous vistas were a constant drain on morale. Ahead lay many long, dark days of the soul, a journey into uncharted personal territory that would draw deep on unplumbed reserves of determination and indomitability. I was levering open the filthy old tins at the back of my ransacked inner pantry, swallowing the iffy contents and waiting to find out if I'd be nourished or poisoned.

Routines, no matter how witless, became comforting to the point of addiction. Whatever I'd been doing had somehow got me this far, so I needed to carry on doing it: yelling the first line of the Beatles' 'Good Morning' every time a cock crowed; entombing my lunch in the Houdini-grade double-elastic-strapped front carrier rather than the quick-release rear panniers; wearing my awful, baggy hi-vis tabard even on an afternoon spent wobbling down a deserted woodland footpath. If it ain't broke, don't fix it; if I ain't dead, don't kill me.

You put your left leg round, your right leg round, round-round-round-round UNTIL THE DAY YOU DIE. These were the treadmill weeks, when fatigue duked it out with monotony. I'd spent so long imprisoned in the Eurasian boreal forest that its dark, coniferous immensity had long since stopped scaring me: it seemed more appropriate to have learned that 'pining' was derived from the Latin word *poena*, or punishment, and indeed that these woods were named in honour of Boreas, Greek god of the north wind. Wanker.

Self-entertainment became a mounting challenge as I plumb-lined through the parallel pines. The old 'guess how fast you're going without looking at the speedo' game didn't occupy me for long: these days I was never more than 0.5kmh out. An attempt to cultivate an interest in conifer variations stalled at 'those spindly ones with the slightly more orangey bark at the top'. It was no better when the trees opened into a muddy, prone continuum, like a family-sized pack of the flat and featureless square kilometre of Lincolnshire beet-land I once visited to assess the Ordnance Survey's judgement on it as Britain's most boring spot. For mad hours I adapted and loudly delivered lyrical musings on being a real nowhere man riding through his nowhere land, or finding myself several thousand light years from home. My internal jukebox was already down to its dregs, and when a tune got stuck on repeat it was never a good one: I spent a terrible afternoon in the head-scarfed smallholdings with Level 42's 'Lessons in Love' for company. Part of me died that day.

I took to ordering the most dreadful-sounding dishes on the evening menu as a stimulating experiment to probe the interface between hunger and revulsion, but hunger always won: the project was cancelled after I wolfed down a tureen of Grey Latvian Peas in their colour-coded tripe broth. Most productively I finessed the rules of Duomatic Roulette, a diversion I had been dabbling with since the sun came out. You will need: one shit bike, one sore arse, one wit's end and one Fichtel & Sachs Torpedo Duomatic two-speed automatic hub. To play, stand up in the saddle to procure temporary relief of perineal distress, then sit down and recommence pedalling. If you now find yourself in the higher of your two gears, th . . . Actually, scratch that. The reality is that no matter what the laws of probability have to say, you somehow don't ever find yourself in the gear you want to be in, especially on hills, and that to avoid the resultant wobbly humiliation you should therefore never stop pedalling. I agree this doesn't make Duomatic Roulette sound especially rewarding. Nonetheless, I sometimes played it a hundred times a day. Holy Joe Stalin, I was losing it.

The weekends were an even lonelier inducement to pre-senile dementia. I spent one bereft Sunday morning reminiscing about my childhood Raleigh Twenty with such evocative intensity that I found myself twisting the MIFA's handlebar grips for a phantom Sturmey-Archer gear-change. Where was everyone? Even the bigger towns seemed dim and dead on a Friday night, their broad pavements empty and the roads sparsely patrolled by young men in pimped-down old BMWs. Saturdays were slightly better. Families harvesting roadside litter in a very socialistic-era civic spring clean; trim matrons plucking new-season herbs from the footpath edges; a drunk splendidly belting out opera arias outside a supermarket. In Liepaja I passed a groom lugging his hefty bride across a bridge amid a chorus of cheers and horn-parps, in accordance with a tradition that must have been rather less onerous in the under-fed days of yore: the pizza bloke told me that husbands were required to carry their new wives over no less than seven local river crossings.

Most notably, Saturday was the only time I got to ride along with other cyclists, even if they were all six. As I slalomed through all those pink snowsuits and stabilisers, I fancied myself firing many a young imagination: 'Daddy, I'll never forget the morning when you were teaching me to ride, and that man went past us on a little bike with oven gloves on the handlebars, and you said: "If you try, if you really push yourself, one day you'll be able to buy a car and never, ever have to look that utterly desperate and pathetic."'

8. LITHUANIA AND KALININGRAD

The Curonian Spit has always intrigued me on the map, a slender appendage curving out from the Lithuanian coast like a hundred-kilometre comma. A beguiling wreath of greasy mist hardly diminished the enigma. I wound between murky pines huddled beneath a steepling dune that hid the undiscovered remains of a great Viking city. Beyond lay one of the world's longest beaches, but when curiosity drove me to climb up the soft sand mountain for a peek, everything was swallowed in fog. Further along I rode through a dry-iced graveyard of blackened trunks, the aftermath of a huge forest fire (suggested headline: SPIT ROASTED). It was wonderfully eerie and as ever I had it all to myself.

This was once the northern tip of the German Reich, a colossal empire that at its 1918 peak padded out the big fat Fatherland with most of Poland and great chunks of the Baltic states. Frederick the Great settled 300,000 Prussian colonists along this coast in the late eighteenth century, and the more enterprising amongst them invented seaside holidays as we know them today: grand hotels and lodges lured Teutonic aristos and industrialists with the now-traditional promise of a brief and bracing toe-dip, rewarded by days of fat-faced indulgence. When the Soviets swallowed the spit, so to speak, they refashioned it as a people's playground, but rather pleasingly repurposed most of the old buildings rather than knocking them down. The Communist authorities' sensitive respect for cultural heritage was a perennial surprise. Warsaw's shattered medieval old town, for instance, was rebuilt with pains-taking attention to detail: 'The house I was born in had been violently destroyed,' wrote one astonished resident, 'but I can now go into the bedroom I had as a boy, and look out at the exact same window at the exact same house across the courtyard. There's even a lamp bracket with a curious twist hanging in the same place.' A Stalin-led invasion of post-war Britain might not have been entirely welcome, but had it happened we'd all be much less fat and Coventry would look a lot better.

In the immediate post-war period, the Soviets made what would later seem rather poignant efforts to win hearts and minds in their satellite states: having freed them from Nazi oppression and rebuilt their cities with sensitivity for the past and the hope of a brighter, communal future, they not unreasonably expected some gratitude at the ballot box. The mood seemed to be shifting across Europe: after the 1945 French general election, the Communists emerged as the largest party. But when the first free elections were held in Soviet-occupied lands, the results were disastrous. In November 1945, the Hungarian Communists won just 17 per cent of the vote, humiliated by the principal centre-right party, which romped home with 56 per cent. The year after, Berlin's first post-war election saw the Communists beaten into a distant third place.

Stalin must have felt as confused and betrayed as Churchill, whose reward for winning the war was a crushing electoral defeat by Labour. But unlike Churchill he had a few options, and chose the one marked 'bollocks to democracy': the Red Army came in to, um, oversee all future elections across his empire, rival parties were nullified and any display of dissidence ruthlessly punished. No matter how trivial – after a fourteen-year-old East German schoolgirl admitted putting lipstick on the portrait of Stalin in her classroom, she spent eight years in prison. (The GDR just loved to incarcerate naughty schoolkids: in 1950, a group of young boys in Jena received ten years each for throwing stink bombs during a celebration of the president's birthday, and the day after the Berlin Wall went up in 1961, a seventeen-year-old boy who wore black to school in protest was sent down for five years.)

I stayed at Juodkrantė, in a four-square, dark-wood Germanic chalet hotel with fog-fuzzed views of vintage gables, decorative balconies, a smear of Baltic and the looming concrete angles of a derelict Soviet leisure complex. Or so I assumed: lovingly careful as they were when restoring old buildings, Communist architects had a gift for imbuing their every new one – even the seaside fun palaces – with a certain hulking malevolence. Their creations weren't so much designed for communities as inflicted upon them; on the holiday spectrum, this example suggested a retirement home for tanks. Some day, perhaps, such buildings will find a new life of their own, though in the age of consumer choice that day may not be imminent.

My hotel's downbeat but approachable manager was an ethnic Russian with an embattled outlook. 'Our president hates Russia and all Russians, she speak of us like dogs. But we remember in socialistic era she study in Leningrad and for many years was member of Communist Party.' He glowered at the mist-haloed streetlights outside and I wished I hadn't brought the subject up. Except I had to, really, as this was a fact-finding discourse for my morning date with destiny: the next day Comrade Timoteya would ride again – deep breath, girding slap on both cheeks – into the Russian enclave of Kaliningrad.

Fear and fascination had battled it out when I learned my journey would take me into this anomalous Cold War relic; the former claimed victory after an initial online route-plan through Kaliningrad turned up the legend, RESTRICTED AREA, NO ACCESS POSSIBLE. The hotel manager assured me this was a false alarm, but otherwise went easy on the succour. 'For sure, the drivers there will try to kill you,' he said, smiling for the first and only time. Together we looked at the MIFA, chained to a picket fence outside

 Tim Moore
@mrtimmoore

Lunched in this sylvan haven behind the dunes. Jacket STAYED OFF.

reception, and his smile widened. 'But even a Russian, I think, will not steal this bicycle.'

The border straddled the spit two hours south. The first full-beam summer's morning of my trip had burned the fog away before I got there; with the Lithuanian frontier post in sight I pulled over to Russia-proof the MIFA. For want of *Ben Hur* wheel spikes and a pannier cannon I pumped up the tyres (for the first time since Finland), gaffer-taped the wobbly front carrier to the head-tube and tightened a perpetually recalcitrant mudguard bolt so hard it sheared straight through the thin aluminium. Right: once more unto the breachski.

In fact, it took longer to get out of Lithuania than back into Russia. Putin-side, I stood before a glass window so heavily smoked as to be impenetrable: all I saw was a pair of immaculately mani-cured and very expressive hands working away in the small gap beneath it, bidding me with wordless efficiency to hand over my documents, remove my helmet, and then in very short order to proceed into the motherland's disembodied western extremity.

The road at once narrowed and decayed; the sandy forest around was a mess of toppled, mossy trunks, suffused with a smell of mulchy neglect. At regular intervals this unappealing hinterland was impaled with stern multilingual warnings: ENTRY BY SPECIAL PERMIT ONLY — NO ECONOMIC OR RECREATIONAL ACTIVITIES. It hardly seemed an exhaustive ban: 'It's all right, officer, I'm spying.' A gigantic hare lolloped out of the trees, and the building heat brought some curious companions to the tarmac: there can't be many places where red squirrels and lizards cross the road together. For a long while there was no traffic, and I harvested endless facefuls of gossamer spider threads, like Scooby Doo running through a haunted mansion.

My death-averse route guide had discouraged EV13-ers from even entering Russia proper, and urged them to cross as much of Kaliningrad as possible with their bikes in a railway carriage. Given this and the hotelier's jauntily morbid counsel it was no surprise when corroded Ladas began to crowd the road and brush me off it. Even here in a national park the verge was clustered with death-shrines. But at Zelenogradsk, a rather fetching seaside town full of ice creams and strappy tops, my spirits rose and the traffic largely vanished, siphoned off down a new motorway. Two hours later I was, I'm afraid, eating a Big Mac with a load of sailors in the Kaliningrad city sunshine.

Ensconced in our little island under the banner INVASION-FREE SINCE 1066, it's hard for us to envisage the ethno-political ebbs and flows that have swept through continental Europe. And I'm not talking about the migration of the Celts or some other distant shuffling of ancient cultures: over recent centuries, huge folds of Europe's indigenous fabric have been torn to shreds and stitched randomly back together. After the last war, the ethnic cleansing went on a boil wash: entire peoples abruptly fled their homelands or were forcibly herded out. Let us try to imagine, by way of example, the population of South Wales being shipped out en masse to Denmark, and replaced with Belgians – all in the space of a couple of years. For any number of reasons – a Lego Huw Edwards prominent amongst them – it's inconceivable, yet in terms of numbers and distance this is precisely what happened to Kaliningrad.

Until 1946 this was Königsberg, longstanding home to an almost entirely German populace. The city had been the capital of Prussia for more than 200 years; the very German philosopher Immanuel Kant was born and died here (and in between never travelled more than 10 miles from the place). In 1944 things took a war-shaped

heroes and Cyrillic slogans fervently rounded off with exclamation marks. The main square, a totalitarian expanse of North Korean magnitude, was girdled with Communist flags and dominated by a soaring column topped with a bronze Soviet star. A monumental Mother Russia gazed down at a parade ground planted with orderly ranks of garish red tulips, like one of those clumsily over-coloured glory-of-socialism postcards we sent home in 1990. Coming hard on the heels of Russia's annexation of Crimea, the message was loud and clear and freshly redecorated: We're back, and we're winning wars again.

'Maybe one repeat beer?'

It wasn't the first time the waiter had asked, nor would it be the last. I was in no mood to return soon or sober to my vacuous, marble-floored suite at a gated 'biznizman' hotel, whose staff had greeted me and the MIFA with unblinking stares of mute horror (as advised by my Lithuanian friend, I had booked it online the night before; the receptionist's 'there must be some mistake' look as her eyes darted from the confirmation email to my grubby, helmet-topped face and back was in vain). The restaurant I had somehow wound up in was a rustic pastiche with chunky Camelot furniture and staff dressed like off-duty musketeers, tucked away in a corner of the only shopping centre I've ever been to with a door policy: after I walked in the bouncers stepped forward to thwart a presentable young man who evidently didn't look as if he'd be spending enough. My menu was awash with appetite-shrivelling translations: Breath of Italy, Stewed Neck of Own Production, Big Man's Snack with Rap-Rap Sauce and Pork Ears. I ordered several dumplings and a succession of soupy, potent dark ales, then at length reeled out past the security guards with a rippling belch.

The promenading families were long gone now, replaced by an after-hours cast of chest-out tough-guys, disfigured beggars and two-bit oligarchs waddling across wide, dim pavements to their scuffed BMWs. I looked up at the war banners and felt a wave of righteous drunken fury course through me. Don't any of you lot think this whole business is getting a bit out of hand? Even in reflective sobriety Putin's worship of all things Soviet had begun to trouble me deeply of late. How alarming to learn that Stalin, a murderous dictator airbrushed from history by his appalled successors, was now being rehabilitated: a museum had just opened in his birthplace, telling a cosy, atrocity-stripped story of Uncle Joe's life, and a recent poll found that only 20 per cent of Russians harboured 'negative feelings' about a man demonstrably to blame for the peace-time deaths of several million of their own countrymen.

Just before leaving home I had watched a new film about Stalingrad, an effectively official account by a staunchly Putin-ite director. At least I tried to – half an hour of the insufferably macho glorification of war and its noble Soviet practitioners proved more than enough. Did you know that Vladimir Putin recently made it a criminal offence to criticise any aspect of the Red Army's wartime conduct? If, as I shall do now, you mention the well-documented mass rapes carried out by Russian troops as they marched towards Berlin, you will be liable, as I apparently now am, to five years' imprisonment. I pondered this as I stumbled through scabby *Khrushchyovka* tenements held together with what looked like giant strips of gaffer tape, and at length pitched up at my hotel compound's entry intercom. 'Come on, Vlad,' I drawled into it after punching the button, 'you'll never take me alive!' But then – bzzzz, click, burp – that's the beauty of polonium.

*

The road out of Kaliningrad was a barrel of laughs, only with the laughs emptied out and replaced with liquidised shopping cyclist. Here was the homicidal traffic I had been warned about, along with the weather I hadn't been. The morning before it had been 22 degrees; it was now 5, and bulleting down. The world always hates the hungover.

Gutters gurgled and frothed; old ladies scuttled between shop doorways, bags and newspapers held uselessly over their heads. Every passing vehicle slapped a full-length iron curtain of chilled rain over me at point-blank range. I stopped under a bus shelter when the downpour built to a ridiculous, machine-gun crescendo. This can't last, I thought, but it did, and as I really, really wanted to get out of Kaliningrad I remounted. Within seconds I was the squelchy embodiment of one of the great fancy-that biological facts: did you know the human body is 108 per cent water?

I'd had regular previous cause to celebrate my MIFA's mudguards – this was the first large-scale ride I had ever undertaken with frame-fitted weather protection – but with a veritable torrent of rainwater rushing down my gutter zone, they were soon irrelevant. I began to tackle the deeper stretches of standing water with my feet high off the pedals and splayed hugely apart, vainly hoping to spare them the front wheel's bow-wave. These were perhaps the daftest and least dignified moments in a trip festooned with daft indignities. Pointless, too: my flat-soled mountain-bike/après-cycling hybrids were already drenched through. They had cost twice as much as my MIFA, and were at least seven times as shit, eagerly blotting up sweat from within and rain from without, and clinging stubbornly to a malodorous distillation of both overnight.

As the border approached, the smeary buildings along the road acquired a steadily more military aspect, guarded with razor wire and sentry boxes. The related vehicles busily displacing rain from tarmac to cyclist grew larger, greener, meaner. It was down to 3 degrees now; every downstroke on the pedals forced cold soup between my toes, a soup that came garnished with carpet-tack croutons as numbness took hold. The strafing rain stripped trees bare and blasted the verge to bits. Multicoloured flecks of gravel and grit, thick wodges of leaf mulch and other plant matter were spattered and clotted together in my sodden leg hairs, all over the bike, my panniers and that stupid yellow tabard. Every so often my ale-damaged skull and innards would add their discordant drone to the whole wretched, blaring symphony of torment. Slooshing listlessly through no man's land I didn't look, or feel, as if I'd ridden through a storm. I looked, and felt, as if God had been sick on me.

'Stop!'

I'd begun to assume that the gormless, hi-vis innocence of my bike and outfit would see me waved dismissively through every frontier crossing. This assumption would not survive my seventh border. At the first booth my documents and I had been subjected to an unusually prolonged Dead-Eyed Stare of Towering Bureaucratic Indifference. This was followed at the second by the classically Russian feminine repertoire of huffy head-shakes and incredulous squinting, and by the time I reclaimed my paperwork the litres of filthy rain had stopped evaporating from my hot, bare legs in steamy coils. Now I was shuddering miserably before a thin-faced young guard in a huge military cap, who had just rapped my front wheel with a mirror-ended stick normally employed for inspecting the undersides of vehicles.

'*Otkryt!*'

A tap on the MIFA's nearside rear; I levered the bike up onto its twin-leg stand and effortlessly unclipped the designated pannier.

'*Otkryt!*'

Accompanied by another brisk stick-flick, I understood this as an order to disgorge its contents. The guard stepped back under the border post's concrete canopy and observed as I bent over the pannier in rain of undiminished vigour, hauling armfuls of clothing and maps out and piling them up on the puddled, scabby tarmac.

'*Otkryt!*'

As I disembowelled the other pannier on request it became clear that the guard was increasingly preoccupied with my demeanour. By now I was shivering uncontrollably and noisily drawing in wet air through chattering teeth, displaying all the pale-faced symptoms of extreme cold that unhelpfully mirrored those of extreme guilt, and indeed withdrawal from class-A narcotics. My frozen fingers soon struggled to dance to the tune of his mirror stick, and when he rapped the tightly double-strapped front carrier it was a frosted fiddle too far. The meaty GDR strap, a challenge in any conditions, proved an insurmountable one in a state of compromised dexterity.

'*Otkryt! Otkryt!*' After a tattoo of stick-taps I dropped to my wet knees and yanked desperately at the strap with clawed and useless hands; it didn't budge but the bike keeled over. A tiny, broken whimper escaped my white lips; I looked beseechingly at the guard and met a mask of cast iron. '*Otkryt,*' it said.

I levered the strap off with a screwdriver in the end, then stood in a juddering hunch as he flicked his stick impassively through a tarmac harvest of soggy snack wrappings and toiletries. How dearly I wished to injure him. When the poking unearthed a forgotten stash of Pro Plus pills his expression hardened; he bent down and picked up the crumpled foil sachet between a gloved thumb and forefinger.

'It's only a stimul . . . it just kind of makes you feel . . .'

With a maturity beyond his years he allowed his features to settle into the look of beatific calm that comes over experienced enforcement officials when they sense a babbling suspect is about to incriminate himself.

'Look, no, really, it's just caffeine. Coffee.'

'Corfyeah,' he said, nodding slowly at least twenty times. Then he dropped the sachet into my damp belongings and flicked his stick towards Poland.

9. POLAND

I was too far gone to celebrate the many ways in which Poland was not Russia. Before slipping into the groggy indifference of under-nourished hypothermia, there was only time to rue the principal fashion in which it was not all the other countries I'd been through: the Poles don't have the euro. How cruel to see the Steaming Kebab of Salvation brusquely whipped from the counter on sight of my debit card and a soggy mess of non-zloty notes. And how wonderful when at sodden, hollowed length I sloshed woodenly into a fish shop in the little port of Frombork, offered a wodge of rouble pulp to the sweet young woman behind the till, and presently found myself installed by a blazing wood burner with a big plate of fried sea stuff in my steaming lap. It was an act of humbling and very unRussian kindness, and one which I chose to reward by removing nearly all of my clothes, wringing them out behind the kindling bucket and draping the lot over the stove. I fell asleep in my shorts and was woken by the smell of molten gardening glove.

But the rain didn't get bored, and throughout the afternoon much of it was delivered in a permeating suspension of fog. A downpour finale plastered me in a coat of mulched catkin, and I presented myself at a rather smart townhouse hotel on Elbląg's cathedral square looking as if I'd swum through a river of muesli to get there. The receptionist blinked bravely at my approach, and recoiled a little when my rain-bloated passport hit her desk with a fishmonger's slap. How enduringly grateful I was that at this time of year no hotel could even pretend to be full.

My room was briefly delightful; in minutes I had spattered its gleaming, down-lit shower in hosed-off pannier detritus and blocked the free-standing dome basin with plant matter and bits of Russia. The complimentary fruit bowl was reduced to pips and skin in a dozen savage bites, and the sleek wenge furniture disappeared beneath dank belongings: literally everything I owned had been drenched during my border ordeal, and was also, I now noted, deeply infused with the muscular scents of woodsmoke and fried fish. I had to bag-up before going out to eat, and it would be three full days before my shoes dried.

Over breakfast I learned I was now in Pomerania, which sounded like a carefree story-book kingdom, but in the harsh light of an après-deluge morning didn't look like one. I had by now regularly fallen foul of an ongoing power struggle to determine the precise passage of EV13; my hard-copy route guide was in a three-way fight with online maps and the sparse signage. A compromise between many suggested options now cast me across a fallow plain of sunlit mud, skidding ponderously and pushing the MIFA for two hours through unnavigable sections that made brown foot-balls of my feet. On days like this it seemed I had spent most of my life bouncing and rattling with painful sloth towards some desolate horizon of snow, sand or mud, passing the very occasional incredulous local with his hands on his hips and a sagging jaw.

It was one of those lonely tribulations that empties the human head, then fills it with daft rage. I gazed at skeletal trees clotted with thriving mistletoe tumours and developed a sudden hatred

Tim Moore
@mrtimmoore

There's an ongoing power struggle to determine the route of EV13. As ever the endurance shopping cyclist is the loser.

for this sap-sucking parasite. How had it inveigled itself into our festive celebrations? We might as well snog Vladimir Putin under a sprig of swastikas. And what about all the cuckoos I kept hearing of late? 'The cuckoo's a fine bird, he sings as he flies; he brings us good tidings, he tells us no lies.' So I had sung at primary school, and so I now bellowed across the churned nothingness. In adulterated form, to reflect the fact that the cuckoo wasn't a fine bird, and that the perpetrator of some of the animal kingdom's most appalling behaviour might be more accurately described as a massive wanker. It didn't scan too well, but my word it felt good. Did you know that if a host bird expels a cuckoo's egg from its nest, the cuckoo's mum comes back and metes out the revenge atrocity of 'total clutch destruction'?

At length I emerged from parasitical metaphors for Soviet occupation into more concrete reminders, passing social-realist monoliths that welcomed me into towns ringed with *Khrushchyovka* tenement blocks. Words familiar from a generation of Polish influence in Britain looked down from commercial awnings and rang out through the open doors beneath: *sklep, dziękuję, kiełbasa, dzień dobry* – shop, thank you, sausage, good morning – and the ubiquitous epithet *kurwa*. After my two-decade dealings with ex-pat tradesmen and cleaners, it felt strange to encounter Poles who didn't speak a word of English and exhibited only a patchy eagerness to please. The captain of a river ferry perpetrated the most shameless, clumsy attempt at short-changing I have ever experienced, clearly confident that foreigners were all so boundlessly stupid that any answer to the conundrum of subtracting five from 100 would satisfy them. I shook my head and kept shaking it until his condescending smile faded and, zloty by grudging zloty, he filled my outstretched hand with the requisite coinage. After disembarking I treated him to a word that wasn't sausage.

For some hours I trundled across a flat, wet and very Dutch landscape, pedalling along raised dykes beneath a big blue sky and crossing wide, straight bodies of water by chain ferry. Then a distant jostle of petrochemical chimneys and dockside cranes poked up from the sun-spangled horizon: Gdańsk, home to more defining moments in recent history than any other city in Europe. The Nazi bombardment of its eastern waterfront on 1 September 1939 marked the start of the Second World War; forty-one years later those same docksides saw the birth of Lech Wałęsa's Solidarity movement, the inspirational beginning of the end for one-party Communist rule across the Eastern Bloc.

Poles have always seemed a little more adventurous than their regional rivals. On our 1990 trip we started seeing their tiny little Polski Fiats in Denmark, labouring under the wheel-splaying weight of human numbers and mercantile cargo. After that they were everywhere, boldly going where for fifty years no East European had ever gone: out in the Swedish fields harvesting produce, by the Austrian roadside flogging home-made pickles, a dominant presence at every car-boot sale from Bergen to Bergamo. Their itinerant quest for a fast buck knew no bounds in every sense, with regard to the deckchair pimps we spotted outside a row of Warsaw-plated caravans bucking about in the corner of a Berlin car park. We even saw Polish tat-traders in desperate, foodless Romania, making a very slow buck. It was a pioneering display of the venturesome enterprise that would later make them the first-wave East Europeans to arrive in Britain.

Old Gdańsk was the venerable incarnation of this spirit, a colourful parade of slender, lofty merchant homes topped with scalloped gables and grand, elaborate civic structures clustered in finials and clock towers, handsomely restored legacies of its sixteenth-century heyday as the Hanseatic League's richest port. I weaved the mud-slathered MIFA through the tourists and came out of the cobbles onto an urban expressway. It went on for hours, endlessly flanked by office and apartment blocks that would deny me a closer glimpse of what were once the Lenin shipyards, where in the 1980s a different sort of Pole pushed a different sort of boundary.

Poland was the biggest of the Soviet's satellite states, and the most perennially bothersome. When bad things happened, Poles made a serious fuss with little regard for the repressive conse-quences: in 1956, an uprising in Poznań against pay cuts left fifty-six protestors dead. There was rarely a shortage of bad things to fuss about. A hushed-up 1970s research project by native econo-mists established that the average Polish woman of working age woke at 5 a.m., and padded out her 9–5 job with two daily hours of commuting, ninety minutes of cooking and housework, plus fifty-three minutes in food queues. Being Polish, she didn't suffer in silence: when in 1970 the nation's woes were compounded by a 36 per cent hike in food prices, more protests swept the nation. In Gdańsk forty-four people were shot dead.

By 1980 most Warsaw Pact colonies were functionally bank-rupt, and with all those weapons to build and stockpile the mother-land was in no position to bail them out. Poland was the brokest of the broke: its foreign debt doubled every year, and in 1981 hit sixty-six billion dollars. Further huge rises in food prices ensued, stoking further unrest. The Solidarity trade union was formed in the Gdańsk shipyards after a strike in the summer of 1980: within eight weeks it had eight million members across the country, more than twice as many as the Communist Party. In the good old, bad old days the Russians would have sent in the tanks, but by 1981 they had lost 2,000 men in Afghanistan and had no appetite for meddling beyond their borders. The Polish authorities imposed martial law: for eighteen months a curfew held, and men in uniforms read the TV news. But without Soviet back-up their hearts weren't really in it, and in 1986 they opened negotiations with Solidarity that paved the way for free elections. How curiously ironic that the first true workers' revolution in history should effectively overthrow a Communist state.

A busy roadside bike path delivered me at non-contemplative speed through this seat of the anti-Soviet revolution, and the drawn-out balance of the Three Cities conurbation: Gdańsk and its industrial-dockside partner Gdynia bookend the seaside resort of Sopot, where that terrible Commie Song Contest was held. The sun was now low and huge, casting a comely golden light on even the dreariest distribution centre, but I took almost nothing in. While lunching outside the gates of a refinery I'd remembered the Pro Plus that had nearly bagged me a border strip-search, and for no obvious reason necked down four with my new afternoon refreshment of choice: Magic Man energy drink. The combined effect, when it took full hold, was that of an adrenaline enema; thus wired I had made a blur of the Sopot boardwalk and Gdynia's crane forest, my unblinking eyes fixed on the odometer. The path fairly swarmed with the Three Cities' many student cyclists, but this wasn't about wheel-to-wheel combat. Perhaps it might have been if I'd had any hope of victory. Then my route peeled away towards the quieter north-east coast, and as the blossom-flecked trees pushed shadows far across the gilded hillsides I settled into the brainless, pinprick-pupilled accumulation of distance.

'I am sorry for my English, is ah—'

I had hit Władysławowo's Blackpool-ish b. & b. belt deep into twilight, a desperate, pallid man astride a bike clagged with sun-baked mud and creaking in exhausted sympathy. Simon, as the

chubby young man at the desk of the first guest house had introduced himself, spoke a language whose long, wondering pauses
made it poorly suited for my predicament. I had asked him if there
was a restaurant in town and now interrupted to ask him again.

'Ah . . . *restauracja* . . . yes, but I think is, ah . . . close at nine.'

I checked my watch; it was 8.40, the latest I would ever finish.

'So, ah, tomorrow breakfast here from eight o'clock, down the
stairs in . . . how is room called? Room where people must eat, like
in, ah . . . office or ah . . . ah . . . I apologise again for my English,
I learn in school bu—'

I cut in with the measured urgency of a man who has just ridden
133km on a shopping bike, the last half of them on Pro Plus and
carbonated taurine.

'Simon,' I said, clamping my white hand to his shoulder, 'you
must tell me where this restaurant is, and you must tell me now.'

With a nervous smile he obliged, and I tore raggedly down the
off-season streets like a drunk ghost. A young woman was polishing
glasses behind an empty counter when I staggered in and executed
an unusually theatrical rendition of my eating mime.

'I'm sorry, I can see that you're hungry but I'm afraid our kitchen
is closed. Maybe you could try the kebab café in the centre?' As I
ricocheted out of the door I looked back and saw her re-enacting
my performance to the loud amusement of unseen men.

I often wonder what would happen if I ever fail to source calories in these situations; this one, for instance, could have ended
very badly for Simon's succulent jowls. But somehow, perhaps
because of the many great deeds and acts of kindness I have
carried out in this life and its predecessors, it always works out. I
successfully located the kebab shop, and there laid waste to an
open roadkill sandwich and several Specjal beers, watching a
succession of progressively more dishevelled locals weave in from

the night, drunk moths drawn to that flaming bollard of flesh. I went to bed feeling oily, replete and very at home.

For three blowy, blue-skied days I tracked Poland's Baltic coast, trying to forget that every westward pedal stroke was taking me further away from my Black Sea goal to the distant south-east. After countless false dawns, spring had sprung: Poles were getting noisy with lawnmowers and strimmers, spraying crap and nitrates over fields and riding bicycles en masse for the purposes of leisure. How pleasing to have learned that the Polish for bike was *rowery*, in unique tribute to the Rover Safety Bicycle, a nineteenth-century British creation that conquered the world and set a design template that still endures. And how regrettable, after the thick end of 4,000km, to be indirectly introduced to the MIFA's final short-coming: big wheels were not just faster, but hugely more comfort-able. The couples and families that wheeled smoothly along the sun-splashed forest paths offered a serene counterpoint to the hectic, deafening progress of my all-action judderfest. And though these wandering trails of cinders and gravel made an aesthetically agreeable environment for a pootle down the Baltic coast, in terms of speed and navigational directness they did few favours for anyone attempting to ride the entire length of continental Europe before dying of boredom or old age.

It was a long holiday weekend. Back in Moscow, Putin was getting ready to cast his sinister, beady gaze across the biggest military parade in Russian history, and the Baltic resorts were at last coming to life. Every couple of hours the pines parted and I found myself winding through a clutch of refreshment stands and seaside-crap shacks, most topped with national flags slapping themselves silly in the wind. Much more rarely I would catch a glimpse of soft sand and rough water. Seaside holidays might have been invented on this coast, but those frigid gusts mean the Baltic's resorts generally shelter behind dunes and windbreak pine glades. Out on the beaches, everyone was hunkered down in stripy-canopied, two-seat enclosures arrestingly positioned with their backs to the sea and its incoming blasts of chilled air. What an odd spectacle they made, less like holidaymakers than telephone engineers working over a thousand open manholes.

These were days of radish-heavy breakfasts, of shades-on sun and good-natured public drunkenness, of distance-blitzing Magic Man afternoons and herring suppers. The wind was stiff and capricious, obliging me on occasion to underlay my gardening gloves with disposable produce-handling mitts nicked from a supermarket. I regularly lost my way, lugging the MIFA for miles through raw sand and brambly brush with my retreat-from-Moscow face on. At length, with blood spotting my socks and shoes full of grit, I would generally emerge at some forgotten entrance to a derelict Soviet army base. So many were strung along the coast, reduced now to weed-pierced asphalt, mossy piles of rubble and the odd rusted sentry barrier with 'CTOП!' on it in brine-blistered red letters. The service roads between these places were invariably laid with miles of liver-loosening cobbles, a punishing ordeal for the smaller-wheeled gentleman tourist. I had to take my watch off when the reverberating crown wheel threatened to gouge through my wrist flesh. More than once I stopped to allow a bout of nausea to pass.

Poland's holiday drinkers got to work early. I saw one young couple taking bottle-toting selfies at 9.15 a.m., but there were none of the rheumy, grazed-knuckled trouble-seekers who had patrolled small-town Poland back in 1990. Indeed, the mood was almost overbearingly convivial. The coastal paths were full of primary-school outings, and every single member of every single one reflexively hailed me with a wave, a smile or a squeaky 'Dzień dobry!' In the evenings, the streets and sands were dense with hand-holders: grandparents, young lovers, even teenage boys and their mothers. It was all very heart-warming, and entirely unexpected. The bloke who retiled our bathroom last year hardly ever held my hand.

The resorts were an intriguing blend of crumbly stucco, smart new boutique hotels and the odd Soviet leisure monstrosity, sometimes unconvincingly made-over with coppered glass and a portico, sometimes left to rot where it stood. The pavements offered an introduction to East Europe's remarkable tolerance of infant recklessness and its handmaiden, sozzled parental negligence: all thronged with whooping toddlers on battery-powered trikes, zipping waywardly through the crowds at lethal speed. From here on, almost every former Communist settlement I passed through would have its main public spaces terrorised after dark by children of similar age at the wheels of rented electric racing cars.

Inland, most non-holiday towns were ingrained with the stubborn patina of Communism, all grimy concrete, battered streets and parade-ready public spaces suffused with the smell of damp plaster and stuff being burned that shouldn't be. The dominant commercial outlet throughout was the *sklep*, a Russian-pattern grocery shed run almost round the clock by a little old lady who stood guard before a couple of well-stocked shelves and a chiller cabinet. It was a very homely set-up, and one that helped me develop some seriously advanced pointing skills. Almost every old dear, in *sklep* and on street, had a grandchild or two under her skirts; Polish women still work as hard as they did in the socialistic era, but these days they don't get any state childcare. Almost every old man was down by some unpromising industrial waterway with a rod and a bottle of beer. This would become one of my ride's stock spectacles. Sometimes they weren't even fishing: an awful lot of retirements in these countries are seen out sitting on the dock of the bay.

Only gradually did I take stock of all the church towers, features so conspicuously absent from most small-town skylines in Russia and the Baltics. Catholicism has always been entrenched in Polish life; for days I followed a trail of those seashell pilgrimage signs that had pointed my way when I dragged a donkey to Santiago de Compostela. The Soviets were always slightly scared of their stroppiest satellite, and after an initial Stalin-era crackdown they allowed the Polish Catholic Church an unusually free hand.

Elsewhere across their empire, spires were toppled and pastors taken away to break rocks or build dams. A troublesome Hungarian cardinal was tortured until he confessed to an impressive range of crimes, amongst them plotting to steal the crown jewels. When an East German priest went through the records after 1990, he found that he'd been spied on by forty different Stasi officers, and that of the seven people who regularly attended his masses, six were informers. The Stasi's campaign against him was impressively broad: 'The meanest thing they did was throw stink bombs into a full church.'

But in Poland the churches were left largely in peace, and when in 1979 Pope John Paul II expressed a wish to visit his homeland, the Soviet authorities felt obliged to grant permission. They probably shouldn't have, though, as a third of the Polish population came out to see their Pope, establishing an unhelpful tradition of mass gatherings that became even more unhelpful after John Paul hit it off with Lech Wałęsa. It's now generally agreed that the Pope's Polish tour catalysed the creation of Solidarity, and (less generally) that John Paul II thus brought down Communism singlehanded.

Everything grew steadily more German as I rode on: trim lawns and hanging baskets, regimental ranks of static caravans, shiny plastic pantiles and intriguingly hideous gnome-heavy garden tableaux. Every wrinkled hand now clutched a tippy-tappy hiking pole, an apparently compulsory accessory for the over sixties across most of northern Europe west of the old curtain. Soon every other number plate was German, and every other voice.

I was waiting at a set of lights in Kołobrzeg, a novel seaside-resort/cargo-terminal hybrid just east of the border, when a crop-haired young man on a rubbish mountain bike pulled up alongside. Shamefully I had yet to hose off the MIFA, and its incongruous topcoat of Russian road porridge and Somme-grade Pomeranian mud clumps had attracted regular attention in such scenarios all week. But the skinhead beside me was surveying the bike, and then its rider, with a new sort of expression. No confusion or pity, no smirking contempt. As the lights changed he nodded, lofted a thumb, and offered me a small smile of approval. Without words, he said: 'That is a really daft thing to be doing, but fair play for doing it.' After six weeks I had finally encountered someone who got it, someone who understood; I smiled back and we rode together hand in hand towards the sunset, or definitely should have.

10. THE GERMAN BALTIC

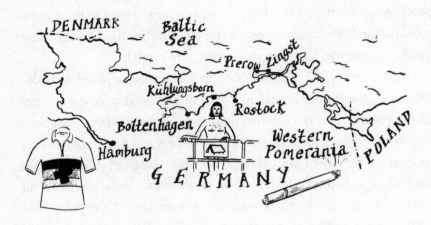

After its memorable and heroic three-month absence, my MIFA came home without ceremony. One minute I was rattling down a boulevard flanked with stalls flogging cheap fags and fake football shirts to cross-border Germans; then came a blink-and-miss-it roadside round-up of national speed limits, and I was in. At once the full parade of stereotypes – the lazy, the patronising, the offensive – marched out around me. Spotless cars drove down velvet roads with a careful obedience that was hard to attune to: I approached one of those digital watch-your-speed displays in a 40 zone and saw it clocked at 38, 39, 39, 38, 38, 11 (me). The hedges were clipped and the pavements almost shone. The farms looked like parks and everyone was wearing lederhosen made out of sausages. After weeks of potholed shonkiness it seemed unreal, like a model village.

And this was, or until recently had been, East Germany – just a Commie knock-off of the real thing. I had to look hard for evidence.

The five-floor tenement blocks were a giveaway, but even these bore little resemblance to those perpetrated by Soviet Russia elsewhere across its empire. Each had a homely pitched roof and pastel-painted walls that didn't seem to have been fashioned from cardboard pulp and asbestos. But then the GDR was the Soviet poster girl, its flagship western outpost, the one place where their brand of Communism almost made it. No one here ever queued for food or went hungry. Welfare provisions were a class above any East European neighbours, indeed the envy of many in the West: education standards ranked amongst the highest in the world, and eighteen million citizens were generally over-qualified for the blue-collar jobs that most ended up in. In 1984, the World Bank rated the GDR as the world's twelfth strongest economy, and the CIA told Reagan it was poised to overtake West Germany. A nation that wasn't even recognised by the International Olympic Committee until 1968 established immediate sporting dominance: from 1972 onwards they finished every Olympic Games, summer and winter, in the top three on the medals table.

It was another crisp, bright afternoon, and I bowled down a series of sun-stippled clifftop paths threaded with pensioners on electric bikes, kicking some serious old arse along the way. Strange as it felt to think of all these German retirees as former Communists – much stranger than it had amongst elderly Russians, Balts or Poles – now that I thought about it, the clichéd Teutonic mentality seemed uniquely well suited to the Soviet ethos. Hard work and healthy play, reliable efficiency, wholesale compliance and the readiness to denounce those who betrayed it . . . Even that hearty, no-funny-business approach to naturism was a good fit.

The path was punctuated with GDR-vintage campsites, most still up and running and mercifully fully clothed. I was interested to note the number of static caravans flying the German flag:

displays of national pride were understandably a bit iffy in the post-war decades, and flags weren't waved en masse in Germany until the country hosted the 2006 World Cup. Thus inspired I coasted to a halt at the edge of a campsite and rummaged portentously through my right-hand pannier. When my wife went home with most of my winter wardrobe she handed over my summer one – an outfit dominated by the jersey I now pulled down over my concave, pasty torso for the first time. Pale blue, ringed with the red, yellow and black national stripes, and there, emblazoned across the front – was this really OK? – the strident emblem of the German Democratic Republic, a corn-ringed hammer and compasses.

I decided that on balance it looked a bit much, and was putting my anorak on over it when I gazed along the row of trees that marked the campsite boundary, and spotted a small lime-green bicycle propped distantly against one. Even at that range I somehow knew what it was; I pedalled breathlessly through the sandy tussocks and found I was right. A MIFA, and not just a MIFA but a twin-racked, caliper-braked 904! A single exclamation mark does scant justice to this historic and emotion-charged reunion. And to think it was happening here, at a campsite that was every MIFA's natural habitat. Blinking out tears I tore off my anorak and struck a Comrade Timoteya pose, beefed up with a glare of Germanic purpose. Had I known that this would be the only time my MIFA met one of his three million stunted brethren I would have taken even more bike-on-bike photographs, and some even weirder ones.

The life expectancy of a bicycle is apparently around 9,000km, the distance typically accumulated in five years of regular commuter riding. And that's a proper bike, with durable components made to exacting modern standards. Pedalling away from my MIFA's long-lost brother – a bike that flaunted its modest territorial expectations, with a plastic bag wrapped over the saddle and two

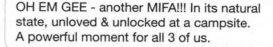

Tim Moore
@mrtimmoore

OH EM GEE - another MIFA!!! In its natural state, unloved & unlocked at a campsite. A powerful moment for all 3 of us.

wire-frame shopping baskets lashed to the carriers – I pondered an ongoing miracle: this twenty-five-year-old campsite potterer, built by bored Communists out of melted-down coat hangers, was on course to better that lifetime total in no more than a few brutal months. How little had gone wrong with it, and how little that was thanks to me. I hadn't even attempted to diagnose the grating creaks that had accompanied me since Russia. This tiny old dear had been left to look after itself, coping with the worst weather and roads our continent has to offer, confounding cynics – especially deaf cynics – for fun.

*

My first night in Germany cast an enduring template: dark wood, bolster pillows, a gold-rimmed *weissbier* glass with an integral drip-doily round the stem, and a plate buried under a Sky-dish schnitzel and a hill of potatoes. This genteel gluttony, and its starchy, subdued environment, would end most of my days in the MIFA's homeland, give or take the odd in-room Aldi pasta-salad rite if I missed the restaurant – they generally closed before eight – or felt the need to restore my financial morale (I'm looking at you, Herr 'eighty euro vissout breakfast' Gasthaus-Swindler). Nobody foreign came up here; half the service operatives couldn't speak a word of English, and there was no menu option beyond Hearty German Fayre. But what a rare joy, in this easyJet age, to find myself on a bona fide voyage of discovery right here on my continental door-step, exploring a huge swathe of Europe I would never otherwise have dreamed of going near. Good old bicycle.

I tracked the Baltic north-west then south, up and down through holiday homes, commercial ports and windswept coastal plains. A million geese honked it up across the flatlands and – here we go – a billion midges met their maker in my face-holes. From a distance the seaside was an alluring Mediterranean combo of twinkly azure and soft white sand, but when the path took me closer I saw children chasing after cartwheeling buckets and other windborne leisure accessories, watched through slitted eyes by parents blanketed up in those stripy weather-proof bench-shelters. So many vistas recalled the old MIFA brochure shots I'd found online, young couples in nylon clothing gathered around a shiny 900 by a wooden jetty or a beach hut, with expressions that suggested a grey-faced man in a dark raincoat was standing behind the camera holding up a sign that said: SMILE CLASSIFICATION: COLLECTIVE ENJOYMENT B2.

Western Pomerania was a great flat blanket, woven in bright green and garish yellow: oilseed rape in vibrant full bloom and a plague of dandelions bursting gloriously through the meadows. Huge-eared hares cavorted wildly across the fields, doing their mad March thing a month or two late; lone fishermen stood transfixed by marshy bulrush glades. My nostrils twitched to a complex perfume of brine, blossom and fresh-mown grass. How very distant the sterile Arctic wastes now seemed. If you'd tried to explain to me what a butterfly was back in the middle of Finland, I'd have grunted sceptically. Then torn your throat open and supped deep on your warm, life-giving blood.

I rode through settlements ticking boxes in my *Observer's Book of Commie Relics*, a Karl-Marx-strasse or a Friedrich-Engels-allee, a concrete-slab path of period military origin (*per-dum-ba-dank-per-tonk-buh-tink* – what a literal pain in the arse they always were), a town hall that suggested a ventilation shaft for some giant underground car park. Very rarely I'd spot a bricked-up ruin: a column-fronted *Kulturhaus* with the T hanging down at an angle, or one of those *Cyanide with Rosie* agricultural mega-structures that looked like tractor prisons, or interrogation centres for subversive cattle. But in general, the Germans had erased the evidence with customary rigour. The country we drove through in 1990 was tired and grubby, mired in a cancerous fug of brown-coal smoke and two-stroke exhaust fumes. Now everything seemed clean, fresh and stridently sustainable, with a windfarm on every other bright green hillside and a rank of shiny black photovoltaic tiles on every other roof. In four days I saw a single Trabant, though it did have its bonnet up with three male heads wedged in the hole, one per moving part. The allotments were neater and better tended than most nation's front gardens, and everyone's exterior woodwork gleamed.

Of the many lost freedoms reclaimed after the Wall came down, the inalienable right to civic slobbery was not one of them. As much as I appreciated all this smartness and order, I didn't feel qualified to envy it – in the words of that great sage Harry Callahan, a man's gotta know his limitations, and I simply lack the house-proud discipline required to cut my lawn in the designated hours between twelve and two on Saturday, or to repaint my shutters every three years by mayoral decree. What would you do if you saw a van with a blue light on the roof and the word *Ordnungsamt* on the side? Not much, perhaps, until someone explained that *Ordnungsamt* meant 'office of order', and that this vehicle was on hand to speed to any emergency contravention of the civil code, which – to take some genuine examples – might include a neighbour's failure to weed the pavement in front of his house, or to stop his pond-frogs croaking on a Sunday. Then you might sneak up behind this van and draw a nob on it.

After all those weeks of nothing and Russia, public decorum was a challenge. For the first time on this trip I felt self-conscious about flobbing into hedgerows, and indeed whipping down my shorts to anoint a roadside tree. Previously there had never been anyone around, and even when there had been they couldn't have cared less. Now my route was fairly well lined with the world's most responsible and censorious citizens. Miraculously, I only got hooted at twice in Germany: once after I overtook a car at 22kmh in a 20 zone, and once when I knocked over and killed two elderly pedestrians on the wrong Tuesday.

Out by the full-fat, blustery Baltic, then back through the dunes to the calm and slightly fetid lagoons behind. Every lunch was a path-side homage to the straight-bat national cuisine, cramming bread rolls with smoked and processed incitements to bowel cancer. The cockerels had been silenced by law and not once was I menaced by a dog. If a German lets his dog loose on the public highway, the diktats of *Ordnungsamt* permit you to electrocute his youngest child.

Prerow, Zingst, Wieck: trim and forgivably twee resorts well-stocked with pensioners and their immaculate cottages, all thatched with roofs that appeared to have been washed and combed that morning. Every mailbox had a lighthouse or a salty old sea dog painted on it. Elderly couples were out on matching bikes in matching tracksuits, often in comradely pelotons of a dozen or more, exuding an air of perpetual, bracingly active retirement and gentle, communal pleasure. These places had doubtless been their recreational stamping grounds since the GDR days, and were probably much the same now, just with better cars and shops. With a start I realised that half these retired Communists looked barely older than I did: a tribute to all those invigorating formative decades spent breathing sulphur and spying on each other. And to all those ongoing current decades of smoking their tits off.

When former West German chancellor Helmut Schmidt died, a few months after my return, the BBC's *10 O'clock News* obituary concluded that his people would remember him 'wreathed in a cloud of his beloved cigarette smoke'. I thought that seemed a little off as the farewell to a grand statesman, but Schmidt – who extraordinarily lived to ninety-six after smoking fifty a day for the thick end of eighty years – really was the poster boy for a vigorously wholesome and salubrious nation with a curious weakness for little white death-sticks. They cheered when Helmut lit up on chat shows – he once got through thirteen fags in a single TV interview – and booed when a Hamburg prosecutor tried to charge him for smoking in a city theatre. In 2013, after the EU announced a ban on flavoured cigarettes, Schmidt immediately stockpiled 38,000 of his favourite Reyno Menthols. He was ninety-four at the time. Coincidentally or not, and assuming adherence to his lifelong rate of consumption, he coughed it in the very month this hoard would have been exhausted.

When did you last see someone smoking on a bike? I saw three puffing wobblers on my first day in Germany, all well-presented men of middle years. The cheerily fag-faced hiker is another staple on the nation's cycle paths and forest trails; my top spot was a rambling nicotine enthusiast in a rauchfrei.de stop-smoking T-shirt. In such a healthful country it was most jarring. There were cigarette vending machines on every other street corner, and the Germans haven't just failed to ban tobacco advertising – they seem to cherish it. Entire towns were dominated by gigantic people waving fags around at glamorous parties, in the sort of themed bill-board profusion you only usually encounter in the run-up to a general election. More than one in three German men smoke, almost 50 per cent higher than the British rate.

The reason for this remarkable idiosyncrasy? Hitler. That's right. The Nazis, you see, were pioneering anti-smokers: their public-health inspectorate made the connection between tobacco consumption and lung cancer some fifteen years before anyone else did. (For the record, they were also trail-blazingly down on asbestos, white bread and food additives.) The Führer personally set up an Institute for the Struggle Against Tobacco, which banned smoking in cinemas and discouraged it in the workplace. Advertising was heavily restricted. They even invented nicotine gum to help people give up. Hitler loved pointing out that he, Mussolini and Franco were all non-smokers, in contrast to the wheezing Allied triumvirate of Stalin (pipe), Churchill (cigar) and Roosevelt (bong).

So when a backpacked German rambler lights up, he isn't just shortening his lifespan and making astonished foreign cyclists swerve into trees – he's making a stand for democracy and righting the terrible wrongs of his forefathers. After the German authorities banned smoking in bars, tobacco activists protested in T-shirts bearing the yellow Star of David with 'SMOKER' printed across them – seeking to remind people, in the most clumsily offensive manner imaginable, that the head of Hitler's anti-fag institute was a fervently anti-Semitic SS officer who killed himself rather than face trial.

It rained, sometimes with merciless intensity, and accompanied on one occasion by a tornado, which laid waste to a village I passed very close to. (I didn't actually see it but nonetheless watched the roof-stripped buildings on TV that night with a certain flinty pride. I accept this doesn't sound great, but nobody died.) Now that it was warmer I stopped bothering to hide from the rain, taking blustery skipfuls of sky water full in the face and revelling in the awed stares of shell shocked Berghaus couples taking cover under picnic shelters. At least traffic-swash was never a hazard: the vast bulk of my ride through Germany was played out on bespoke bike paths. The natives really do a tremendous amount of cycling, and I encountered several unfamiliar new breeds: hausfraus pedalling home with the weekly shop bulging their panniers, boys towing the family dog in a weather-proof trailer. The unhelpful common denominator was pottering sloth; on a bike with almost no brakes I could hardly afford to be reckless, but my speedy weaving would routinely elicit 'easy Tiger' tuts and harrumphs.

So rarely do German motorists expect to share the carriageway with cyclists that I could sense their panic when required to. Even dark-glazed, low-riding street machines – the sort of vehicles that in other countries run cyclists off the road on principle – would drop back and wait for several hundred clear metres of tarmac to appear before they dared overtake. Sadly, though, I was never quite far enough from the road to be spared the terrible noise that leaked from every car, soul-wilting, ear-rotting reminders of a nation still unshakably rooted in the High Mullet age. If it wasn't Toto it was Bonnie Tyler. 'The Final Countdown'? What a cruel misnomer – I never heard the last of it. My historical ponderings were routinely interrupted by the mental image of Germans sitting about drumming their fingers and bursting into the odd yodel, just filling time before someone invented the power ballad.

To cut the nation some slack, perhaps they're ju . . . no, I can't do it. When I reflect on my portentous ride through Germany, the nation that more than any other defined what my journey was about, one moment stubbornly bullies itself to the front of my mind. I'm freewheeling into a sumptuous, sunlit valley, alone in the world, when a drunken yell bursts raggedly from a roadside clump of trees: 'Woah-oh, ve're HALF-VAY ZERE!' I veer wildly across the tarmac in alarm, then glance down at the odometer and think: Well, look at that – so ve are.

I crossed Rostock harbour on a ferry, gazing without envy at cruise liners stacked with deck after deck of egg-box cabins, like Commie resort hotels laid on their side. Heiligendamm, Europe's most venerable spa resort, had spent the socialistic era with its grand white mansions requisitioned for holidaying forestry workers and war invalids; with very mixed feelings I wheeled past these same buildings, now returned to the elite, lavishly reinvented as the sort of hotels G8 leaders shake hands outside. Again I was presented by the distasteful spectacle of very rich people refusing to look as if they're enjoying themselves: the lounge-suited saunterers out on the manicured lawns were engaged in the usual sombre parade, competing to see who could appear the most wearily blasé about their wonderful surroundings.

How much more fun the forestry workers would have had out here, I thought, feeling a special affinity for this fine body of men and women now that I'd spent – let me see – just over 20 per cent of my fifties within their wooded realm. Apart from anything else, all those lumberjacks would have been striding around with their choppers out: by the 1970s, full nudity was standard on GDR beaches and at holiday camps. Many people took the habit home, and it was commonplace for whole families to strip off when they came back from school and work. Germans, of course, are always keen to stress that there's nothing sexy about nudism. 'I never heard of anybody seeing even one erect penis on a naturist beach,' says Kurt Starke, formerly the GDR's leading sexologist. But Kurt's professional existence, along with the fact that the best-selling book of all time in his defunct nation was a shag manual entitled *Man and Woman Intimately*, speaks of a stiffy-centric society.

Typically enough, the GDR's unexpectedly enthusiastic promotion of free love and hot comrade-on-comrade action was founded on ideology: notions of honour and virginity had no place in a secular state, and great sex was seen as the expression of a happy and equal society. Premarital relations were endorsed to the point of encouragement, with fourteen-year-olds advised merely to avoid 'regular intercourse'. An instructive film shown in schools majored on the female orgasm, and optimal positions in which to achieve it. Starke insists that GDR women had more and better sex than their West German counterparts. 'We studied the difference in orgasm rates among teenage female students in the East and West in the 1980s,' he says, referencing a research project that might attract a very different sort of official interest today. 'Our findings were that 98 to 99 per cent of GDR women aged sixteen to eighteen were able to have orgasms.'

My GDR jersey looked a little different these days. On its debut afternoon, back at the Fully Clothed Campsite Gathering of the MIFAs, that awkward emblem had earned me a few double-takes; pushing the bike over a narrow canal bridge I passed, at uncomfortably close quarters, a man of about sixty who fixed me square in the chest with a stare of incredulous hatred. A very short while later, a much younger man – too young to have been more than a toddler when the Wall came down – gave me an even filthier look. At a stroke I had morphed from hopeless ninny to bastard Stasi apologist; something had to be done. The next morning, and every morning after, I got busy with the gaffer tape, hiding the offending symbol under a big black cross. It looked pretty daft but it did the job – at least until late afternoon, when sweat and the elements began to undo the adhesive. By the time I presented myself at a guest-house reception desk I would be clasping one hand over my heart, like Pavarotti about to belt out an emotional aria.

Tim Moore
@mrtimmoore

MIFA's coming home! Also unveiled my summer wardrobe. GDR jersey guaranteed to mislead and very possibly offend.

I understood what a terrible misjudgement the jersey had been at Kühlungsborn, pushing the MIFA around an outdoor museum at the foot of a GDR-era watchtower. I'd already passed one of these survivors poking balefully above the dunes, a cylindrical shaft topped with a splayed observation deck, like some giant concrete golf tee. Over five million East Germans attempted to flee their homeland in the course of its forty-year existence, nearly all of them before the 'inner German border' was fenced off and fortified in 1961. Thereafter, the tantalising proximity of Denmark and West Germany drew thousands of would-be escapers to these beaches, knowing that freedom lay just a moonlit lilo ride away. But the authorities knew it too: 2,500 border guards were packed into this short stretch of coast, twenty-seven watchtowers erected and long swathes sealed off behind a huge wall. For twenty-eight years the two seaside parties played a game. You could call it cat and mouse, but it was more fist and face.

It was a warm day, but while wandering past the stark exhibits I automatically pulled my anorak on over That Jersey. Soon it was buttoned right up to my neck. There were some truly dreadful GDR propaganda/deterrent photos of the 189 Baltic escape bids that ended in death: bloated, nibbled, washed-up bodies in the shredded remnants of home-made wetsuits, beneath some gloating headline about victims of imperialist ideology. All were young men. One display was filled with mugshots of some of the 4,500 people arrested on the sand or in the water, made to pose pathetically with their DIY submersibles or canvas canoes.

Fewer than 900 escapees made it across the freezing open water, their tales a tribute to determination, ingenuity and sheer dumb luck. Most compelling was the story of Axel Mitbauer, a nineteen-year-old 400m freestyle champion from Leipzig who had already attracted the Stasi after being spotted chatting with West

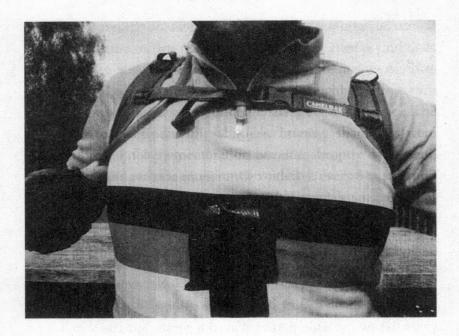

German swimmers at an international event in 1968, an offence that earned him seven weeks of lamp-in-the-face interrogation and a lifetime ban from competitive sport. For a year Mitbauer swam alone in flooded quarries, always under the Stasi's watchful gaze. Then in August 1969, he leapt off a moving train to escape his surveillance team, made his way on foot to the Baltic resort of Boltenhagen, and pitched a tent in a dense copse behind the dunes. After a week-long recce, one warm, clear night he ate two roast chickens, sewed his medals into a pair of flippers and smothered himself in thirty tubes of ersatz Vaseline. You made your own fun in the GDR. But Mitbauer wasn't finished: he crept down to the sand, and waited. Over previous evenings, he had established that the giant searchlights which swept the beach through the hours of darkness were switched off for one minute every hour, to allow them to cool. As soon as the beam died

Mitbauer ran down to the black water and plunged in, clearing a horribly exposed sandbank just before the beam burst back into life and raked across it. Guided by the stars he swam for five hours before fatigue and hypothermia set in; he was saved by clinging to a naval buoy illuminated by an on-board diesel generator whose warmth sustained him until dawn. At 7 a.m., having covered 25km in ten awful hours, Axel Mitbauer was picked up by a West German ferry.

Hooray! Right? Wrong. The Stasi didn't like happy endings, particularly for one of the 600 vilified 'sport-traitors' who fled to the West. One morning, Mitbauer started up the car he'd bought after selling his story to a tabloid, and thought it felt strange: he got out and found all the wheel-nuts had been loosened. After that, and mindful that the Stasi had a history of kidnapping high-profile escapees and defectors and repatriating them, drugged and trussed up in a car boot, he took to sleeping with a chest of drawers pulled across the door. Back in Leipzig, his mother was repeatedly interrogated by Stasi officers, and ultimately ordered to sign a statement that denied her son's existence. After refusing, she immediately lost her job and never worked again.

I pedalled woodenly off down the boardwalk, gazing out at the misty outline of Denmark and the routinely suicidal desperation that had driven so many towards it. If nearly all of them had been young men, then that was only because older ones had wives and children and other escape-deterrent responsibilities, and because women weren't always physically equipped for the challenge. The GDR was as good as Communism got, yet everyone who lived there hated it.

Or not quite everyone. As I'd learned from my nightly reading – my wife had brought out a three-volume library of East European history in exchange for my Winter War book – the Stasi recruited one in six East Germans as informers. Most volunteered without being asked, drawn by what a former Stasi psychologist described as 'the German impulse for order and thoroughness, to make sure your neighbour was doing the right thing'. One in six! Every time I went past a group of old cyclists or a bus full of pensioners I'd look at the faces and wonder which of them once passed the evening with their ears pressed to a wall, notepad in hand. Perhaps that postman had been one of the schoolchildren the Stasi roped in to roam these beaches, reporting on suspicious lingerers. Maybe twinkly-eyed granny over there was a chambermaid who let the Stasi know which guests had brought along an inflatable dinghy. A country full of fear and hate and secrets. What a terrible place to live, the embodiment of that polarising Cold War maxim: you're either with us or against us. No wonder East Germans drank more than twice as much as their hardly abstemious Western brethren.

The Baltic seaside levered itself up into a farewell parade of small hills, then I turned inland and left it behind for ever. Spooling back through our four-week friendship made me feel rather intrepid and resilient: the coastline that had been scattered with slabs of pack ice on our first date was now generously sprinkled with parasols. And then I spooled forward, and felt a little sick. My next scheduled appointment with the sea lay twelve countries and 5,000km away.

11. THE INNER GERMAN BORDER

'From Stettin in the Baltic to Trieste in the Adriatic, an iron curtain has descended across the continent.' Delivered on 6 May 1946, Winston Churchill's address in Fulton, Missouri, introduced what would become a standard coinage for the divide between western Europe and the Soviet-run east. His speech was widely considered the Cold War's opening rhetorical salvo: at the time, most west Europeans were too preoccupied with their own domestic reconstruction to be overly bothered with what the Soviets – still regarded as heroic war-winning allies – were up to over there.

Stettin, for many hundred years a Prussian city, had just been rechristened Szczecin by its newly installed Soviet-sponsored Polish authorities. Trieste, now in Italy, was then a free territory, hard up by the newly declared Socialist Federal Republic of Yugoslavia. Had Churchill's nominal barrier come to fortified fruition, it would have saved me an awful lot of cycling, especially if, as he did,

I chose not to trouble myself with Finland. As it was, over the next three years his metaphorical curtain was yanked hither and thither, ending up hung over a substantially more dilatory border. In 1948, the Yugoslavs split from the Soviets, pushing the curtain east; a year later, it was pushed west through a newly divided Germany.

After the war Germany had been split into four zones, administered by the four principal Allies; not even the feverishly Russophobic Churchill imagined that Stalin would swiftly force through a constitution which established the Soviet zone, covering the entire eastern half of the country, as a separate nation under his effective control. One suspects Winston warmed up for his famous Iron Curtain speech by kicking himself hard and often. At the 1945 Yalta Conference, he and Roosevelt had blithely accepted Stalin's pledge that free post-war elections would be held in all the many East European nations the Red Army had just pushed the Nazis out of. Yalta was intended to fashion a durable peace; instead it provided the Cold War blueprints.

For the first few years of coexistence, East and West Germany shared a fairly open border. But 'Ossis', as Easterners were nicknamed, proved stubbornly resistant to the appeal of a Soviet-ordained way of life, and crossed to the West in ever-thickening droves. For the GDR, fortifying its 1,381km inland frontier represented an admission of ideological and economic defeat, but the scale of the exodus left them no alternative: by the time the Berlin Wall went up on 13 August 1961, 3.5 million East Germans – a sixth of the entire population – had fled to the West.

My first passage across the Iron Curtain proper, the inner-German border as was, came near Schönberg: a beautiful town in name alone. Here the conserved frontier post had been rather clumsily accessorised with a Trabant on its front lawn and a polystyrene sentry mannequin; the museum inside was closed for lunch, but hooding my eyes against the glass doors I read enough captions to understand this crossing's unedifying main business. Throughout the later years of national division, a daily convoy of trucks passed through here from west to east, returning a few hours later. In between, they had been relieved of a cargo of toxic Western waste – from as far away as Italy and Holland – dumped in a ten-million-ton, 100m mountain a couple of miles away, which remains the largest hazardous landfill site in Europe. The whole enterprise was an exercise in cynical irresponsibility: the safe disposal of such material in the West cost around 100 dollars a ton, but Schönberg offered a no-questions-asked service that earned the increasingly impoverished GDR authorities twenty dollars a ton in hard currency. After unification, appalled inspectors discovered fizzing open pits full of leaky, unmarked barrels that had their Geiger counters clicking themselves silly. A recent study found that the incidence of cancer amongst Schönberg workers stands at 80 per cent above the norm.

How the people of the GDR suffered, taken unpleasant advantage of on all sides from their bastard nation's birth. After the war, the victorious Russians found their prize new territory irresistibly strewn with plump metalworks, ripe blast furnaces and other pick-your-own solutions to their domestic industrialisation problem. In two years, over 4,500 East German plants were carefully dismantled, packed into trains and shipped to the motherland, stripping the new country of half its industrial capacity. Many plants had their entire workforce forcibly transported at the same time, sent out to the middle of Russia to bolt their factories back together and then run them. One afternoon I rode for miles along the bed of a railway that had ferried pre-war tourists to the Baltic resorts: the Russians pinched all the tracks and that was that.

The EV13 signs made a brief reappearance, and as was their wont promptly despatched me across many hours of deserted hilly pasture. But by now the MIFA and I were used to having a bit of rough with our smooth, and we took the verdant juddering in our stride. The abrupt transit from bustling suburb to houseless, rolling greenery was, I soon learned, a sure sign that the former inner border had been crossed: the GDR systematically depopulated its frontier regions, ostensibly to create a secure buffer zone against Western aggression, but in truth to hamper escape bids. Almost every day I'd pass a plaque or memorial that marked the spot of some age-old hamlet the authorities had completely erased. They were still at it deep into the 1980s.

EV13 forever criss-crossed the old border, but I rarely lost my bearings. The West had better tarmac, fewer cobbles, more bike paths and a surviving scatter of that Cold War classic, the little yellow sign telling NATO tanks how fast they could go. The east remained visibly poorer – a young 'Ossi' told me later that his 'Wessi' friends earned twice as much doing similar jobs – and was home to tattier cars, more Aldis and a veritable forest of 'cash paid for your old gold' signs. I also became adept at spotting the very Russian GDR border-guard barracks, windowless four-floor hulks half hidden in overgrowth. The most obvious tell, though, was the squat little hat-wearer who still lets East Germans know when it's safe to cross the road. The red/green 'Ampelmann' has been deliberately retained as a non-emotive nostalgic token of the GDR: 'A positive aspect', in the words of its original designer, 'of a failed social order'. I suppose it's a bit like the Nazi people's car that somehow wound up as Herbie the love bug.

Being blessed with those state-ordained wide-open spaces, the eastern borderlands were also home to an irksome abundance of airborne insects. As dusk approached they would flock to EV13 like moths to a rustic bike path, garnishing my every inhalation with wings and legs and spattering me horribly on the descents, like flung handfuls of boiled rice. On one such late afternoon, my phone buzzed while I was palming thorax pulp off my thighs at the foot of a big green hill. A text message: two of my oldest friends had arrived in Berlin to stay with a third who lived there, and were asking if I wished to join them for a halfway spot of rest and recuperation.

I frowned pensively at the screen, smeared an aphid across my cheek, gazed around at the plump and empty hillsides, then thought: Yeah, all right. And with that I pedalled into a lazy sunset with the invigorated air of a man about to get drunk for four days, and who doesn't yet know that there's a national rail strike on, which will require him to spend one of them cycling very soberly all the way to Hamburg, then lashing his bike to the back of a long-distance coach.

On 21 September 1990, my wife and I crossed from Poland into what was still – just – the GDR, our passports stamped with a treasured Cold War souvenir by a demob-happy old border guard, offloading a good thirty years' worth of pent-up smiling. We bumped onwards through the East German night down a Nazi-era concrete-slab motorway and hit West Berlin, our journal records, at 4.45 a.m. What a thrilling shock to the system after weeks of grey, washed-out meagreness, of dumplings and cratered streets that died after dark. In East Berlin people were shuffling groggily out to work. Across what was left of the Wall, they were shuffling groggily back to bed. Swept up by this manic, cosmopolitan blurt of twenty-four-hour neon decadence we went to the Intercontinental Hotel to cash a traveller's cheque – what a gigantic pain those things were – then proceeded directly to an all-night café-bar and ordered a meal whose written description is smudged by my wife's grateful tears: 'Fresh rolls, parma ham, watermelon balls on a bed of ice cubes, brought to us by an enormous gay punk.' We slept in the car for two hours, and then did something I still can't quite believe.

A couple of weeks earlier, a sighting of another copy of Comrade Shoestring on a neighbouring Polish breakfast table had led us into conversation with an expansive American named Ron. He'd just come from Berlin, and had stayed there in an apartment belonging to a journalist called Werner who was currently abroad: 'I don't know him at all, it was a friend-of-a-friend thing. An old guy next door has the key, Herr Dumke. If you can sweet-talk him I'd recommend it.' Can you imagine? We tutted for days after at Ron's shamelessness. But our morals were clearly loosened by exhaustion and the reckless Berlin vibe, because off we drove to the appointed low-rise apartment block and knocked up Old Man Dumke.

Having made the mistake of passing her German O level, my wife did the talking. Her words were few and none of them diminished the craggy Herr Dumke's towering scepticism; an already painful situation took an agonising turn when another passing resident butted into our doorstep negotiations in fluent English. 'But Werner is almost *more* than a friend to us,' I heard myself tell him. 'Really sort of a brother. And what a journalist. We keep all Werner's articles in a special red box.' The resident nodded, then exchanged words for a series of elaborate scoffing sounds with Herr Dumke. 'He tells me that Werner is the last name of his neighbour. Your sort-of-a-brother's first name in fact is Johannes.' How very pleased he looked. Perhaps too pleased, because to everyone's astonishment Herr Dumke immediately snatched a key from his hallway shelf and dropped it into my wife's hand.

We stayed there for two nights, ringing JW's lovely bath with accumulated Communism and staining his sofa with sweet-and-sour sauce during takeaway-lapped evenings before his massive TV. Then we belatedly came to our senses, and checked into a suburban campsite before our friend three times removed whistled in through his front door and forced us into a Goldilocks-pattern escape.

The campsite backed onto the Berlin Wall – away from the city centre, its 155km perimeter remained largely intact – and I was thrilled when our tent-neighbours, two young British miners, led me to a man-sized cleft someone had battered through it. The barbed wire had been removed from the yawning swathe of death-strip behind, but the watchtowers and searchlights were still in place, along with the patrol paths and a wide ribbon of footprint-spotting sand. 'Just think of all the people who were killed right here,' mused one of the miners, though in fact not that many had been – fewer than a hundred would-be escapees were shot dead trying to cross the GDR's best-defended border, typically young men acting on a drunken whim.

The miners had driven their Morris Ital all the way from Durham to pay homage to history and its victims. It was the first time either of them had left the country, and they were always getting lost. 'I know I'm laughing, because you've got to laugh, see, or else you'll cry,' said one after a five-hour return drive to the campsite from the city's Reichstag museum. 'And I can't be crying.' Yet they remained endlessly moved by their pilgrimage, and one night read us a poem they'd written at Checkpoint Charlie, which I regret to confess is unkindly reviewed in our journal.

On Christmas Eve 1989, the iconic Brandenburg Gate was opened after forty years marooned in no man's land: one of our friends jumped in his car and drove all the way to Berlin, and when we watched the New Year's Eve celebrations on telly, there he was on top of it, cavorting amongst the mulleted throng. Ten months on that inebriated headiness still hung in the air, and my wife and I spent a slightly dizzy few days trying to process Berlin's chaotic changing of the guard. Enterprising East Germans had turned their front rooms into bars and cafés. Poles hawked Russian vodka and hunks of demolished wall on trestle tables. Every street was home to a scatter of abandoned Trabants the colour of brown coal and concrete, and Checkpoint Charlie had been smashed to pieces. Then the weather took a tent-unfriendly turn for the worse, and a department-store cashier snapped my credit card in two before my eyes. It seemed a very New Berlin cue to move on.

I suppose we thought that soon everywhere in Eastern Europe would be like Berlin, but if we did we were wrong. In fact, Berlin wasn't like anywhere else even then, and still isn't today – least of all like anywhere else in Germany. Throughout my halfway mini-break, my friends and I were surrounded by hip young urbanites in a completely mullet-*frei* environment. It must be the world capital of bearded vaping. Everyone I met worked in new media or music, or said they did – whenever we invited people to come out for brunch or an early-evening beer they seemed suspiciously available. In *Peep Show* terms, Berlin is a city of Jeremys marooned in a nation of Marks. My friends and I awkwardly straddled both camps, drinking at lunchtime, mooching about parks with kebabs in hand, then photographing war memorials and staying up until 8.45 a.m. to audit the ongoing British general election with our reading glasses pressed to a data-wall of screens.

They were all rather taken aback by my appearance, with especial reference to an advanced state of emaciation – I now weighed less than I did when we'd all left school – and that blistered, plum-nosed wino tan. The MIFA's all-round poxy tininess was if anything a greater shock. All three of them had a quick go up the crowded pavement and two nearly came to grief, scattering hipsters into the gutter. None could even begin to understand how I had successfully ridden this thing so very, very far. Watching the slapstick struggles of my closest peers I could have almost doubted it myself. Almost. In truth, I've always been a significantly more impressive character than any of them, in one case embarrassingly so.

On my final full day we took the MIFA – by tram – to the fabled Russian war memorial in Treptower Park, a last enclave of Soviet ceremonial might. Having passed through Gdańsk, where the war started, I was keen to visit the place that more compellingly than any other marked its European end. I had imagined us pushing my bike across forsaken granite parade grounds drifted with last year's leaves, and was therefore more than slightly surprised to find the approaching streets noisily alive with people and honking cars. The surprise was magnified when it became clear that the crowds surging in through the park's monumental gates were almost exclusively Russian, many waving national flags old and new. Somehow – let's blame the brain-draining horror of George Osborne's triumphant smirk – I had completely failed to grasp that this visit coincided with the seventieth anniversary of Victory Day.

Inside, the grounds were filled with babushka folk songs and traditional costume. The grassy slopes up to the colossal centre-piece statue – a sword-wielding Red Army hero with a rescued child in his arms and a splintered swastika under a mighty bronze boot – lay buried under scarlet bouquets and banners. Where had all these Russians come from, and who had brought them here? KGB Major V. Putin had been stationed in Dresden for five years when the Wall fell, and as an unusually fervent Soviet loyalist must have been shattered by the experience. Putin has claimed that when a mob gathered around his office – directly opposite the city's Stasi HQ – he strode out brandishing a revolver and repelled them singlehanded. 'This is Soviet territory and you're standing on our border,' he quotes himself shouting. 'I'm serious when I say that I will shoot trespassers!' That's his story. In mine he dresses up as a nun, hides in a cupboard and wets himself. But Vlad's version of the truth is probably more significant than the reality: let us just agree that in the context of his formative experiences in the service of a doomed empire and its showpiece colony, here is a man with issues.

By an accident happy or otherwise, we had pitched up at Trep-tower Park on the most auspicious Berlin day since the Wall came down. Perhaps in the memorial's entire history, for the unregulated public celebration around us bore no resemblance to the GDR era's dourly regimented Victory Day parades, depicted in archive photographs dotted about the grounds. It was a most confusing spectacle, and I struggled to distribute my emotions proportionately. Sympathy, of course, for the 80,000 Soviet troops who died in the house-to-house Battle of Berlin, a futile end-game tragedy with Hitler already bunkered down on his sofa with Eva B and a cocked pistol. Relief for a city – a nation, a continent, a planet – saved from Nazism; we saw a banner in German thanking their Russian liberators in these precise terms. But also a distinct unease at the mood of tub-thumping Russian patriotism, a far cry from the sombre, lest-we-forget Cenotaph vibe, which implanted a suspicion that the crowds were here not just to mourn those who died defeating Hitler, but their resurgent nation's recent conquest of Crimea, however notionally indirect.

For the elderly Berliners out here in the eastern suburbs, how strange it must have felt to see their overlords parading the streets once more. Not just rubbing their noses in those stinky old Stasi memories, but reminding them once again that all this was their own fault, for starting a really terrible war and losing it. Awk-ward! In the weeks ahead I would often wonder if the joy of unification had been tempered by Germany's difficult history: hooray, we're all together again, let's relive those special days when we were last one big happ . . . Actually, let's not do that.

But there wasn't a hint of trouble with the Russians, because Berlin is a city of well-trained amnesiacs. It's easier to forget than forgive. That evening we went to a bar that told its long history in a multilingual wall chart, beginning in 1500 and proceeding in regular instalments until Mrs Muller took over behind the beer taps in 1927. Then a conspicuous void before 1989, when the director Sergio Leone popped in for a pint. This was a city with an awful lot of bad shit to gloss over, and the Return of the Russians simply called for another coat of mental whitewash. Most locals I talked to even struggled to remember exactly where the wall had run. I can only assume I was infected, because on Sunday afternoon I pulled the MIFA off a train at Boizenburg, pedalled tentatively out through the lengthening, small-town shadows and wondered what on earth I was up to.

'Hello, I am sorry to say this but you are late.'

It was 7.30 p.m., and I had very recently established that the River Elbe was not, as my maps implied, crossed at this lonely point by a bridge, but by a ferry which had stopped running ninety minutes previously. I was in the old East, and the only hotels across a generous radius lay in Hitzacker, in the old West, whose half-timbered homes sat soaking up the last golden rays of sunset across the spangled water. Since setting off I'd only had a single rest day prior to the Berlin Hiatus; how difficult it was to readjust my mind and body after a ninety-six-hour reboot. I rejoined the route wearing civvies, and in body and soul felt like I ought to be pootling blearily home from a friend's house after an all-nighter. Instead, I had ridden 42km with a vestigial hangover while wodges of underpant inveigled themselves into every tender fold and valley; now I learned that hitting the sack in Hitzacker would require an additional 35km round trip via a definite actual bridge, a prospect that caused me to desecrate this peaceful and becoming scene with an unhinged Viking battle roar. This had attracted the attention of a tubby old gent in socks and sandals, who pattered up the jetty and responded with undeserved temperance.

What followed should be a lesson to all travellers in need: deafening self-pity is your friend. The old man beckoned me to follow him down to the water's edge, where a battered little tin dinghy bobbed among the reeds. He clambered in, relieved it of several bucketfuls of brown water and on the fifth attempt tugged the outboard motor into smoky, spluttering life. 'Please,' he shouted, holding out an oily hand. I heaved the MIFA in then followed it, and off we buzzed through the sunlit, lightly misted waters, across what for most of his life had been the most fiercely defended, lethal stretch of aquatic no man's land in the whole of Europe. The GDR operated a fleet of thirty high-speed patrol boats to police the Elbe's share of the border, captained by men in leather trench coats who thought nothing of mowing down west-bound swimmers. More than 200 East Germans died trying to cross frontier rivers.

My ferryman deposited me at Hitzacker's quayside; I offered him effusive thanks and a crumpled ten-euro note. He frowned at this evidently unanticipated reward for a while, then swept it into his pocket and said: 'If you are here again, and ferry is finish, you know where is my boat.' An hour before, struggling to relearn the art of long-term leg rotation, I wondered if I'd ever reacclimatise to life on EV13. An hour later, sitting behind a *kalbsschnitzel* the size of a MIFA wheel in a dining-room filled with murmuring pensioners, it was as if I'd never been away.

*

I followed the broad, lazy Elbe and its successors for a bright and blustery few days, criss-crossing from east to west on a succession of ferries. With the river largely out of bounds, the dead-end settlements on either side had withered dramatically in the Cold War years; one or two especially vulnerable towns on the eastern bank had been entirely walled in like pocket Berlins, to deter escapees. A few late-era observation towers survived and I climbed up one, a 10m stub of concrete with a row of metal-framed windows round the top. It was predictably cheerless in there: cramped, bleak and cold, with streaked and greasy views of the sunlit realm of free-roaming plenty it was nominally built to monitor. You'd imagine that the 47,000-odd GDR border guards who sat cooped up for long and miserable years in places like this must routinely have hatched schemes to flee to that tantalising promised land, and you'd be right. More than 2,500 border troops escaped, despite (or perhaps because of) a rolling programme of ideological indoctrination that filled an extraordinary 50 per cent of their training schedule.

My favourite related story was that of Jürgen Lange, a teenage border guard on national service. One night in May 1969, patrolling a remote and mountainous stretch of death-strip with his sergeant – guards were never trusted out alone – Lange watched in horror as the older man suddenly scooted off and began to shin up the last-line mesh fence. Border troops were under strict orders to shoot to kill in these situations, and had no excuse for missing: all had passed an advanced marksmanship test requiring them to hit two moving targets with four shots at a range of 200m, by day or night. At least thirty-seven guards were fatally gunned down by colleagues in the act of escape. On dutiful reflex, Lange raised his rifle; then lowered it, and watched the sergeant drop down and disappear into the darkened land of opportunity. He himself had never even thought about escaping, but having failed to shoot his errant colleague knew he'd now face imprisonment and a lifetime of menial disgrace. After an agonising ten minutes, Lange set off in the sergeant's footsteps. When the West Germans picked him up and took away his gun, they found it wouldn't fire: the sergeant had taken the precaution of disabling it before the pair went out on patrol.

Calves and foals were stumbling about and meadows were being mown; nesting storks spread their impressive wings atop every other chimney and telegraph pole. A tireless headwind chased painterly white clouds across the blue sky and sent me down into a crouch, the MIFA's chorus of groans and shrieks singing through the frame at close quarters. With starvation and violent death a less pressing concern these days, I had to make do with a cocktail of humdrum irritants. Why (oh why oh why) had the proprietors of even the humblest guest house subscribed to that inexplicable fashion for topping their every bed with an artful cairn of decorative pillows? It was impossible to relocate these plump stupidities anywhere that didn't result in a nocturnal prat-fall and a faceful of beaded velvet. And why did hotel curtains never quite meet? I was forever coming to in the small hours with a piercing shaft of streetlight playing across my face, and had a recurring dream at the end of which I woke up in a shop window.

Travelling through rural Germany in May delivered an improb-able further nemesis: asparagus. It was two weeks since 'SPARGEL!' began appearing on roadside shacks manned by some careworn farmer's wife; by now the word was scrawled with abandon across every restaurant chalkboard, and poised to trip from every waiter's tongue. Now, no one appreciates a frothing stream of heavily tainted urine more than I do, and it was certainly welcome to be offered a food group that wasn't pork or potato. Except *spargel* was never an offer. It simply appeared unbidden on every plate, served with an almost pornographic leer and announced with wet-lipped,

sibilant relish: '... *mit spargel*'. It didn't help that the native preference is for white asparagus reared under plastic black-out tunnels,
so my schnitzel was never garnished with wholesome greenery, but
buried under a sheaf of flaccid corpse fingers. They even stuck it
all over my breakfast, and I came to dread parting filled rolls. It
was soggy and bitter and made my pee reek like a tyre fire. But at
the same time it was More Food, so in it all went.

The settlements grew sparser and lonelier, their elderly residents supplied by mobile butchers and bakers whose vans would
pull up outside the church, honk horns and wait for business. In
the old West, towns that hadn't been worth an Allied bombardment were full of colourful medieval homes, their timbers appealingly decorated with religious homilies in elaborate Gothic script.

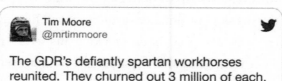

Tim Moore
@mrtimmoore

The GDR's defiantly spartan workhorses
reunited. They churned out 3 million of each.

Over the old border, the GDR trappings lingered: enamel-shaded streetlights like something out of the Gulag, smutted-porridge house render, a lost colony of Trabants in a concrete barn. And an awful lot of cobbles, which doubtless predated the Communists but must surely have appealed to them, with their spartan durability and no-pain-no-gain administration of progress. By mid-morning everything from my brain to my breakfast would be shaken into a pulpy coalescence that settled just above the buttocks.

Two or three times a day I'd wheel past a surviving watchtower or some other big-picture souvenir, a sprawling rank of derelict checkpoints by a former motorway crossing, or the huge and hideous scar of an open-cast brown-coal mine. There was usually a big stark sign to let you know where the old border had lain, saying something like 'Germany and Europe were divided here until 7 September 1991' (with 1.4 million mines to clear, the authorities didn't reconnect some areas until 1994). If there wasn't, I'd often find a memorial to somebody who died crossing it. One of the most affecting honoured Kurt Lichtenstein, a fifty-year-old West German journalist killed in October 1961 while compiling a report on the ongoing erection of what the GDR always referred to as 'the Anti-Fascist Protection Rampart'. Lichtenstein was a lifelong hard-left socialist disillusioned by the increasingly authoritarian East German regime, and well known to them as a result – there is nothing a Commie despises more than a red of a different stripe. When Lichtenstein stepped across a shallow trench near an unfinished stretch of wall he was machine-gunned by guards who had been tracking his every movement, falling dead with his head and shoulders in western territory. The next morning's GDR press honoured the guard who fired the fatal shots with a smiling portrait and the headline, 'Well done Peter!'

Most border-zone villages had opted, quite forgivably, to eradicate all evidence of the hated, bloodstained wall, but I rode past occasional sections nobly preserved as A Warning From History. The first, at Hötensleben, caught me unawares: I rounded a parade of suburban homes and suddenly found myself in the death-strip, looking down a long, broad grass corridor studded with girder-pyramid tank traps and observation towers, hemmed in by mesh fences and that whitewashed concrete final frontier. I dismounted and pushed the MIFA up the concrete dog-handler path, by turns alarmed, sobered and thrilled. I wasn't alone: how bizarre to see the Anti-Fascist Protection Rampart patrolled by very different people walking very different dogs. Ignoring the loud inner voice that urged restraint and respect, I propped the MIFA against the wall proper, balanced my camera on a tank trap and trotted back to the bike.

I had blundered across my camera's voice-activated shutter option one lonely, long-ago night in a Finnish log cabin, and since employed it with selfie-tastic abandon. Its Korean programmers had endowed this feature with a three-word trigger vocabulary; the inexplicable 'whisky' had never once worked. I struck a dramatic pose, one hand on the MIFA's saddle and my granite stare fixed on a distant watchtower, then uttered the most dependable shutter cue.

'Shoot.'

Nothing. I tried the other.

'Capture.'

A windy day such as this generally demanded a raised voice; I upped the volume and tried again.

'SHOOT.' Silence. 'CAPTURE!' Nope. 'SHOOT! SHOOT! SHOOOOOOOT!'

I can't explain why it took me so long to grasp that these weren't the words for a man in a GDR shirt to be yelling across a death-strip dotted with elderly dog-walkers. By the time I did, though, I had bellowed them each at least a dozen times, rising in a spittle-flecked crescendo of furious decibels. The precise moment of realisation coincided with the shutter's overdue click. It is difficult to describe the crumpled contrition apparent in the resultant photo, because there isn't any: I'm laughing hysterically.

Tim Moore
@mrtimmoore

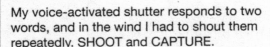

My voice-activated shutter responds to two words, and in the wind I had to shout them repeatedly. SHOOT and CAPTURE.

The terrain had been limbering up for a while – a hill here, a valley there – and one afternoon it suddenly leapt to its feet and started doing star-jumps. My German editor Rainer had warned me about the Harz Mountains, and after all that Finno–Baltic flatness it was certainly novel to find myself up in the saddle through villages stacked either side of a gushing Alpine torrent, with background toots from a narrow-gauge railway. Having looked reasonably sensible for weeks my MIFA seemed once more comically unfit for purpose, but to give the bike its due it conquered the hairpins with something near assurance: as later climbs confirmed, in low gear I could now ride up a 10 per cent slope for hours, albeit with immense sloth.

'SHOOT!'

Just look at our happy faces by that 600m sign: the highest my little MIFA had been in its life, I fancied, forgetting it had recently been in an aeroplane.

At the top, EV13's embarrassment of rogue route-planners lured me off down a logging trail that opened into a buttercup-strewn, Julie-Andrews-ready mountain pasture. I was utterly lost and a misty twilight had begun to creep up from the lowlands of Saxony; a day that had started with sun cream was ending in goose-pimples. Yet somehow I knew that Germany wouldn't let me down. I whistled bumpily down the tilted meadow and there, at its loneliest fundament, stood a little white bench with HOTEL GRÜNE TANNE painted on it in Gothic script. A trail of further benches strung out through a steeply pitched forest led me improbably to the eponymous establishment, and an hour later a waitress in an embroidered dirndl was coaxing pallid stalks of *spargel* between my helpless lips.

What kind of Communist would I have been? Popping out of the womb in 1964 would have made me a born and bred state socialist, with twenty-five years of formative indoctrination to look forward to. It was a thought that had accompanied me for months, and crystallised as I walked through the homespun border museum in a village hall at Tettenborn, still breathless from a wild 54kmh descent that had loosened my handlebars. On the one hand I'm a bit of a coward, so active rebellion would never have been on the agenda. Neither would escape. One diorama detailed a local man's attempt to drive his family through a heavily fortified railway frontier in a lumber truck clad in home-made armour plating: I looked at its stricken scale representation, peppered in bullet holes with a wheel sheared off, and knew that man would not have been me. But on the other hand, I've been insubordinate from a very young age. My earliest primary school memory is being told by a teacher to hold my tongue, and obliging with a thumb and forefinger and a horrible sarky grin. I can't see that sort of business going down well in the GDR's semi-compulsory state-run junior organisations, the Young Pioneers and the Free German Youth: from the age of six upwards, two-thirds of East German children spent a couple of evenings a week grassing up neighbours for watching Western telly and pledging en masse to 'deepen friendship with the Soviet Union and defend socialism against imperialist attack'.

I found one possible metier in a display case full of GDR propaganda magazines, stuffed by the thousand into aluminium 'hand rockets' that shed their load over the West with the aim of demoralising border guards. A photo of Brian Jones from the Rolling Stones in an SS uniform above a no doubt jauntily withering caption. A beckoning comrade dolly-bird on one side of a double-page spread; a threatening Soviet mega-missile on the other. Within the constraints of the system I could have had some fun working on these, I thought: an appealingly surreal office environment, with no harm done except to the enemy litter patrols – in forty-five years, precisely one West German border guard defected. But in truth I'd never have got the job without that vital state-approved youth background. In all likelihood, I would have wound up doing something menial and harmless, making MIFAs by day and getting through the evenings with a few half-litres of sour pilsner. Nude.

The museum was a one-stop encapsulation of the GDR's creepy, timeless weirdness. A case full of cheap children's toys and toilet-paper comics told a tale of impoverished stagnation; everything seemed rooted in some 1960s pound-shop dystopia. And how painful for Germans of all people to live with the unevolving shoddiness, the two-stroke Trabants and spoon-brake MIFAs. I learned here that those cylindrical-shafted golf-tee observation towers were made from stacked sewer-pipe segments, and regularly toppled over. The Stasi reports that wallpapered one room bore dates that spanned the nation's five-decade existence, yet all seemed to have been banged out on the same forms using the same typewriter.

'Trust is good, but surveillance is better.' The Stasi's unofficial motto kept 97,000 employees – a workforce one and a half times the size of the army – very busy for forty years. They monitored a third of all East Germans, some six million people, and in doing so accumulated files that required 125 miles of shelf space: seventeen million sheets of paper per mile, with a total weight of 6,250 tons. In a few brief decades, the Stasi filed more documented records than the whole of Germany had managed to accrue since the Middle Ages.

Dissident groups were so densely infiltrated that by the mid-1980s every other demonstrator was a spy, creating an impression of gathering public discontent that began to concern many senior officers. Still they couldn't stop themselves. The scale of surveillance, and its petrifying, lunatic scope, knew no bounds.

After the Wall came down and the archives were laid bare, people learned that two-thirds of the nation's church leaders had been informers. They found entire rooms stacked with neatly labelled jam jars, each containing a shred of fabric: the Stasi had kept a national 'scent database' of unreliable citizens, enabling them to send sniffer dogs into suspected meeting areas and establish who had been there. Some samples were obtained from swabs placed on chairs in Stasi interview rooms, others from socks and underwear stolen from suspects' apartments. For good measure, while the Stasi spooks were in the flat, they would often spray the floor with a radioactive tracking substance that has since been linked to several deaths.

But even interesting people lead fundamentally banal lives, and Stasi surveillance was all about quantity, not quality. Here is a representative sample from the minders who tracked Lutz Rathenow, a dissident writer:

Rathenow then crossed the street and ordered a sausage at a kiosk. The following conversation occurred:

RATHENOW: A sausage, please.
VENDOR: With or without a roll?
RATHENOW: With, please.
VENDOR: And mustard?
RATHENOW: Yes, please.
Further exchanges did not occur.

When peace activist Vera Lengsfeld looked through her liberated Stasi files, she discovered that a record had been kept of her preferred washing-up liquid (of the two brands available in the GDR). She discovered that a jar of her odoriferous essence had been stored on a shelf. And on the list of sixty Stasi officers who had been permanently assigned to track her every move, she discovered the father of her two sons, a poet she had been married to for thirteen years. When she confronted him, he admitted that he had been working for the Stasi since his teenage years, and had met, wooed and wed her on their orders.

Outside the museum I tightened the handlebars beneath a huge plastic GDR emblem, and concluded that anyone reared in East Germany had earned the right to hate everyone and everything, and to take that wounded bitterness to the grave. Yet here's the extraordinary thing: having threaded this way and that over the old border for so long, I'd established that East Germans of all ages were notably cheerier than their western counterparts. When someone shouted encouragement from a bus stop, or slipped an extra bread roll into my bakery bag with a wink, or offered me a boat ride over the Elbe, I knew which side of the old border I was on. More than once in the old East my breakfast came accompanied with a *'Guten tag, Herr Moore,'* an unheard of personalised honour for the fly-by-night touring cyclist. If you were in a long supermarket queue, and the sweaty foreign cyclist in front of you dopily failed to notice that a cashier had just opened another till, what would you do? No offence, but unless you're East German I can't see you tapping him politely on the shoulder to bring it to his attention. Perhaps it was a legacy of the comrade days; perhaps an outpouring of post-Stasi bonhomie. Either way it was most welcome.

The contrast was especially marked when I ran into an almost unbroken procession of bank holidays. In the old West they took their front doors off and repainted them on trestle tables. In the old East they pulled trolleys full of beer very loudly into the woods. Late one sunny afternoon I clattered down a barley field – thanks, EV13 – shot through a gap in the hedgerow and ran straight into a gathering of farmers and their families, busy emptying a tractor-trailer piled high with booze. I dare say more sober, more Western people might have found this encounter less amusing. An hour or so afterwards I enjoyed that stubbornly unforgettable Bon Jovi serenade, at least I think I did. To be frank my recall of these days is tinged with delirium: the shops were rarely open and for the thick end of a week I got by on petrol-station snacks. Once even the petrol stations were shut and I rode all day on two warm cans of Magic Man and a forgotten, pannier-matured salami roll. From then on I sidled shiftily along the guest-house buffets with an open rucksack and a reedy hum: 'On the twelfth day of breakfast, the cyclist stole from me . . .'

I was a connoisseur of frontier porn by now, a hopeless border-phile. I'd ride past a farm and note that its sheep were fenced in by recycled sheets of Anti-Fascist Protection Rampart mesh. I could cast an expert eye across the land and chart out the border by colour alone: the twenty-five-year-old trees that had annexed the death-strip were a conspicuously paler green than their senior neighbours. In another twenty-five the watchtowers might have all been swallowed by trunks and leaves, but for now they stood clear. One point for a second-generation BT-9; two if it still had its searchlight. Yet even in trainspotting mode it was impossible to tune out the jarring malevolence of such structures in this land-scape of plump and cheerful hills: Big Brother keeping tabs on the Teletubbies. The contrast was turned up to eleven when harmonious old witch-hat castle towers began to partner them on every other horizon.

Sometimes – OK, once – the border threw up a cheeringly human story with a happy ending. Most escape bids, even the successful ones, were breathless dramas full of bullets and barking Alsatians. But the border-side village of Böseckendorf produced a two-part Ealing comedy: in 1961 and 1963, more than a quarter of its residents sauntered cheekily into the West completely undetected, when heavy snowfall buried the minefields and all but the top few feet of the fences. I didn't have long to savour this jaunty tale. A couple of hours later, I paused at a memorial to a

GDR border guard killed in 1962 during a confused confrontation with Western counterparts. An everyday tragedy with a shocking epilogue: in 1998, the West German guard who had fired the fatal shot was found dead near his car with a bullet hole above his right eye, the precise injury suffered by his victim. Some months earlier, a former Stasi officer had unsuccessfully attempted to launch a prosecution against the guard over the 1962 incident. The murder remains unsolved.

The blue-skied bank holidays brought a million bikes out to play, clotting the towpaths along what my EV13 route guide winningly billed as 'The Salty Werra'. I later passed the extraordinary, sparkling hills of white potash slag that explain why this river ranks amongst the most polluted in Europe – one of them so huge it was marked on my map as Monte Kali, after the mining firm that piled it up there. You won't be astonished to learn on which side of the old border this towering alien spoil-heap is located, but you might be to hear that it's still growing by 900 tons an hour. For days the air was thick with a not displeasing tang of phosphates, and the Werra's poisoned waters tumbled appealingly over weirs and wound past hillside castles. Throughout the afternoons my fellow cyclists would pull over and haul picnics from their panniers, offering cautious nods as I barrelled past. What different breeds we were, Pootling Couples versus Man on a Mission. No contest: for a week I was never once overtaken, in a race that no one else knew they were in.

The MIFA's stunted gawkiness remained an enduring burden. I would shuffle into a guest-house reception and meet a good-hearted welcome from a proprietor curious to know what had brought a foreign cyclist to his or her door; then they'd come out to show me where to put the bike for the night, and helplessly glaze over the minute they saw it. I'd carry on talking but their nods and hums were automatic, as if the MIFA had told them all they needed to know: this guy's story isn't worth hearing. Until one afternoon, when someone very gratifyingly decided it was.

'I think u are cycling thru Coburg. We are in Sangerhausen, that's not too far. Would be a pleasure to welcome u here!! I am Peter by the way.'

As one of 493 million diehard me fanatics around the world, Peter had been following my progress on Twitter. The first message he delivered through this medium was pleasing enough as it stood, but those that followed ramped my excitement up to critical levels. The 'we' in question was the Mitteldeutsche Fahrradwerke, referred to henceforth by Peter as 'the MIFA'. Incredibly, they were still making bikes at the same factory that churned out my 900 all those years before; delightfully, they wished me to bring it along for a tour. So on a silent, small-town Sunday, beneath a hot, blue sky gently streaked with cirrus, there we were alone at Pressig station, waiting for the first of three trains that would take me and my plucky little bike to meet its maker.

Sangerhausen lay deep in the old East – much further from my route than Peter had cheerfully implied – and the ponderous journey there exposed me for the first time to the hard-core, full-strength GDR, away from those borderlands diluted by proximity to the old West. The stations we clanked through were arrestingly grubby and decrepit, and the passengers who got on at them incrementally more impoverished: I saw my first pairs of scuffed German trainers, and an unshaven man with holes in his tracksuit knees. Outside the window a parade of dead factories and warehouses slid past, their lower reaches smothered in half-arsed aerosol doodling. It was the most at home I'd felt since setting off.

Sangerhausen announced itself with pyramids of mining slag and an invasive sense of heavy-industrial decline; I wheeled the bike into a cavernous ticket hall dominated by a faintly psychedelic Communist mosaic of multicoloured coal miners, tractor drivers and – yay! – road-race cyclists working together, self-evidently in vain, for a better future. A young man with a happy face and a fag in his fist waved from the doorway, and thus was I introduced to the very splendid Peter Meyer, MIFA's PR and social-media manager. We shook hands, wedged my MIFA into the boot of his car and set off for the hotel I was most kindly being put up at, in order to refresh myself for whatever was expected of me at the following day's factory tour.

On the way, driving past rows and rows of *Khrushchyovka* tenements, Peter gave me a rundown of Sangerhausen's post-unification travails: after the mainstay coal mines closed down, most young people had moved west in search of jobs and better pay. In twenty-five years the population had fallen by almost half, to 25,000. The one chink of light, rather wonderfully, was 'the MIFA' – with 800 workers, the bike plant was now the largest employer in town. To my immense satisfaction, as he dropped me off in the hotel car park Peter confirmed that the factory retained the address that had leapt out at me during my scattergun pre-departure Googling: 33, Juri-Gagarin-strasse. With a toot he was off; I patted my 900 on the saddle and we exchanged a silent vow not to show each other up in the morning.

'That's OK, that's OK.'

This was Peter's favourite English phrase, and twelve hours later he gave it an extended airing as we launched our tour in undignified fashion, bundling my MIFA over its birthplace's 8-foot perimeter fence after failing to wedge it through the staff-entrance turnstile. My bike's grubby dishevelment was OK, my cheeky request for a complimentary factory-workshop service was OK, and my light blue GDR jersey was OK.

'Yes, that colour was national sport colour of DDR, but today we don't care.' Peter shrugged blithely, then pulled a very large camera from his holdall and asked me and the bike to pose before the disappointingly bland white concrete sheds that housed 'the MIFA'. 'That's history, that's OK.'

'I'm very glad to hear you say so,' I said, and ripped off a curling strip of gaffer tape to lay bare the notorious emblem, looking around in vain for a plinth mounted with the three millionth 900, or a colossal hero worker holding a 20-inch wheel aloft in his tarnished fist.

When I looked back at Peter I saw him frozen with his face to the viewfinder.

'You have maybe a jacket?' he asked at length.

My jersey had suddenly become much less OK. As I pulled a fleece from my rucksack Peter mumbled something about creating a correct impression for his social-media publicity, and evidently harboured more immediate concerns: when we walked towards the reception area a while later, he motioned at me rather animatedly to zip the fleece tight up to my neck.

My bike was whisked away by a man in a boiler suit, and as we wandered into the factory Peter filled me in on MIFA's improbable survival. Following the most recent of many flirtations with bankruptcy, the firm had been rescued by an old-school industrialist who had, I gathered, made a fortune from fan belts. His turnaround formula was in evidence all around us: electric bikes, high-end off-roaders and other niche machines, dangling by their front wheels from a production conveyor lined with diligent unisex technicians. In common with almost every other European bicycle producer, MIFA is an assembler rather than a manufacturer: it doesn't make any bike bits at all, but rather bolts together Far Eastern components. The shiny floors and muted hums and tinkles associated with this process imparted an almost surgical vibe, distantly removed from the oil-stained cacophony that would have reigned in the slapdash, mass-production age of the MIFA 900.

We repaired to a down-lit executive meeting room, and over coffee I reminded Peter how very keen I was to interview a veteran employee – a living link with my bike. The night before, at my prompting, Peter had told me that quite a few MIFA staff from the old GDR days still worked at the plant, but he appeared to have regretted saying so ever since. 'That's OK,' he now told me, with a face that said otherwise; a while later he returned with a man of about my age, who wore a smile, a suit and a pair of frameless glasses.

'This is our sales manager Dieter, he is working here for thirty years.'

Like most Germans, Dieter seemed painstakingly normal, a *vorsprung durch* technocrat. There was, however, a very weird tinge to our ensuing chat, and not simply because it was conducted through the medium of Peter, the sole bilinguist amongst us.

Q: 'So when you started at MIFA, what was your job?'

A: 'Since year of unity, 1990, he is the sales manager.'

Q: 'Yes, but before that, before 1990?'

A: 'That's OK, Dieter is now my boss. You will write about Grace e-bikes and Steppenwolf MTBs? These are my brands at the MIFA.'

And so it went on. I'd ask how things had changed since he started working here, and listen to the masterfully evasive Dieter-Peter tell me at length about the recent global resurgence of local bike shops and their influence on retail strategy. A query on the MIFA 900 series spawned an address on the domestic electric-bike market. As Dieter-Peter held smoothly forth on something else I hadn't asked about, I glazed over and began picturing the MIFA sales office in the years of centralised monopoly: a lot of graphs with 'SO WHAT?' and 'WHO CARES?' scrawled up each axis, and a wall-chart headed 'THE COMPETITION' showing one stick-man pushing another around in a wheelbarrow. When I refocused the room was silent; I cleared my throat and gave it one last shot.

'Dieter, I really want to know what it was like here at, um, at the MIFA before 1990. In the Communist era. In the DDR. Please tell me.'

Peter shifted a little in his leather-backed swivel chair before translating my query.

'*Tarvashure!*'

Dieter's blurted response unleashed such a burst of hilarity – even the multiply-pierced social-media assistant who had just joined us slapped at the artfully distressed denim sheathing his thighs – that I automatically joined in.

'It's funny, yes?' said Peter, when he had regained his composure. 'Because . . . Gustav Schur, we call him Täve, Täve Schur, he was big DDR legend of bicycle racing – you know him, of course?'

I laughed again, alone this time, then stopped quite suddenly and said: 'No. No I don't.'

'That's OK,' said Peter, a little awkwardly. Then Dieter rose to his feet, shook my hand and left. The elephant in the room must have followed him out, because Peter at once relaxed.

'So, now you come outside – I think your bike is ready and we have some surprises!'

I confess that I had been rather ashamed of my MIFA when I brought it back in through – or rather back over – the factory gates. What would its creators have to say about its abused filth, and most particularly about all those authenticity-sapping adulterations? I imagined a stern-faced old hand staring in disgusted betrayal at the bolt-on crossbar and that Fichtel & Sachs hub, running a forensic gaze over the replacement pedals and mongrel bar grips before crossing his arms and giving me a look that said: If I wasn't German, I'd spit on the floor now.

The boiler-suited whistler who now reappeared pushing my bike was not this man. Via Peter, I learned of the running repairs his team had most generously effected: the ill-disciplined headset knob had been very forcefully tightened, and the self-loosening coaster-brake bracket fashioned by Pub Quiz Peter from my ancient parts bin was no more, replaced by a proper chrome thing that would give me no further trouble (rather soppily, I miss the old one to this day). The tyres pinged when I flicked them and they'd given everything a good clean.

My *danke-schön* festival was cut short by Peter, who excitedly gestured at the trio now approaching us through the MIFA car park. One carried a camera, one a notebook and the last – a splendidly upright old gent in a tweedy brown suit and gleaming brogues who immediately put me in mind of Paddy Ashdown – was pushing a small black bicycle. The first two had been sent by a regional newspaper to compile a pictorial interview that survives online under the deathless Google-translated headline, BRITISH CYCLING IN MIFA SADDLE THE BOSPORUS. (*'Always on my little tyre,'* the *Englishman says with a grin. 'This is simply the best.'*) The third was Heinrich von Nathusius, septuagenarian MIFA CEO and fan-belt magnate.

Hands were shaken and I fielded the reporter's gentle questions. When the photographer got to work, the proud figure of Paddy von Fanbelt strode magnificently into shot and together we posed with our small bicycles, exchanging mutually incomprehensible pleasantries, which, as I note from the photographs Peter later forwarded, appear to have entertained me to the verge of lunacy.

'So our boss has an idea,' he said now. 'He will give you this new MIFA folding bicycle to continue with your journey. That's OK!'

I looked around at a sea of Christmas grins, and down at the bike Paddy was proffering expectantly. It had an embarrassment of gears, an alloy frame and a general air of purposeful, pocket-sized competence that was borne out by a test ride around the car park. How dizzying to be reacquainted with the ability to build speed so smoothly and shed it on a sixpence. But also how pointlessly frustrating.

'That's so, so kind of you,' I said to Paddy via Peter as I climbed off the saddle. 'What a lovely bicycle. But . . . my journey is about history, about the days of my old MIFA 900, so I must . . . you know . . .'

I gestured helplessly at the chunky little state socialist propped up on its stand between us, before faces furrowed in confusion. Paddy von Fanbelt seemed particularly puzzled; I fear he believed that I was only riding this pitiful old relic because I couldn't afford anything better. For a moment I wondered if my gift-spurning ingratitude might earn me a firm, round slap, captured by the photographer and splashed across the *Mitteldeutsche Zeitung* under a righteous headline: THANKS FOR NOTHING, TOMMY THE COMMIE! Instead, Paddy ruminatively rubbed his ruddy chin, then spoke at length to Peter.

'Our boss is a real enthusiast for bicycles and for history,' I was soon informed. 'He builds a new museum in Magdeburg for old bicycles, and would be very happy to have your MIFA there after you finish your ride. We will deliver to your house this new little MIFA and take the old one for our museum. That's OK?'

I didn't know what to say. Actually, I did. A bike, what I rode, in a museum? Life doesn't get much more OK than that. I grasped Paddy von Fanbelt by his mighty oaken hand and croaked out a stream of humbled unworthiness, which Peter didn't need to translate. There were more photographs and handshakes, then Paddy looked at his watch and with a brisk farewell nod headed off across the sunlit tarmac.

An hour later, as my train clanked back past the benighted stations and warehouses, I struggled to make sense of an extraordinary day. The Dieter-Peter Conundrum had taught me that for many in the old GDR – perhaps most at 'the MIFA', one of its few institutional survivors – today was still Too Soon. Dieter came of age in a land of spies and lies, reared to toe the line and keep schtum: when I read up on his old road-race hero, I found that Täve Schur still denies that the GDR doped its athletes, despite ample hard evidence of the most systematic and damaging performance-enhancing substance programme in sporting history (one former GDR skiing champion has estimated that for every gold medallist, 350 athletes were left as invalids). Peter was a young man but he was old enough to remember, indeed old enough to have been a Young Pioneer.

On one level, the salutary tale of that Western border guard assassinated in 1998 by retired Stasi hitmen had shown me that the GDR's darkest powers exerted a reach beyond the nation's grave. On another, all that stuff about smell-jar archives and records of washing-up liquid preference was just so shamefully absurd. When Anna Funder, an Australian-born journalist working in Berlin, talked to older colleagues while researching her excellent book *Stasiland*, fear tied fewer tongues than humiliation. 'The whole Stasi thing,' said one. 'It's just kind of . . . embarrassing.' Funder became accustomed to her interviewees adopting a very particular facial expression while reliving their GDR pasts: 'not knowing whether to laugh or throw up'.

And bearing all that in mind, I probably shouldn't have been as saddened as I was that beyond their insurmountable reluctance to discuss the old days, not one MIFA employee had expressed even the tiniest curiosity in my bike. Not a single prod or query, not even a second glance: an ugly duckling rejected by its own mother. I had confidently imagined that my 900's back-to-its-roots pilgrimage would have meant as much to its creators as it did to me, picturing veteran employees massed around it with rueful smiles, inspecting their humble handiwork with a blend of pride and embarrassment and sharing bitter-sweet reminiscences of Five Year Plans and boozy lunch-breaks. Instead, they had all gazed right through what was evidently an uncomfortable reminder of an unhappy past. Right until the very last minute, when their boss had suddenly insisted on putting it on reverential public display. It was all most confusing.

The morning matured into a gorgeous, balmy afternoon, and after hauling my freshly serviced MIFA off the train at Pressig I rolled up warm tarmac to Probstzella. Its curious name had leapt off the map, and in a long and lazy sunset its looks matched. Low rays gilded the flanks of pine and Thuringian slate that hemmed Probstzella in, and cast a flattering glow over its winding straggle of grimy old homes. Opposite them lay the ghostly bulk of a red-brick railway station – one of the few that had linked East and West Germany in the old days, and in consequence now surrounded by a derelict sprawl of windowless buildings and weed-fractured concrete. And above everything, looking down on this unpeopled scene, an extraordinary red eminence sprouting angular pavilions and topped with a Gotham City turret.

The Haus des Volkes was built in 1927 by Bauhaus architect Alfred Arndt, for Franz Itting, a philanthropist who had chosen to endow this remote and modest slate-mining community with a cathedral-sized community centre. By way of thanks, Itting was imprisoned before the war by the Nazis as a socialist, and after it by the Soviets as a capitalist.

As a GDR border town, Probstzella found itself declared an exclusion zone: 'untrustworthy elements' were banished from the town, and the ideologically sound comrades allowed to stay were effectively cut off from the rest of the country. Travelling out of these areas was awkward enough, but visiting friends or family marooned inside them – even for a cup of tea – demanded a permit that had to be applied for eight weeks in advance, and was turned down four times out of five. In consequence, just twenty years after it had welcomed its first workers, Itting's Haus des Volkes was shuttered up.

Following a long, dust-gathering vigil it reopened in 2008 as a hotel, though off season you'd hardly have guessed it: I rang a phone number stuck to the bolted door, and was given a code that accessed the key box alongside. Then I went in and didn't see a soul until breakfast. I wandered alone down corridors and epic stairwells lined with shriekingly vibrant modernist murals, peering into the original bowling alley and a trapezium-vaulted, thousand-seat theatre, savouring all five floors of hard lines, smooth curves and lofty, slender windows. The grounds were similarly deserted and no less splendid, strewn with copper-roofed refreshment kiosks and leaf-scattered bandstands, each a sinuous study in brick and glass, like pocket pre-war Tube stations. It was creepy and wonderful in just the right proportions, and my well-appointed room was graced with a big bowl of complimentary Haribos. Should you ever find yourself in this neglected backwater – realistically by mistake – I would urge you to stay there. As you may already have worked out, it wasn't expensive.

I dined in a discoloured old pub opposite the station, next to a table of brazen smokers playing cards with one of those curious decks the continentals go for, all bells and acorns. Trains squeaked and rattled lethargically by in the warm night; line workers in orange jackets shuffled past the pub's dirty glass doors. Whenever anyone came in or went out they moved through the room rapping a knuckle on every table in turn, mine included, accompanied with a small nod of greeting or valediction. How tremendously endearing, I thought, especially so as I'd just been made aware – courtesy of a phone call from home – that it was my birthday. These things pass you by on the road. By longstanding tradition I mark my special day with a curry, and happily settled for the daft national institution that is *currywurst* – a rare rebellion against Germany's innate culinary conservatism, the resilient inertia of pork, cabbage and spuds. When the barman laid down my dish the card players interrupted their game to join in the bar-wide chorus of *guten appetits*. I toasted them with a doily-stemmed pilsner, then set about smearing my face and a tableful of maps and route guides in aromatic red gloop.

At length I rose with a birthday skinful and a spring in my step, a combo that would in due course make heavy work of the many decorous staircases that separated me from my bed. I strode over to the card players, rapped an overbearing farewell on their table and breezed expansively out into the night. On previous evenings I had always been too exhausted – and frankly too scared – to plan beyond the next overnight stop, at the most the one after. But this had been a short day and in various ways an inspiring one: with a plinth in Paddy von Fanbelt's museum of two-wheeled heroes on offer for completing this ride, I had breathed deep, drunk deeper, and made a big, crumply audit of the remaining distance.

Many moons before (in fact only four of them, but still), Ed Lancaster had warned me that EV13 was thought to run 10,400km from the Barents Sea to the Black. By rights I was barely more than halfway, but the navigational aids bundled messily under my arm had given me the most wonderful present a drunken long-distance shopping cyclist could ask for: somehow, I appeared to be almost a thousand miles closer to the end than I should have been.

Two hours after I shelled out fourteen euros on sun cream, I discovered why the German for weather is *wetter*. For many days thence I frothed inside my anorak, toiling up heavy slabs of hill-side in a dank world of grey: concrete watchtowers, whole villages faced from top to toe in local slate, pewter windfarms, the leaden, leaking skies. Two months of hard labour had deformed my legs into hourglasses of muscle pinched in at the knee, but they still only had one big climb a day in them. Every incline after that was a rain-faced Calvary of gurns and steaming death-rasps: one close-up bus-shelter selfie taken at 800m appears to show Bono concluding an especially overwrought chorus in a rubbish sauna. Even my arms suffered, painfully aglow with the strain of yanking up on the bars, like that was going to help. Standing in the saddle of a shopping bike felt pretty stupid, but at least it was an option: had I been half an inch taller my right kneecap would have sliced against the handlebar bell-bracket with every single revolution, rather than every third or fourth.

The descents were a reckless mess, my MIFA's runaway clatter bringing worried old faces to every other window in the valley-side villages. Near the foot of one especially knuckle-blanching plummet, I hazarded a glance at my juddering Garmin screen. I'm pretty sure that 64.7kmh is the fastest I have ever travelled on a bicycle, and entirely certain that this was not the bicycle to do it on. In two days, my almost pristine brake blocks were reduced to smoking nubbins.

I was now into the final run of the inner German border, a region where the nation's richest province, Bavaria, butted up to Thuringia, one of its poorest. Back in the years of division this disparity drew crowds of West German holidaymakers, who climbed up a very particular breed of observation tower to gaze down at their benighted cross-border brethren with a blend of compassion and *schadenfreude*. My sole fellow guests at the Haus des Volkes had been a retired West German couple I met at breakfast, who told me they'd climbed the 150ft Bayernturm – largest of these gloat-decks – thirty years previously. They were near the end of their own walk down what the wife called 'the line of death', and I was fascinated by the pair's enduring fixation with people they clearly thought of as an alien and inferior race.

'It's perhaps their history,' said the husband, 'but the Ossis we still find a little rude, a little bad in education.'

It transpired that we'd eaten in the same pub the night before; they'd seen me but I'd failed to notice them, presumably because they hadn't rapped a hello on my table.

'Did you not find it terrible? Everyone with cigarettes and cards, eating bad food with dirty hands.'

His wife shuddered at the memory of what had been one of my favourite German evenings. 'We really felt we were back in the East, with Honecker in control.'

I thought of them, and my strangely self-censored interviews at the MIFA plant, when I pushed the bike over a stretch of sodden pasture and up to a slatted wooden bridge. A cluster of mossy signs and fingerposts indicated that this was the lonely meeting point of three countries, two of them Germanys, and one of those no more. This was it: my farewell to the erstwhile German Democratic Republic, and its enduringly awkward legacy. I huffed an accumulation of rain off my upper lip, then bucked muddily away through phantom minefields and into the Czech Republic.

12. THE CZECH REPUBLIC, GERMANY AND AUSTRIA

In 1990, Czechoslovakia welcomed us with open arms and hungry wallets, a nation in thrall to the new freedom and its commercial spin-offs. The GDR had petered out into grime and gloom; on our last night we'd slept on a bare mattress in an unheated campsite shed, welcomed in the very loosest sense by a Stasi wannabe who handed us a bent key and seven squares of waxed toilet paper. Then we crossed the border and at once found ourselves on gaily lit streets suffused with an almost palpable spirit of good cheer.

The old state-controlled hotel agencies in every Czech town were anarchically thronged with homeowners hawking their spare rooms at prices even my wife found hard to resist, and we hadn't once regretted taking them up. Never had I encountered such glowingly house-proud hosts, people who sometimes seemed more interested in showing off their well-ordered arsenals of West

European cleaning products than in taking our money. Every menu was a zingy wake-up call to palates withered by days of boiled pallor, and the bustling cafés seemed to have picked up where they left off in the gilded, chocolatey *belle époque*. I must also pay special tribute to The Miracle of Wenceslaus Square, wherein Prague's most fabled public space was lined with tankers full of Pilsner Urquell, dispensed by white-coated brewery technicians into half-litre glasses for which they asked the equivalent of 3p. The afternoon that unfolded here spawned one of our journal's most worrisome entries: 'Got tanked up and bullied a cab driver.'

Czechoslovakia is long gone, of course, cleaved in two shortly after our return by mutual consent. Since then I'd been back to Prague twice, but had never revisited the Czech provinces and was keen to see if they retained that infectious *joie de vivre*. After a lengthy approach through the still unpeopled exclusion zone, I found my two-letter answer in a two-letter town.

'*Besahlen*! *BE-SAH-LEN!*'

The Hotel Goethe in Aš had attracted me with its shabby-chic art nouveau façade, one of the town's many noble but haggard survivors from Bohemia's turn-of-the-century golden age. Now, through dense veils of tobacco smoke at the panelled entrance lobby's dingy fundament, I was being ordered – in loud and terrible German – to pay up front, by a blubbery, ageing skinhead who didn't seem likely to show me his prized collection of anti-bacterial surface cleaners any time soon.

Upstairs I sat on my bed, which sagged gently down to the hair-balled carpet amid a chorus of geriatric groans. How very far I had come in an hour and a bit. The disorderly streets of Aš had presented an abrupt departure from well-entrenched civic norms, sparingly dotted with people who were younger, gaunter and conspicuously more laidback – more aimless – than the typical townsperson I had

TIM MOORE

pedalled past for the previous thousand miles. The bike paths were
gone and so was half the tarmac; the muddy front yards were strewn
with battered children's toys in a manner unthinkable, indeed probably unlawful, back over the border. Everything – clothes, apartment blocks, cars – looked cheap and worn-out. Half the shop
names had missing letters, their dusty windows thinly scattered
with sun-bleached merchandise. I couldn't even make a puerile
joke at this sorry dump's expense, because it's actually pronounced
'ash'. Not for the first time – or the last – I wondered how on earth
our pocket continent preserves such startling cheek-by-jowl diversity in this age of globalised convergence.

The compact hotel restaurant was heaving with noisy diners in
matching tracksuits who appeared to be members of some sort of
competitive smoking club, and staffed by a harassed duo in stained
red waistcoats. As I made my way towards the only empty table,
the younger female half of this pair barged waywardly out through
the kitchen doors with one hand over her face, then ducked down
behind the bar. For a while I could hear her heaving sobs above
the tracksuit gang's racket, but I never saw her again. Her superior,
a paunchy middle-aged man with a yellowing moustache and a
medieval rash poking out above his grimy shirt collar, glanced
briefly behind the bar with an expression far removed from
sympathy, then returned to his business. This principally involved
the dead-eyed, desultory transport of full and empty bottles of
beer to and from the tracksuit tables. After ten minutes he flicked
a menu into my lap on his way past; after another ten he sparingly
thinned out the forest of empties I was sharing my table with. My
expectant cough and lofted finger went ignored on this and
umpteen subsequent occasions. I was about to stick out a foot and
floor him when he stopped before me with an open notepad and a
very Russian expression.

230

'OK, so, um, could I maybe start with *salat*?'

The menu was entirely in Czech, and though after 131 steep, wet kilometres I hardly cared what I ate as long as there was a lot of it, it seemed prudent to kick-off with a familiarity. I pressed a finger to the relevant menu entry, then watched as the bill of fare was removed from my grasp with great speed and no little violence. This mysterious and arresting turn of events was accompanied by a shrill burst of z-centric words, delivered into my face at close quarters along with a generous splash of spittle.

'Sounds good,' I said to the waiter's rapidly retreating back. 'I'll have it medium-rare with chips.'

Then, my ears still ringing and my face aflame, I picked my way through the suddenly silent tracksuits and went up the road to a Thai-run sushi steakhouse, where I had a pizza and wondered what on earth had gone wrong with this country.

If nothing else, EV13 was commendably well signposted in the Czech Republic. The next morning I blankly followed it through wet towns full of lorries, and over wet hillsides full of mud. I'd been kept awake half the night by death-watch plumbing creaks and a host of rival noises off, further reminders of how spoiled I'd been by weeks of subservient motorists and well-balanced service staff, of hotel guests who didn't spend the small hours washing dogs in their baths or holding corridor football tournaments.

Come back, Germany, I thought, head down at the brimming potholes, all is forgiven. I pedalled on and ever upwards, watching my sodden red trainers rise and fall, rise and fall, and thinking that thought didn't sound quite right. OK, most is forgiven. Then I looked up and saw a sign informing me that I had reached the Mittelpunkt Europa, and understood that my wish had been granted.

This was the start of a long round of the EV13 hokey-cokey: for a fortnight I would weave across borders with dizzying frequency, left leg in, right leg out, never spending consecutive nights in the same country. There would generally be some token indication of the frontier, an old border hut or a metal sign with the facing nations on either side of it, but sometimes there was nothing. In twenty-five short years we've gone from an iron curtain to a blown-down garden fence.

My first reacquaintance with Germany, welcome as it most surely was, came at a price. The rain intensified and the hills swelled so loftily that some came topped with a ski station. In a single week I had doubled my entire trip's Garmin-archived accumulation of vertical distance. And my word it was cold, so cold that smoke once more coiled forth from every cottage chimney and hung thickly in the wet air. Helmut Schmidt would have loved it at least: blended with powerful wafts of new-growth pine, every inhalation was a drag of high-tar menthol.

In 1990 we stopped at Auschwitz-Birkenau, back then a sparsely attended site and as such perhaps more haunted and harrowing than it is today, with one and a half million annual visitors. No matter how much you think you know about such places, confronting the horror first hand is always a draining ordeal. For good measure I was going down with my inaugural kidney stone, which added a top note of physical pain to the emotional anguish. Auschwitz must surely be the most terrible place on earth, but the Nazis provided plenty of competition. Between 1933 and 1945, they operated more than 20,000 concentration camps – a scarcely fathomable total, and one that made an encounter along my route inevitable.

On a shiversome, bedraggled afternoon, the remains of Konzentrationslager Flossenbürg exuded a grimly appropriate air of misery.

And a jolt of shock – the site lay at the heart of a trim little town, and I later noted with quiet horror that several parades of post-war homes had been built directly on to the foundations of the old prison huts. Flossenbürg was a labour camp rather than an extermination facility like Birkenau, but what with it being run by the SS, over 30,000 inmates – most of them political prisoners – still perished here: worked to death in a neighbouring quarry, starved to death in those long, low huts, hung at dawn for trying to escape or not being Nazis.

What remained of the site has been sombrely conserved, with the old kitchen block now home to a museum. I was dourly processing its dreadful revelations – the encyclopaedic registers whose last column neatly displayed every prisoner's 'date of release', the on-site SS casino, the post-war repurposing of the camp's largest hut as a toy factory – when a female voice called out from the entrance. There were a dozen of us inside, but when I looked up I saw a woman with a laminated badge round her neck beckoning me directly.

'I must ask you please to remove your bicycle,' she said coldly. I'd left the MIFA propped on its stand behind the kitchen block, which I now learned represented a transgression of the site's code of respect: a sign she led me to bracketed bicycles with picnics, unleashed dogs and racist insignia on the roll-call of the banished. 'You see, we have rules here.' This seemed an unfortunate statement in the circumstances, but I resisted a regrettable riposte and slunk away through a teenage school group, who parted before me in silent opprobrium.

I spent the balance of an extremely challenging afternoon clearing rain from the Garmin screen with a weary swipe of gardening glove, watching the altitude rise and the temperature fall. In these conditions, I had finally learned, the key was to keep going, indeed to speed up when your aching, refrigerated body begged you to pack it in. By five o'clock I was blotted, numb and spent, barely able to uncurl my clawed fingers from the handlebars. Yet with the wet air now chilled to 4 degrees, I knew that any drop in pace would multiply every woe, and that if my engine cooled down I might not get it started again. This was a tough enough ask on tilted tarmac, and a frankly ludicrous one when an ill-fated dalliance with Google Maps led me down a dark and dwindling forest trail. Waist-high brambles and toppled trunks obliged me to gather the MIFA up in my arms and lug it blindly through the world's stupidest assault course for almost an hour; I staggered out on to the road looking like a rubbish fireman wondering why he'd just rescued a shopping bike from a mudslide. As a rule I quite enjoyed getting massively lost: the relief at eventually rediscovering the true path was always more profound than the initial dismay of mislaying it, so I garnered a net morale boost from the experience. This episode was an exception to that rule.

Eslarn, where I'd planned to stay, was liberally dotted with pensions and guest houses, but their doors were all locked and my ever more ragged knocking and letter-box bellows didn't open any of them. Shuddering like a coal-fired Trabant I toiled on to Schönsee, the next cluster of roofs and bulbous church spires, where at tearful length I was eventually ushered in through a pension threshold. When someone rescues you from cold, wet hunger, it's extremely difficult not to smother them in grateful kisses, even if you're paying for the privilege and they're a big, bald Dutchman.

The borderland hills wouldn't lie down, pumping themselves up into thousand-metre monsters that tapped into rich new seams of pain. My back began to squirt out wincing pulses of bruised agony,

as if instead of spending his evening offering tips on route planning and historical research, that lovely Dutchman had bent me
over his knee and whacked me all night with a clog. My forearms
burned, my splayed knees shrieked, my right ankle yammered out
its duller woes like a nutter on the bus, and below them all the
MIFA's hopeless little pram wheels revolved with ever more
wobbly reluctance. More than once I was bullied off the bike and
into the Push of Shame, gazing with wet, wan eyes at the retreating
ranks of conifers below and all around, wreathed in smoky mist as
if the latest downpour had just extinguished a hundred forest fires.

The German mountain villages were the usual studies in sober
discipline, counterbalanced with radioactive bad taste. Every lawn
was a fanatically marshalled putting surface, with a garden hose
coiled tight and true as a big green slinky in one corner, and in the
other some garish monstrosity, a cluster of giant, polychromic
baubles or a plastic snail the size of an Alsatian. The gnomes were
large and many, and generally engaged en masse in something
unexpected, like ganging up on a purple stork or masturbating.

In vivid contrast, the Czech settlements were sparse and ghostly,
sometimes nothing but five roofless cottages and a stray dog. My
Dutchman had offered the explanation: as I should have remembered from History O level, this was the Czech Sudetenland, a
region of ethnic Germans fatefully annexed by Hitler in 1938.
When the Soviets set up shop in Czechoslovakia after the war,
they inevitably took a dim view of the Sudetenland's inhabitants,
and set about making their lives a misery. Ethnic Germans were
forced to wear white armbands, and prevented from sitting on
park benches or even walking on pavements. Almost 6,000 of
them committed suicide in 1946 alone, and millions more were
deported with merciless efficiency. By 1950, just 150,000 Germans
remained of the three million who had called the Sudetenland

home before the war. One village I went through started the 1940s with 2,500 residents, and ended them with fifty-two. Even by the standards of the age this was ethnic cleansing on a shocking scale: today, just 40,000 Czech citizens claim German heritage. Aš, I was chastened to learn, had lived most of its life as Asch, the Sudetenland's most completely German town. In October 1945, the entire population was herded into twenty-seven trains and taken away, and seventy years on the poor place had barely begun to recover.

These were days of damp feet and cuckoo-clock chalets, of early nights spent festering dankly in bed with a belly full of stodge and ale, rain clattering the black windows. I squelched uphill through the buttercupped mountain meadows with such painful lethargy that more than once I'd stop at the top and find a spider assembling a dewy web across the front carrier bracket. Then a lunatic plunge between dark walls of spruce and pine beside a frothy Alpine torrent, shotblasted by stinging pellets of rain before rolling to a halt at the valley bottom, and draining a Magic Man in a bus shelter. A night on the Czech side brought me a pound-a-pint dinner of goulash and dumplings, and the sort of hotel where they hand you a TV remote sheathed in sticky cling film along with your room key. After turning in I'd watch Commie-era native films, heavy on slapstick and sideburns, and fiddle with the radiators. Uselessly: my clothes and possessions stayed wet for a week. In Germany everything was thrice the price but twice as nice, and generally twelve times weirder. I spent my last night there in the honeymoon suite of a *'wellness und bier'* hotel, sleeping in the left ventricle of a heart-shaped barrel.

Tim Moore
@mrtimmoore

I'm now in the honeymoon suite at a beer hotel.

Brinelling – now there's a verb to conjure with. It has a faintly shameful ring to it, perhaps an activity you might see trouserless figurines practising in the corner of a German garden (no matter how dearly we all wish I'd been joking about the self-pleasuring gnomes, I'm afraid I wasn't). In fact, Brinelling refers to the permanent indentation of a hard surface, named after the Swedish engineer who devised the relevant assessment test, by riding a sub-standard bicycle for several thousand kilometres without adequate maintenance.

I had been inadvertently dabbling with this phenomenon for some days, mystified by the MIFA's slight but ever more obvious reluctance to turn corners. On my approach to the wellness and beer hotel, navigation became aptly if alarmingly wayward: the handlebars developed a powerful urge to centre themselves on some invisible tramline, and I was soon fighting my auto-piloting bike round the bends, tackling each in a series of very short straight lines, like the perimeter of a dodecagon.

Curled up in my love-barrel, I Googled away into the small hours for a diagnosis. A consensus emerged just after I tore open the pillow chocolate for a midnight snack, to find a honeymoon condom sliding horridly into my hands. The ball bearings in that ever bothersome headset, it appeared, had ejected all their grease; heated by friction to the point of malleable incandescence in the rattling descents, they had eroded each other into dimpled, interlocking semi-spheres.

'We have a very great bicycle man in Neureichenau,' said the desk manager when I checked out and explained my predicament as best I could. He was a slightly over-familiar chap with the booming, wide-eyed manner of a children's TV presenter and a predilection, which I now endured once more, for snatching guests' reading glasses off their heads and giving them a wipe down with a cloth drawn from his top pocket. 'He works at the garage for Honda cars, but he will have the instrument to correct your little balls.'

If he did he was playing with it at home; it was Saturday and I found the garage dark and shuttered. Instead, trying to bully the bearings free by weaving about the road like an F1 driver warming his tyres on a parade lap, I pressed on up the moist green hills and almost at once found myself in Austria. Ten countries down, nine to go.

I'd imagined rural Austria would be trim and prosperous Germany turned up to eleven, but in fact it was a cheerfully unapologetic shambles. The farms smelled of crap rather than sweet, fresh hay and many of the cars were in a state of red-neck dilapidation. It's fair to say that the people of Austria haven't had a great press in recent years, what with that ex-Wehrmacht president of theirs and the whole Josef Fritzl incest-cellar business, but they did me proud from the off. Just outside the first town I passed through, I spotted two young men fixing a moped in a driveway; I pulled over, jiggled my self-centring handlebars at them and within moments one was going at the MIFA with a vast adjustable wrench.

'You drive this to *Turkey*?' chortled his friend when I detailed my mission, the italics stridently audible. 'How many years you are taking?!' Admittedly their remedial efforts did no more than tone down the symptoms: we agreed that my little balls needed replacement, but even then I sensed this would never happen, and that Brinelling would hereon join taurine abuse and public urination as one of the immovable cornerstones of my life on the road. Nonetheless, on another damp day in the big hills these jolly fellows were a cheering ray of sunshine, seeing me off with a tribute that put the wind in my wheels:

'Good travel for a great guy!'

More glad tidings were dispensed a few hours later in improbable circumstances. In the late morning I re-entered the Czech Republic in daft and dangerous fashion, lugging the MIFA across some forsaken mountaintop log flume deeply flanked by sodden, waist-high vegetation. (That night I learned that this historic eighteenth-century waterway, the Schwarzenberg Schwemmkanal, linked the Black Sea and North Sea watersheds and their mightiest navigable rivers: my giant leap for bike-kind might instead have been a disastrous slither, sweeping me halfway home like a very unfortunate turn of snakes and ladders.) Now, after a full ten rounds with the rain-flicking, flesh-pricking brambles, I had at last stumbled out onto asphalt, and was celebrating with a ragged, lunatic yodel when a red Audi with German plates overtook and pulled up.

'It is you, yes?'

'Um, is it?'

'Of course!'

The two middle-aged men who had leapt from the car and splashed eagerly up to me seemed almost dangerously excited; I set my expression to Constrained Delight, a face that has done good service over the years when tasting cakes baked by my children.

'I tell my friend it is you, he don't believe me!'

The one with the Begbie tache turned to his associate, who responded with a happily sheepish shrug. 'Please – a photo, it's OK for you?'

Without waiting for an answer, Begbie smoothed his mullet into order, wiped rain off a cheek and put his arm round my shoulder.

'I can't believe it is you,' he said, shaking his head as his friend began snapping away with a phone camera. 'Incredible.'

I smiled uneasily into the tiny lens, then cracked, and asked a question I hadn't asked aloud since the loneliest, mind-messing depths of Finland.

'I'm sorry, but who am I?'

Begbie's answer thoughtfully overlooked any existential predicaments. 'Come on, it is you, the Englischer with the little MIFA,' he said, waving a hand first at me and then at my bike. 'We are from Sangerhausen; we read your story and see your photo in our newspaper!'

Enlightenment drained all discomfort from my features. How remarkable, and how very splendid, that we three should congregate on this silent, soaking hillside so very far from all our homes. ('Small bicycle,' chirped Begbie, 'small world!') We took more photos and chatted a while; I learned they were ex-miners, enjoying an early-redundancy road trip to Budapest. Then the rain abruptly intensified, and after some hurried handshakes, they scuttled back to their Audi.

As you may have gathered, I've got history with the Eurovision Song Contest; as you may not have, I am an impervious, goal-driven machine of a man. At any rate, it was finals night, Austria were the hosts, and I had that morning made a rash vow to re-consummate my love-hate Eurovision relationship with a nation-appropriate telly vigil. The conditions I conquered in fulfilling this ridiculous oath were unstintingly terrible. After the miners went I was 88km shy of Gmund, the next Austrian town on my route, and every last one of these metric bastards did its best to sadden and hurt me.

The rain fell in sheets, smearing out a world of hills and lubricating the MIFA's steel rims so profusely that my front brakes gave up, which along with the resurgent steering issues made an adventure of every downhill corner. The niggle in my right ankle blossomed into a searing, export-strength torment; on the steeper inclines, it seemed as if my Achilles tendon was about to snap like a dry twig with every revolution. ('If you experience ankle soreness,' the internet later helpfully advised me, 'try using a lower gear cycling uphill.') How useful, on days like this, to have a bulging repository of even more awful recent tribulations to dredge up, putting my current misery into flattering perspective. With those memories finally exhausted, all I could do was double-up on the Magic Man, and ride things out on that brittle, tinny high, shivering and wax-faced. I soon felt strange and desperate and must have looked it too, because for the first time in my entire life, a motorist pulled over and offered me a lift.

'How many you go?'

Not too many by then; I turned him down. Though I might not have done had his car been less completely crammed with garden furniture.

The border approach was marked by a ramshackle commercial parade of outlets offering Austrians stuff they can't get at home, such as life-sized garden wolves and topless barmaids. Then I sloshed heavy-lidded through the unmanned customs sheds and into Gmund, in no fit state to appreciate or even notice the immaculate loveliness of its principal square: when I saddled up and went out in the morning, the fanned cobbles, tightly stacked, colourful old townhouses and embarrassment of mahogany and brass cafés all came as a wonderful surprise. Instead, I dully noted the word HOTEL above a door, battered it open with the MIFA's front wheel, and presently found myself dribbling brown water and death-sweat all over a lobby crammed with elegant wedding guests holding champagne flutes and bouquets. Everyone looked round and two uniformed receptionists weaved speedily towards me through the throng. It suddenly felt like the end scene of some turdy rom-com, my cue to deliver a bumbling declaration of love and rescue the bride from a faithless cad, before riding away together on our bicycle made for none.

The Hotel Goldener Stern, one of the finest buildings on that delightful old square, would have been out of my league on the best of days, and as this absolutely wasn't amongst them I must credit its staff for their courteous, helpful hospitality, and all-round failure to grab me by the wet shoulders and throw me back out from whence I came. What had happened to Austria? One waist-coated functionary wheeled my filthy MIFA away through the reception party (I found it in the morning propped against a speaker in the function room), and another ushered me gently to a seat near the bar, where I blotted expensive upholstery and shuddered unappealingly for a while, before a waiter laid an unbidden but tearfully welcome pot of tea before me with a gracious flourish. Presently I heard that my room had now been readied, and was accompanied to it by a young woman whose expression welled with such profound concern that I genuinely feared she might ask if I needed a wheelchair. It was like being in a five-star hospice. Admittedly they stuck me in the attic and charged me ruinously for that tea, and later politely declined to turn the heating on. In consequence I was obliged to gaffer-tape the hairdryer button down on turbo mode and convert my en suite into a cacophonous kit-drying chamber, in full compliance with environmental best practice and fire regulations. It worked a treat, but also completely drowned out the Eurovision final. What a truly terrible shame.

The Soviets never trusted Czechoslovakia. Before the war, it had ranked amongst the world's most technically advanced countries; afterwards, still better off and better educated than any other on its side of the curtain, the nation was picked on as a hotbed of bourgeois intellectualism. More than 400 Czechoslovak dissidents and undesirables were executed after the Soviet empire's most brutal post-war show trials, the bloody sharp end of a uniquely intensive crackdown: at the age of twelve, future post-revolutionary president Václav Havel was identified as a class traitor and thereafter struggled to find any educational establishment willing to accept him. It didn't work, of course, and the Czechoslovakian Communist Party's famously ill-fated dalliance with economic and political liberalisation in 1968 attracted the tanks. A hard-line regime was installed, and obediently persecuted its own people with scatter-gun mindlessness. For years after, appearing in public with long hair was enough to earn young men a police beating. Yet the stoic, thoughtful Czechoslovaks never succumbed to the temptations of violence and revenge: when the time came, their 1989 'Velvet Revolution' overturned forty-one years of Soviet rule in ten bloodless days.

I offer this condensed tribute to a now-divided land's relevant history as a pointlessly overdue personal wake-up call: the Czech

Republic was passing me by. In truth, as countries came and went with what passes for dizzying speed on a MIFA 900, such wholesale, nation-grade oversights would from now on become a recurring issue. But the Czechs deserved better, and I felt a little guilty for having cold-shouldered their land on the back of one bad night with two rude men at the Hotel Goethe in Aš. That and 12,000 years of biblical rain. Happily, the country had the decency and good sense to see me off with clear skies and the city of Znojmo.

I arrived at its outskirts damp and done in, wearied after a long day slooshing between castle-topped Austro-Moravian hill towns, my progress either ponderous or breakneck. Of late the larger Czech settlements had been dispiritingly girdled with a scattering of bedraggled roadside prostitutes, and my heart sank when a huddle of figures appeared around Znojmo's city-limits sign. But happily, all were local farmers hawking bottled Moravian produce: pickles, jams and – joy of joys – wine. Wine! Sun-ripened nectar of southern Europe, the essence of long, hot summers and not being anywhere near Finland. More so than that log-flume mountain border, this felt like a defining watershed. When I looked up the clouds had fractured, and before me Znojmo's squat and slender spires glowed in a sheaf of golden rays.

I bagged a cosy little room under an ancient roof, overlooking one of the many undulating cobbled alleys that graced Znojmo, then showered and laundered, and with an expectant whistle fluttering from my unaccustomed lips, struck out into the warm night to reacquaint myself with the half-remembered pleasure of alfresco evenings. What a civilised thrill to walk into a city you have never previously heard of, confident that it is poised to delight you. Znojmo duly offered up half a millennium's worth of appealing architecture, much of it laid out around two tilting squares of extravagant proportion. I paced around the larger for almost half an hour, watching the last slabs of sunlight retreat across the meaty old cobbles. Its sides were lined with baroque porticos and pastel-stuccoed Habsburg mansions; one end was guarded by a four-square, pointy-roofed medieval turret, and the other – woah! – by a low-slung, open-mouthed Communist town hall, like some enormous concrete video-cassette recorder. This brazen excrescence was inflicted on Znojmo's most graceful space in 1969, effectively as a punishment for the nation's indiscretions the year before. I stared at it for a full five minutes, more stunned than appalled, looking around for someone to share this outrageous spectacle. Only then did I realise that I had the square almost entirely to myself. Here was a scene crying out for an Italian-pattern mass nocturnal walkabout, but it was Sunday and everyone but a distant pair of teenage couples had gone home. It took me half an hour to track down the vegan café that was Znojmo's only open restaurant, and half that to put away four plates of spartan nourishment.

For a welcome while the landscape lay flat on its back and sunbathed. Farmers were out pruning and tethering vine tendrils in poppy-speckled fields, brought to attention by the MIFA's whirring clunks and hoisting secateurs in greeting. At my last Czech town, I successfully spent all my remaining korunas on a dozen cigar-shaped rolls and three cans of an energy drink compellingly named in honour of a notorious native invention. Red Bull gives you wings; Semtex blows them off. Then it was back into Austria, heading south along the Slovakian border down a flood plain scattered with village-idiot hamlets: Dorfles, Dürnkrut, Grub.

These places were uniformly charmless, full of grey-rendered bungalows and heavy with the stench of boiled food and boredom.

Every mantelpiece supported a carriage clock and a pair of ceramic spaniels, and when I nipped into a bar for a splash-and-dash coffee/pee, I found its rosewood jukebox topped and tailed by Rick Astley and Roger Whittaker. The town of Laa an der Thaya was lethargically gearing up for an onion festival; an air of drab, Mittel European stolidity pervaded throughout.

I began to wonder if these borderlands had been made so unappealing by design, to discourage invasion by the Communists who once surrounded Austria on three sides: seriously, comrades, are we worth it? I was almost right. In fact, the towns had all been laid out to Soviet blueprints in the early 1950s, and afterwards left studiously unembellished to avoid antagonising the neighbours.

Poking so deeply into the Soviet empire – Vienna lies way east of Prague – Austria, much like Finland, had to play a very careful hand in the Cold War. Having culled most (OK, all) of my relevant historical knowledge from *The Third Man*, I knew that Vienna had been split into Allied sectors in 1945, on the Berlin model, but hadn't previously realised that the whole nation was divided for ten long years. The Soviets governed and reconstructed the entire eastern half, my bit, and at the time it was generally assumed that this chunk at least was fated to wind up behind the Iron Curtain for good, forming a neat continuum between the Czech and Hungarian borders. But Stalin's death induced a certain giddiness amongst the Soviet top brass, and in 1955 they abruptly offered Austria full independence on the condition of neutrality. Hands were proverbially bitten off and Austria settled into five decades of low-profile mollification, painting their bungalows grey and waiting for the Cold War to blow over. At the same time, that precarious front-line geography ingrained a quiet sense of paranoia. Over 30 per cent of Austrians had access to a nuclear fallout shelter, and no one batted an eyelid when in 1978 Josef Fritzl applied for permission to build one under his garden. In fact, the local council even gave him a two-grand grant.

Slovakia had a full five hours to make a good impression, and failed miserably. A lone raindrop plopped into the River March as my border ferry bumped to a halt, and an eager throng of its friends were soon rushing down to greet me. With EV13's riverside route an unnavigable mud-bath, I reeled Bratislava miserably in along a thin and cratered road filled with thunderous, sluicing traffic. Armies of pylons marched across saturated, rain-smudged flatlands; the rotting *Khrushchyovka* tenements were back, and the ear-scratching bus-shelter idlers. It was all very Russian, inestimably more Soviet than the Czech Republic had been. Bratislava passed by in a dreary smear of stack-a-prole blocks and trams, then it was over the mighty, swollen Danube and back into Austria.

Then Hungary. Then Austria again. Central Europe's shattered-mirror geography had my phone bleating out welcome texts like a cornered lamb. A cornered lamb with a phone.

I was almost out of small-town Austria and it remained a conundrum. In theory, it was awful: expensive, dull and politically horrid. There was an election coming up, and the verges were clustered with stake-mounted placards depicting blotchy, snaggle-toothed right-wing populists, each one screaming out for a marker-pen toothbrush moustache, above some shouty slogan about border controls or Austrian jobs for Austrians. It could have been worse: the late Jörg Haider, former head of the Freedom Party, which provided the creepiest roadside faces and currently holds a quarter of the seats in the national parliament, once described SS veterans as 'decent people who stuck to their beliefs'. I've often wondered if they'll ever get bored with this stuff here, and concluded they probably won't after reading an interview with Felix Baumgartner, the mild-mannered Austrian skydiver who memorably fell to earth from a platform at the edge of space. 'You can't do anything in a democracy,' young Felix later told an interviewer, who'd only asked if he'd ever been scared of heights. 'What we need is a dictator.'

Austrians, considered as a collective whole, were an unappealing people. Yet one-to-one, they had proved almost unfailingly wonderful – the most consistently helpful nationals I had encountered. During a break in the weather I stopped to clean and oil the MIFA's chain, suddenly aware that 2,000 filthy, wet kilometres had elapsed since I had last done so, and concluding that this oversight might at least partly explain those awful grating shrieks (I was wrong: it completely explained them). I carried out this service on a back road so quiet that in twenty minutes, only five motorists passed; but of these, three pulled up and volunteered assistance. An hour later, poking cheese slices into tiny Czech rolls at a war memorial in Deutsch Jahrndorf (Austria's eastern-most town, it says here), I glanced up and saw a bespectacled old lady trotting up the road with a wodge of bulky textile clutched to her chest. For a moment I feared I was about to be stuffed into a sack and punished for my disrespectful picnic. But her burden was a pair of fleece tracksuit bottoms, which she proffered with a volley of concerned-sounding words and a beseeching look at my drizzle-tipped, goose-pimpled leg hairs. In every sense, I didn't know what to say.

'*Danke* . . . but, um, *nein danke.*' I left her with her arms full of thermal polyester and a forlorn face that said the next time she saw me would be in the *Deutsch Jahrndorf Zeitung*, below a tragic headline.

The rain came and went, and the gently billowing landscape was stealthily annexed by smart vineyards. Stoats and weasels scampered across the road and an eagle flew right over my head, so close I felt the beat of its mighty wings. An auspicious encounter, for soon after I was riding through ancient gates topped majesti-cally with sandstone representations of this regal bird. The night before, I had shared a concrete shoebox of a motel with a billion ants, whose doughtier patrols were still crawling from my washbag four countries down the line. Now I was booked into the Habs-burg dynasty's imperial summer residence. The instigator of this miraculous promotion was not far behind: her hire car swept to a halt on the gravel half an hour later, with my son at the wheel.

13. HUNGARY, SLOVENIA AND CROATIA

An awfully long time had elapsed since I had waved my wife and son off in Finland, enough from my perspective to have encompassed the rise and fall of a civilisation or two, and from theirs to have drained the dishwasher of rinse-aid. (I always like to imagine my household regressing into loveless, grunting squalor during my protracted absences, but this is generally as good as it gets.) They were, though, gratifyingly disturbed by my weather-beaten, hollow-cheeked degeneration: the scales in our magnificent bathroom would show that I now weighed a kilogram less than my slimline, twenty-one-year-old son. As instructed, my wife had brought out the old 1970s Peugeot jersey I wore while riding around France fifteen years previously – the fun had gone out of distressing survivors of Soviet-era oppression, and my GDR top would be returning home with her. The Peugeot jersey was tight even in 2000, and I hadn't dared put it on since; I did so now, and it slid loosely over my concave torso with alarming ease.

My support team stayed for three more nights and three more countries. They brought the sun and a tailwind so fierce I could hardly keep up with it, pedals a blur through the Austro-Hungarian vineyards and elder trees. We would arrange to meet twice a day, at lunchtime and our end-point hotel, and I always set – and met – preposterously ambitious targets for both, out of nothing more than dumb macho pride. Fifty-one years old, and still showing off to women and children.

On their first day I covered 159km across Hungary, speeding past poppy-speckled cornfields as the wind swept pretty patterns through their deep, silvery pile. The road surface steadily deteriorated, the start of my long goodbye to smooth and diligently maintained tarmac: there were no Austrias or Germanys left from here to the Black Sea. Some of the villages were arrestingly medieval, scraggy ribbons of hovels and thatch-roofed bus shelters, laid out along the road for half a mile or more. Men were out in the fields with scythes and sickles, and the bicycle was a beast of burden, pushed along the verge with buckets slung from its rusty handlebars or rakes laid across them. Hungarians have a reputation as a bit of a rum bunch, and my presence was acknowledged with a stony-faced hauteur that offered a distinctive departure from months of total indifference, snide hostility and the odd waving infant. Though in fact, now that I cast my mind back to the dawn of time, it was strongly reminiscent of my standard reception in Finland, with whom the Magyars share a distant ethnic identity and a weakness for mad vowels.

The history round here was big and often brutal. I flew through Fertőd, catching no more than a regal glimpse of the rococo super-palace that has been called the Hungarian Versailles; my wife stopped for a tour, and told me that the nearby quarry which provided most of its limestone was requisitioned by the Nazis as an execution site, its rocky walls still riddled with bullet holes as testimony to the thousands of Hungarian Jews who died there. At Andau, hard up by the Austrian border, I poked fruitlessly about in the hedgerows trying to find the little wooden bridge that 70,000 Hungarians had desperately stampeded across during the 1956 anti-Soviet uprising – amongst them my late, lamented next-door neighbour Stephan, just seventeen at the time, who wound up splashing through the swampy water beneath.

And then there was the borderland hilltop north of Sopron, where a picnic proved the unlikely beginning of the end for

 **Tim Moore**
@mrtimmoore

Austro-Hungarian border. Thought better of getting in there for a jaunty selfie.

the Soviet empire. I met the support crew up there and we wandered together through a clearing studded with artworks and information boards, a commemorative site opened with a fanfare by child-of-the-GDR Angela Merkel on the Pan-European Picnic's twentieth anniversary. Six years on everything stood forlornly knee-deep in weeds, a sad fate for a site of such import.

Hungary was always a black sheep in the Soviet flock, even before the revolt that left 700 Russian soldiers dead on the streets of Budapest. You get the impression that the Russians were always a bit freaked out by their barking-mad language and hardwired moodiness, and after a post-1956 crackdown they steadily allowed the recalcitrant Magyars a longer, looser leash. By the Seventies, Hungarians were allowed to run their own small businesses and buy Western goods; by the mid-Eighties, they could travel freely across the Curtain. The reciprocal freedom for Westerners to enter the other way soon attracted hordes of East German holiday-makers to Hungary, the one place where they could meet up with West German relatives.

So thousands of suntanned Ossis were already in Hungary in the summer of 1989, when the native authorities rather boldly announced that they would henceforth be de-fortifying their border with Austria, on the pretext that they couldn't afford the upkeep. When the Hungarians upped the ante, and told the world that as a 'symbolic gesture' the border crossing at Sopron would be opened for two hours on 19 August, a great crocodile of chugging Trabants converged there for a self-styled 'Pan-European Picnic'. As the information boards confirmed, no one quite knew what to expect, least of all the Hungarian border guards who later revealed that they'd been given no orders to countermand the default shoot-to-kill mandate. When an official unlatched a tiny wooden gate, the crowd hesitated, a fearful, Stasi-reared generation who figured there had to be a catch. But when the border guards merely shrugged, tentative sidling erupted into a gleeful stampede, and 700-odd East Germans dashed across no man's land and off into Austria.

The hectic scene was memorably captured in the commemorative site's photographic panels: what with the hair and the clothes, it looks like the opening of an unusually good-natured Black Friday sale, *circa* 1974. 'We're making history!' one of the 700 remembered shouting as he squeezed through the gate. He wasn't wrong. Before the Pan-European Picnic, the Iron Curtain's fate still hung in the balance; afterwards, its days were numbered.

The Hungarian border bosses were initially appalled by this anarchic moment of madness, and in the days ahead over 5,000 East Germans were arrested trying to cross the border around Sopron. The father of one family group was tragically shot dead. But encouraged by the West German authorities, who reputedly offered to write off a few hundred million in debts as a quid pro quo, the Magyars soon began dismantling fences and control posts; within a couple of months, over 60,000 East Germans had fled to the West through Hungary, and the Soviet empire's end was nigh. At Sopron and elsewhere the borderlands were left strewn with hastily abandoned Trabants and Wartburgs, all later acquisitioned by locals and to this day a conspicuous feature on Hungarian roads – I saw more Communist cars here than anywhere else.

My family's visit presented a strange, dreamy interlude. We lunched together beneath strip-lights in a Tesco cafeteria, and under parasols on a rose-bushed Habsburg terrace; we slept in dusty old hotels and ritzy designer apartments. In between I rode with a manic intensity, flicking through kilometres like calendar pages in a time-flies movie montage, as if the faster and further I went, the longer they would stay. With my panniers in the support vehicle and a kind wind the MIFA fairly flew along, though shorn of expeditionary luggage and pedalling like a dervish I cut an even madder figure than usual, a man taking a ride down the shops way too seriously.

After festering in my own filthy, mad juices for so long it was difficult to process my wife's helpful reminders of what constituted acceptable human conduct, and more particularly what didn't, such as the retention of fortnight-old leftovers, keeping foreign currencies in separate sanitary-product disposal bags and humming 10cc all through dinner. Through her eyes I belatedly grasped the inherently weird ickiness of the CamelBak hydration system, how all the bladders and tubing I sluiced out and slung up to dry every night suggested paraphernalia concerned with the draining of human fluids, rather than their replenishment. 'Don't you feel odd suckling away from that thing?' she asked as I strapped it on one morning. 'I bet people think you're drinking your own wee.'

Slovenia spent the Cold War as part of Marshal Tito's Yugoslavia, the renegade, semi-Westernised Communist state that wasn't so much behind an iron curtain as a plastic trellis. The little nation managed to extricate itself from the post-Tito Balkan mess without bloodshed, and around me the Slovenian landscape exuded the appealing essence of peaceable good-living: a rolling vision of mellow fruitfulness under a cirrus-flecked blue sky, the hillsides trimly planted with orchards and ripening cereal crops, interrupted here and there by a neat collation of terracotta roofs. The roads were broad and the drivers sympathetic, and the sunset so flattering that I mistook a cement factory for a castle. We stayed at

Moravske Toplice, a restful spa town that offered us the condensed cream of Slovenia's surrounding influences: Italian food, Austrian cleanliness, Hungarian roses and Croatian lymphatic-drainage massage. But Slovenia was as tiny as it was lovely, and by mid-morning I was out the other side.

I hate having my hair cut and in nine weeks hadn't bothered, oblivious to the bouffant grizzle wafting stupidly out from under my helmet on all sides until my wife repeatedly pointed it out. On our last evening, at a hotel overlooking the crevassed sludge plain that had been Croatia's largest lake before it sprang a catastrophic leak, she ordered remedial action. Off I went, with my son for company, into the gently flyblown centre of Prelog, where we presently found ourselves sharing a hair-floored front room with a bespectacled, white-bearded barber, three artillery shell-cases and a very happy man with five teeth.

The barber was less a stylist than an engineer, who went to work with the military precision befitting his souvenirs. One of the dozen-odd implements he would wield was a metal ruler, employed to assess the geometry of his cut along my collar line. That diligent focus was soon challenged, however, by the antics of his dentally imbalanced next customer. This fellow had bounded in through the door with a joyous blare of salutation, and at once settled down on the waiting bench extremely close to my son, who had just selected a periodical from the barber's coffee-table stack. In the mirror before me I watched our new friend relieve my progeny of his newspaper with a matey wink, before riffling clumsily through it until he reached a large photograph of a young woman who had forgotten to put her top on. A lascivious cackle filled the room; leering horribly he introduced this image to my son's face at a range of about four inches and lofted a grubby thumb.

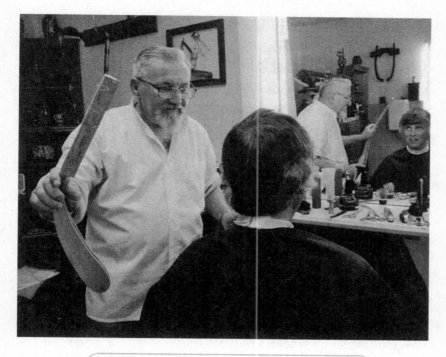

Tim Moore
@mrtimmoore

Finally had a trim, in style with this madcap
Col Sanders. 'First cut, then drink!' Out came
his homebrew slivovice.

'Sorry,' murmured the barber, slicing the tip off a single hair above my left ear, 'maybe he a little bit drinking.'

It's a fair bet that any Croat with a collection of spent ordnance knows how to work amid noisy distraction, and the barber stoically snipped away through a barrage of brays, belches and bared bosoms that sent my eldest child wanly recoiling ever further down the bench. His tonsorial work was almost done when Freddy Five Teeth launched into a spirited anthem of nationalistic aspect, keeping time with hearty slaps on my son's shoulder. Enough was

257

enough: the barber sighed heavily, downed tools and filled a plastic beaker from a bottle of water nestled amongst his blades and brushes. This was sternly presented to Freddy, who accepted it without protest as his final raucous stanza died away. After sweeping a last cull of grey hair from my caped shoulders, the barber allowed me to admire my severe and precise parade-ground coiffure in a handheld mirror, and then filled three further beakers from the bottle.

'Fuck da Coke,' he told my son, handing him the first.

'Fuck da pizza,' he told me, proffering the second.

The third he held aloft, gazing at it reverentially before concluding his rhyming ditty with a gusto that brought Freddy to his unsteady feet, beaker raised. 'All we need is *Šljivovica!*'

The ensuing communal toast informed my oesophagus that this fluid was very much not water; when my son, who had chauffeured me there, declined to participate with his hands on an imaginary steering wheel, Freddy responded with a loud scoff and a clearly well-informed mime of the delights of drunken driving. We left very shortly after, but not before the barber had progressed with impressive haste through several stages of inebriation. One minute he was chuntering on about the EU; the next he was chasing us around with a pantomime-prop cut-throat razor, three feet of cardboard and silver foil.

My wife had recoiled slightly when I came back reeking of moonshine with a conscript's crewcut, and did so more extravagantly the next morning, when my CamelBak leaked all over her during our farewell hug in the car park. 'You're so thin I thought I'd burst you,' she said, blotting her blouse with a sleeve. Then doors were slammed, tears blinked back and my support crew were off, on a drive to Vienna airport during which they would impressively accrue 510 euros in motoring fines.

It was a broiled and airless morning, the tipping point of full-on summer. By 10.30 a.m. the digital mercury hit 27 degrees, and after all those months of steering into patches of sunlight for warmth, I now weaved ponderously about in search of shade. For a long while I tracked the Drava, a yawning aquatic corridor that was nonetheless a mere tributary of the Danube, its dappled banks dotted with brown-bellied old anglers in Speedos, fag in one hand, rod in the other. Either side of this immense river stretched a rich alluvial plain, its cornfields crowned here and there with a grain silo or the silvered sphere of a water tower, wobbling up out of the heat haze.

In a generally successful bid to keep my bereft blubbering at bay, I counted the upsides of being alone on the road once more, a man on a very solitary mission. Earlier starts, shorn of familial faffing. An end to the contamination of my painstakingly ritual- ised, male-pattern capsule unpacking system, honed over six dozen nights to minimise the unthinkable horror of leaving some- thing vital behind. The departure of a recidivist corner cutter, who was forever waggling a finger over one of EV13's border-hugging cartographical meanders with the temptingly subversive catch- phrase, 'Why bother with that bit?' (I may as well confess now that to satisfy my support team's capricious desire to spend each night at a nice place in a different country, of late the route had suffered some drastic tweaking: for three days I had saddled up at the wrong A, and dismounted some way from the right B. And of course all those record-shattering distances I had racked up in their presence came suffixed with a disclaiming asterisk: *without panniers.)

Just as it had after Berlin, the interlude induced a back-to- square-one reboot. I would find myself bumping through a field of lilac opium poppies or slip-streaming a gypsy horse-cart and ask myself, aloud, what the freaking knackers I was up to. By now I had ridden further than my Tour and Giro rides combined, and succumbed to irrational fears as I probed ever deeper into uncharted territory, a bit like those early train passengers convinced that the unheard-of speed would melt their faces. At one point I forgot how to propel a bicycle, and watched in bemusement as my feet repeatedly slipped off the pedals. More often, pedalling seemed so effortless, and the flood-plain horizon so impossibly distant, that I felt I was back up in my attic on the exercise bike, going nowhere fast. And then, without warning, a surge of cock-sure self-belief would course through me: all this last stretch demanded was rhythm and routine, the simple discipline of getting up every morning and knocking out the big clicks, of channelling that Forrest Gump vibe: *Ride, Timmy, ride*. It took me a while to realise that these surges always occurred just after my mid-afternoon refreshment stop. It was the Magic Man talking.

Croatia marked EV13's exit from the EU's passport-schmassport Schengen zone, as I had discovered one morning while attempting to enter it with all my documents distantly locked away in the support vehicle. ('I give you choice,' the border guard cheerfully told me when I ill-advisedly lost my rag. 'One, you stop talking, then wait here for wife and she come with passport. Two, you pay five hundred euro for travel without document, then wait here for wife and she come with passport.') There was a palpable sense that I had broached our continent's outer limits, and gone back the thick end of a century for good measure. Hunched crones in shawls and headscarves dragged hoes across dusty backyards decorated with laundry and roses; tractors trundled past wicker corn cribs, each cab full of uncles and a dozen cousins dangling their feet off the trailer behind. The division of weekend labour in this part of the world was arresting: while women of all ages toiled away in the field, husbands went fishing in their pants and sons hung about by bus stops vacating their nostrils into the gutter.

Accommodation was in ever shorter supply, and from now on I took any bed that turned up after 5 p.m. At Virovitica, a welcome blurt of noise and life, that meant a room above a petrol station; at sleepy Suza, a village guest house on Marshal Tito Street. This tribute to the very Serbian father of socialist Yugoslavia seemed a surprising find in twenty-first-century Croatia, but I didn't fancy asking the sombre, baritone proprietor for an explanation. Hard up against the border with Serbia, Suza lay at the edge of the Croatian municipality of Draž, which took a predictable hit in the Balkan conflict. As Wikipedia blandly has it: 'There are 2,767 inhabitants in the municipality . . . During the Croatian War of Independence (1991–1995), 1,300 were expelled.' Twenty years on, the wounds continue to suppurate: the border between the two countries has yet to be fully defined up in this Danube-divided corner, a dispute in which shots are still occasionally fired.

Mittel Europe, with its stodge and beer, its Bon Jovi and bike paths and drizzle, began to seem very far away. My days now began at a table strewn with little dishes of paprika paste and pork scratchings, beside a big jug of thin white yoghurt that more than once I blearily poured into my coffee. Then it was out under a belting sun through cricket-chorused fields of ripening cherries there for the taking, down scabby roads splattered with careless reptiles. After all those villages shuttered up to keep the heat in, the ones I now rolled through were built to keep it out. And seeping through every other car window and fly curtain from here to journey's end, the hectic, brain-softening ululations of Balkan folk pop.

A long black snake slithered out at alarming speed from the roadside brush and – *per-lomp, ker-domp* – went straight under my wheels. The heat built. I learned how to ask for more chips in Serbo-Croat, from a barman who went outside to inspect the MIFA, then gave me a pat on the back and a beer on the house. A return to Hungary cluttered the verge with crucifixes and the towns with pepper-pot church spires; I overtook eight barefoot men in reflective jackets with 'I Trust in Jesus' on the back, pushing a giant trolley full of bibles down the road. One afternoon I went down with the ominous introductory cramps of a kidney stone, and manfully saw off this potential ride-ender with four litres of water, two hours of hunched distress, and – what the hell – the raw head of a giant cannabis plant I found growing wild by the road. For two days the quieter borderlands were thick with jagged little leaves and potent odours, presumably the legacy of drug shipments abandoned in panic. You couldn't imagine north Europeans tolerating such plantations, even if they had the weather to foster them. I'd passed from the chilly, rule-bound roundhead realm to the broiled and slapdash land of the cavaliers.

I spent my last Hungarian night in Mórahalom, whose proximity to two borders made it a very popular stopover for long-distance truck drivers who didn't fancy a night in Romania or Serbia. Besieged as it was by thunderous heavy traffic, the town still bravely clung to its past as a genteel spa resort – and with evident success, as I bagged the last available room in its largest hotel. Result: the palatially proportioned disabled suite, with a sit-down shower, help-me-up lavatory arms and other blessings for the kidney-bruised, mildly drugged shopping cyclist with 6,738km under his ever looser belt.

Most of the other guests were retired couples – Serbs, Germans, the odd native – and all had the build and bearing of that particular breed of spa visitor whose health cure is a strict regime of frothy wallows, interspersed with the regular stuffing of a fat red face. I left my laundered kit drying out on a twenty-wheelchair balcony, and went down to join them for dinner. This was a first-come, first-served buffet job, and came included in the price: a recipe, with bulky pensioners and me in the mix, for sharp-elbowed conflict. There were ugly scenes around the cutlet trough, and when I snatched the last dumpling from under his bulbous nose, some indignant wobble-chops in a towelling tracksuit called the police. So it seemed at least; in fact, the epaulette-shirted duo who now muscled up to the silver food bins were simply queue-jumping guests. What sort of policeman goes on holiday in his uniform? The cap I spotted on their table provided the answer: a German one.

In the morning I spunked my last forints on fly spray (why?) and a quarter bottle of Partizan vodka, then swapped a fifty-euro note for several thousand Serbian dinars at a bureau de change. I didn't need a reminder that I was about to leave the EU's comfort zone, but the woman behind the glass gave me one anyway.

'Where you go after Serbia?' she asked, unhappily counting note after tuppenny note into a grubby stack.

'Romania.' She pulled a frying-pan/fire face. 'After that on to the Black Sea in Bulgaria.'

'Oh, is nice,' she said, brightening.

'On a bicycle.'

'Is not nice.'

Then I scooped up the mountain of cash, walked out into the already wilting heat and set course for Horgoš, where I would enter a pariah state and pedal blithely past an unfolding humanitarian tragedy.

14. SERBIA

I saw them as I turned down the motorway ramp that would eventually deliver me to the Republic of Serbia, a couple of hundred blurry silhouettes slouched in the shade of a long blue building just inside the Hungarian border at Röszke. Amongst the police vans dotted about the surrounding compound was one with POLIZEI on the side – evidently those buffet-browsers were not on holiday at all, but had come to assist their EU counterparts with border security. Serbia wasn't in the EU, Hungary was; I deduced that the stooped and seated figures were apprehended migrants. But with a thousand roaring, many-wheeled vehicles poised to occupy my thoughts, that was all I deduced.

Horgoš and Röszke were all over the news within weeks, focus of a refugee crisis that shocked the world. The people I saw were Syrians, the first trickle of what would soon be a flood: a month later more than 1,000 were massing here every day. This border pinch-point was the beginning of the end of their long and desperate journey from a war-torn homeland to sanctuary in the EU, or at least the German and Scandinavian bits of it that were willing to take them. (A pleasing postscript: four months after I came home, Syrians began crossing from Russia into Norway up at the Kirkenes border – exploiting a loophole that permitted cyclists free passage. You may imagine my delight when TV news reports showed refugees wobbling up to my departure point through the first snows of winter on their ride of choice: a cheapo kid's bike. Some 5,500 made it over before the Norwegians changed the rules.)

The Hungarians, it has to be said, didn't acquit themselves terribly well. The refugees' sole intent was to proceed straight through the country en route to more sympathetic lands, yet at Röszke they nonetheless found themselves stoned, spat at and hosed down by water cannons. A camerawoman for one of Hungary's many nationalist TV channels, filming refugees in flight from a police baton charge, was photographed kicking two children and tripping up a man carrying his young son.

A few months later, when Hungary erected a 175km razor-wired fence along this border, I remembered all those snide and blotchy roadside nationalists in Austria, and their strident pledges to refortify the frontier. I remembered the Croatian barber who despised the EU, and recalled that every single nation I'd passed through – even placid Finland – was now host to a burgeoning Eurosceptic movement. In Hungary, a poll suggested that two-thirds of the population wanted out. Was the one-Europe dream over so soon? The Iron Curtain Trail had been laid out to celebrate the end of a beastly era of division and hatred, but walls that had come down in 1989 were already going back up. Would EV13 still be around if I returned in twenty-five years? Hard to say: I'd be seventy-six by then and wouldn't recognise a bike path if it hit me in the face, which it repeatedly would.

The motorway border post was despatched without incident, and I shortly found myself in the knocked-about, lethargic countryside that would define much of my passage through Serbia. I had, I confess, been dreading my entry into a maligned and marginalised nation that receives fewer annual visitors than Luxembourg, and generally bags a top ten spot in internet polls of the world's most hated states. By popular international agreement, Serbians are the baddies, the bullies, the ethnic-cleansing war criminals, the Tito-tutored tyrants who just can't cut the cord, who still feel all of Yugoslavia is theirs by right.

The dread reappearance of Cyrillic, rare as it was this far north, didn't help, and nor did the return of totalitarian keepsakes: crumbly white obelisks topped with sun-bleached red stars, dere-lict military compounds where sentry posts and basketball hoops poked above well-established vegetation, a bust of a people's war hero in every funereal village square. The very first Serbian I encountered who wasn't in a border uniform almost flattened me, pulling straight out of a sandy side road obscured in a cloud of his own making.

This was a rare excitement, for the Vojvodina plain now served up a huge, hot slice of nothing. For hours I bumped along a deserted concrete-slab road marooned amid a treeless, houseless sea of scraggy maize and wheat. The crops thinned and the soil blackened; the camomile pot-pourri that had perfumed the hedge-rows for days soured to a putrid miasma of mouldy old towels. My only company across this poisoned prairie were the toads who croaked unseen in the roadside drainage trenches, deep down in the sickly bulrushes.

By mid-morning it was 35 degrees; a fifty-seven-point swing up the Celsius scale from my ride's opposite Lapland extremity. There was a curious affinity with those Arctic wastes, that same sense of having ridden right off the map. Indeed, Finland was lodged in my mind all afternoon once I'd run out of water. All those months ago, as I crawled across iced lakes with a frigid gale ripping in through my balaclava eyeholes, I had scraped together some solace by telling myself there would be times ahead when I would pay good money for a frozen headwind. Here was the first of those times.

'One thing, please,' drawled the Hostel Paparazzo's tattoo-ankled receptionist, laying the dusty MIFA to rest between an ironing board and a Marshall speaker stack. 'You will not drink the water here in Kikinda, never. It is technical water only.'

Hardly a surprise, given the stagnant, sulphurous wafts I had toiled through for hours, but an intriguing phrase nonetheless. A worrisome one too, as just outside Kikinda I had lowered my blistered lips to a village standpipe and gratefully ingested bobbing throatfuls of the stuff.

'You can use for toilet, not in kitchen. Even you take it to 100 Celsius, you will be like this.' With sudden gusto she showered the MIFA's bedroom with imaginary human voidance. 'The boss he will not be happy.'

This gentleman – owner of the Marshall stack and, I suspected, the receptionist's heart – was a local rock-god whose lion-maned, Fender-fondling image had been plastered gigantically all over the lobby, and halfway up the stairs to my airless dormitory. 'If you are lucky he will be here in morning,' the receptionist told me as I headed out an hour later, reeking of technical water.

Kikinda guts, as I brilliantly dubbed it, was a dusty wonder: the Paparazzo lay at the heart of a bustling mess of pastel cathedrals, monumental sculpture and crumbling socialist apartment blocks, which together brought Latin America to mind. Everything from the brown eyes to those filthy wodges of semi-worthless banknotes would have transferred seamlessly to some banana republic. I hadn't felt so foreign since Kaliningrad.

The blistered stucco walls were slowly releasing the day's mighty heat and I cooled myself with a fist-sized ice cream, tonguing it languidly along a leafy boulevard clustered with ambling couples and families. There wasn't a single Western shop sign, and the windows were piled with clumpy shoes and cheap-looking furniture: EU and US sanctions were only recently lifted, and almost everything on sale in Serbia is made locally. I went round a grocery and found its entire stock – fig rolls, drinking yoghurt, shampoo – labelled as produce of the Republika Srbija. Any motorist who recalls the Yugo, subject of a recent monograph entitled *The Rise and Fall of the Worst Car in History*, will tell you that the Republika Srbija isn't very good at making things. Even exported Yugos sometimes came with mismatched front seats – one brown, the other black – and dashboard warning-lights labelled by hand. The shop's rear end was stacked from floor to ceiling with colossal plastic barrels of non-technical water, several of which I had seen being lugged through the streets over an often ancient shoulder. It wasn't a terribly European look. I have just established that the water supply in Vojvodina province is contaminated with our continent's highest levels of bacterial and chemical pollutants, a cocktail that routinely contains threadworms, raw human waste and arsenic. Anyway, drinking half a hogshead of it didn't kill me. In fact, like some fledgling Marvel superhero exposed to toxic radiation, it may have made me stronger.

I had two Lav beers (no – it's too easy) and a pizza in a restaurant full of Balkan pop, sauce-faced kids and smoking parents, then strolled over to the showpiece civic spaces. At 9 p.m. Kikinda was busier, and balmier, than any place I'd walked round after hours since Berlin, and it was here, among the poisoned fountains and dimly lit relics of a complex past, that I first began to fall for Serbia. Toddlers clipped their parents' ankles at the wheels of rented electric go-karts, buzzing between a moribund socialist hotel and a big ochre church. Louder elder siblings were playing unisex football by a boldly abstract 1960s war memorial; the more restrained had gathered at a giant chess set, rubbing chins amongst the waist-high pawns. A couple embraced in the grandly turreted shadow of the Habsburg-vintage city hall, and outside the pockmarked high school that propped up the Paparazzo, a young accordionist was drawing a small crowd. It was infectious and heart-lifting and – cough – unbelievably cheap. The ten-dinar notes I'd been piling up on counters all night, I now calculated, were each worth 6p; the entire evening had set me back under four quid. I was so pleased I phoned my wife to tell her, blissfully unaware that Serbia lies in the same tin-pot, pariah-state telecommunication charge band as North Korea. After I got home I discovered that every minute of this conversation had cost more than my night out.

A little man with sunken eyes and a straggly grey poodle-perm was installed behind the Paparazzo's desk when I stumbled wearily downstairs after a sticky, restless night. At length I connected him with the thrusting axe-merchant staring imperiously down from the walls. As I pushed the MIFA out of his storeroom he lugubriously hoisted the sign of the horns with both hands; I returned the gesture with one and headed out into the blazing sun.

Serbia's towns proved a dependable delight; its countryside bored and burned the pants off me. In the morning I'd stockpile toothsome, cheese-stuffed road-fuel at one of the splendid bakeries that graced every urban street corner, huff wistfully and strike out across a fresh expanse of flyblown, shade-less flatland. As long as I kept pedalling, the self-generated breeze made the heat bearable; whenever I stopped, it was shocking, an oven-baked horse blanket flung rudely over my head. The Garmin topped out at 47.1 degrees in the sun. Tiger-stripes of red began to sear through my deep base tan, and my mind boiled dry. I spent an entire afternoon counting pedal revolutions: 171 per kilometre in top gear, for the record, and 232 in low. The rare and drowsy villages were falling down and half empty, thinly scattered with aged locals stooped in sagging, ancient thresholds or gathered under trees. My appearance aroused a novel sort of attention: for once I wasn't a weirdo on a daft bike, just a stranger, a new kid in town. Old couples would nudge each other and edge forth from their doorways as I jangled by, faces puckered in awe: 'Look – a man.'

In fact, the bike and I didn't get a single funny look in Serbia. As a legacy of distant centralised manufacture and recent economic sanctions, the ancient 20-inch-wheeled shopper was and remains rural Serbia's ride of choice. I'm sure you can imagine our excitement at this discovery, though if you can't I'm happy to send on request a selection of related commemorative selfies. Many of these MIFA-likes supported more than one rustic bottom, the rear carrier ferrying children to school or granddad to the bus stop. And doing so with incredible sloth: the average speed of a Serbian bicycle is roughly 0.3kmh above that at which it would topple over.

Even the scabbiest hamlet was home to a grocery shed with a colourful drinks fridge out the front, and with my CamelBak drained and the last, sweaty pastry gone I would dive in through the fly curtains, queuing up for fluids and waxy Serb chocolate behind some well-built, powerfully aromatic farmhand, trading empty beer bottles for full ones. Every settlement had its name translated into multiple languages on the welcome and farewell signs; I once counted six. Hungarian, German, Serbo-Croat in both Latin and Cyrillic flavours plus the odd mystery guest – evidence of the Balkan region's extraordinary ethnic diaspora, and Serbia's new-found willingness to embrace it.

On I pressed, ever deeper into the Borat moustache belt, past mighty, glinting grain elevators and fields fringed with mounds of smouldering refuse. Whenever an agricultural vehicle chugged by I would put in a catch-up burst and settle gratefully in its slipstream, much to the driver's black-toothed amusement. Late one afternoon I was sucked along for a good hour behind a leaking muck spreader, an instructive exercise in the opposing forces of magnetism.

Come sunset all was forgiven, indeed largely forgotten. By then I would have slung my laundered kit over a wrought-iron balcony, and be out on some broad and well-peopled square, stopping on occasion at an appealing, parasol-fronted bar for a shish kebab or another beer, gazing with weary contentment at my route maps, the girdling of regal façades and in due course the bill. Vršac – which you should pronounce ver-shatz if you find yourself in the area and want to get laughed at less loudly than I was – proved an especial treat. Every vista offered an engaging tangle of history: pointy-topped Ottoman arches, pink and yellow Habsburg stucco, some wilfully monstrous hunk of Communist concrete hard up against the neo-Gothic cathedral's graceful spires. Serbia had been persistently reminding me of another country, and wandering through Vršac I realised which one. The ritual evening stroll, the sons holding hands with their garrulous mothers, the unhelmeted youths careering madly through the traffic on deafening mopeds – I don't think you need any more clues, but if you do, it isn't Norway. From then on, Serbia delivered Italianate cameos with tireless diligence: a bus driver with a phone to his ear and his foot to the floor; a whistling, shameless fly-tipper flinging a bathroom suite into a ditch; a cluster of old men outside a village bar, watching the very small world go by in companionable silence.

After all those stopover settlements left behind without a second thought, I was beginning to find morning departures a wrench. A damp little town in Austria seemed fair game for a loveless one-night stand, but I wanted to go out with Kikinda for at least a couple of weeks, and possibly even marry Vršac. She had the sweetest nature and a cracking set of bakeries. And though I'm slightly regretting this unwholesome analogy, anything had to be better than my next conquest: just up the road I'd be getting down and dirty with EV13's wartiest old hag.

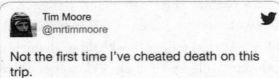

Tim Moore
@mrtimmoore

Not the first time I've cheated death on this trip.

15. ROMANIA

'*Turizam?*'

'Industrial espionage,' I said, nodding brightly.

The Serbian border guard returned my passport, and jabbed a thumb at the Garmin.

'How many you go?'

I cupped the screen to shade out the dazzling sun, and slowly dictated the running total: 'Seven thousand, two hundred and twelve kilometres.' I watched his dark eyes widen. 'About one and a half thousand left.'

'But . . . is *bicikl normalno!*'

What a stirring acclamation, rounded off with the two most beautiful words in the Serbo-Croatian language. One clause of my admittedly sketchy mission statement had been to prove that the bicycle, even in its humblest incarnation, was a go-anywhere, do-anything machine – a shopper would always get you down the shops, even if they were 6,000 miles away. As the border guard summoned his colleagues to pay homage, I mentally ticked that one off. After fourteen nations' worth of derision, I had at last found a country that recognised the MIFA as no more than a bog-standard bike. Regrettably I was leaving it at once. A few short days before, I had left the EU behind with a sense of deep foreboding. How curious to find my heart far heavier as I now prepared to re-enter it.

In 1990, we drove into Romania behind a convoy of Red Cross vans, the only other foreign vehicles we would encounter there beyond a couple of typically foolhardy Polski Fiats. The native border guards were flabbergasted to hear the purpose of our visit. 'You come on *holiday*?' It was ten months since Nicolae Ceaușescu and his wife had been lavishly ventilated by a firing squad, and after twenty-four years of despotic lunacy the country remained ravaged and traumatised. Nonetheless, by then we fancied ourselves battle-hardened, inured to East European squalor and scarcity, ready for anything. Anything but Romania, it almost instantly transpired.

We spent our first night in Deva, just east of Timișoara, where the discontent that would swiftly topple Ceaușescu had first flared up a year before. As we approached Deva's only hotel the whole town went black, almost pitching us into a cavernous void in the road, bereft of any warning furniture and deep enough to swallow a bus. A torch-wielding bell-boy hobbled out on crutches, his eyes nervously scanning the darkness, and beckoned us to drive across the pavement; he kept beckoning until the Saab's front end was literally inside the hotel doors. The lights flickered back on a while later as a waitress led us into the kitchen. With a take-it-or-leave-it shrug, she threw open a fridge that contained three oval slices of bread and a blistered enamel plate with a dozen tiny cubes of cheese scattered across it. What an introduction. It was all down-hill after that.

In the countryside, people grubbed listlessly for roots in the cold autumn mud, sometimes recoiling at our approach as if they'd never seen a car before; we shared the crevassed roads with haywain-hauling horses, and hordes of filth-caked, semi-feral urchins. Both were Ceauşescu legacies. He had banned abortion to boost the nation's birth rate as part of his monomaniac drive to haul Romania into the industrialised twentieth century, and when that went ruinously wrong, punted his bankrupt country back to the nineteenth. In 1986, just four years before our visit, Romania launched a nationwide horse-breeding campaign: tractors had become an unthinkable luxury.

The towns, though, were inestimably worse. Every time we stopped, even briefly at a junction, gaunt zombies would slowly mass around the Saab with their hands out. Whenever we got out of the car, the crowd came suddenly to life and surged forward, blundering hectically around us, like bees around their queen. We had to clear a way through by tossing out Western unobtainables stockpiled in preparation: Biros, oranges, sticks of Wrigley's gum. In the shops, shelves were thinly stocked with hopeless, cracker-novelty crap or stolen goods. One grocery had a counter stacked with tins of Red Cross baby-milk powder. There was a dead dog in the gutter outside.

The hotels were bleak and unheated, forbidden by law to turn the radiators on unless the outside temperature fell below 10 degrees Celsius, which in the official forecast it apparently never did, even when there was ice on the windows. Our rooms were miserably damp and decorated with clumsily hand-painted patterns in the absence of wallpaper. Taps dispensed a chilled fluid that sometimes looked like Bovril, sometimes milky tea. Electricity came and went. The TV, if there was one, offered nothing but monochrome Hollywood obscurities, generally featuring the young Kirk Douglas doing something plausibly socialist, like saving redwoods from a logging conglomerate or punching a ruthless cattle baron on the jaw.

We survived on fizzy green pickled tomatoes, chalky mineral water and ladles of a gristled pottage that our systems promptly rejected one way or another, generally both. One restaurant had food but no cutlery, and we ate our carbonated tomatoes and dog stew with the cocktail sticks provided. Mostly the opposite problem applied. A waiter in an otherwise deserted restaurant would politely show us to a dim table and present a menu, then shake his head regretfully, sometimes after a chin-rubbing rumination, as I ran a finger slowly down its full length. In Gura Humorului, a sizeable settlement which Wikipedia tells me was then home to 17,000 inhabitants, we enacted these silent Monty Python cheese-shop sketches at two restaurants and a café: the whole town had been entirely stripped of edible matter. 'I just used to go on stage and say, "Food",' a Romanian comedian said recently, recalling his experiences on whatever passed for the native stand-up circuit in the 1980s. 'The audience always burst into applause: I was thought so brave for using a forbidden word.'

The only passable nutrition we ingested at any point in Romania was at the Dracula Hotel in Brasov, where to our astonishment a lorry driver on the next table flung his cutlery down after one forkful and stormed into the kitchen to complain. An hour later, I went out to get something from the car and found the chef and two waiters beating him to a pulp.

Every large town was dominated by a vast and ghastly steelworks, the evil, belching embodiment of Ceauşescu's monstrous misrule. Making lots of hard metal was a rite of state-socialist passage, and the fact that Romania – a land blessed with rich soil and an abundance of other natural resources – possessed no native reserves of iron ore wasn't about to put off the Warsaw Pact's most unhinged dictator.

Eastern Bloc leaders were rarely shy of a personality cult – one edition of *Neues Deutschland*, the GDR's national daily paper, contained no fewer than forty-one photographs of Erich Honecker – but only the General Secretary of the Romanian Communist Party went the full North Korea. Nicolae Ceauşescu proclaimed himself a secular god, and built a 'people's palace' that remains the world's second largest building, after the Pentagon. He once delivered a six-hour speech that incorporated 125 standing ovations. Ceauşescu was the megalomaniac's megalomaniac: paranoid, jealous and in most other ways just full-on nuts. He was 5ft 3in and refused to employ anyone taller, being thus preceded by a team of very small functionaries who dabbed down everything he was about to touch – pens, door handles, taps – with surgical alcohol. He never wore any item of clothing, even a pair of shoes, more than twice, and had everything incinerated afterwards. On overseas trips, Ceauşescu took along a tiny chemist whose job it was to destroy his excrement, thereby denying foreign agencies the opportunity to assess his state of health via faecal analysis.

To unwind, he would take a boat out across the Danube delta to inspect the pelican colonies that inhabited its more remote islands. 'Ceauşescu was fascinated by their structured society,' recalled the national security adviser who accompanied him on these trips. 'The old birds always lay up on the front of the beach, close to the water and food supply, with the children and grandchildren behind them in orderly rows. He would tell me he wished Romania had the same rigid social structure. Then he took out an Uzi and gunned them all down.'

It was this sort of business that saw Nicolae Ceauşescu shunned by his less terrifyingly potty Communist brethren. Funding that obsession with steel thus obliged him to buy ore from the Other Side, generally with Western loans, in order to produce rubbish steel that nobody wanted. The spiral drove Romania into catastrophic debt. By the Eighties more than three-quarters of Romania's food production was being sold to the West, an export trade still very visibly active in the stream of heavily laden fruit and veg lorries that wobbled past us to the border in 1990. A land of plenty with nothing to eat.

Our nadir came one crisp, bright afternoon at Bicaz, a town atop a glorious Carpathian gorge rudely stoppered by a hydro-electric dam, built to power the local steelworks. Punctures had become an occupational hazard on roads strewn with horseshoe nails, and I had just laboriously fitted our Saab's spare tyre when a lurch and that dread rumble from below made a bad day worse. Just how much worse is summated by my wife's journal entry: 'T put his head on steering wheel and wept.'

The hours ahead were not my finest. My wife left me blubbering uselessly in the stricken Saab, and set off through the crumbly tenements with a carton of Kent cigarettes down her coat. (These were Romania's default hard currency back then – always bartered, never smoked – and all week we'd been paying for hotel rooms and plates of rancid poison with the forty-odd duty-free packets acquired at the Hungarian border.) An hour later she returned, accompanied by an ogre in vest and braces who would in due course vulcanise a successful tyre repair, to find the Saab besieged by the youth of Bicaz.

The happier outer circle was clicking away at their new retractable ballpoints, cheeks bulging with Wrigley's gum; the luckiest few savoured the more exotic booty that I had fearfully fed through a small gap in the driver's window after our stock of mob-appeasing trinkets was exhausted. Most of it came from my wife's washbag, now hollow and ransacked on the seat beside me. The inner ring, driven to a covetous frenzy by the bottles of shampoo and Country Born hair gel being cradled by their triumphant peers, were now rocking the Saab to and fro, as if trying to shake it loose of fragrant toiletries.

My wife bullied the passenger door open and squeezed in, to find me wedging the sleeve of her Levi's jacket through my window gap. She snatched it clear from five dozen grubby fingertips, then firmly wound the window shut. The rocking resumed, accompanied now by a chant of irony or the very cruellest delusion: 'Por-sche, Por-sche!' Our eyes met and we came to a wordless understanding. Ten hours later, after a non-stop drive through the night past Bucharest and many other intended stops on our Romanian itinerary, we slipped a border guard twenty Kent and a five-dollar bill to jump the queue, then sloshed into Bulgaria through a trough of disinfectant.

DRUM BUN.

The sign that saw me off from the Romanian border post raised a smile: it was everywhere in 1990, a tilted, rusty farewell outside every town that literally meant 'good road', adopted by us as a catchphrase tribute to the percussive, month-old bread rolls that comprised the typical hotel breakfast ('It's a drum; it's a bun!').

I knew Romania couldn't possibly be as bad as it had been in 1990, though its fearsome rep clearly lingered. EV13 tracked the Serbo-Romanian border for several hundred kilometres, but whoever decided its precise path had conspicuously favoured the Tito side; I would merely swerve into a country that remained of evident concern to the responsible elders of cross-continental cycling. My EV13 route guide warned of dogs, terrible driving and towns that 'greet the visitor with poor road conditions'; the chap who rented me a room in Vršac spoke succinctly of '*beeeeg* danger'. What no one mentioned were the huge, hot hills that reared up straight from the border, the first 3D geography I had tackled for an age. The flies couldn't get enough of my leaking face, and the desiccated roadside brush was alive with reptilian scuttles and thrashes; I dropped my gaze and sustained myself with yet another lingering appraisal of those frankly magnificent new legs of mine, tanned and toned and winsomely aglow with perspiration.

The villages, when at last I swept gratefully down into them, were no worse than cheerily ramshackle. Garish little houses faced in shiny pink tiles glittered through the dust thrown up by tractors. Shirtless men were splitting logs on the pavement; a tortoise inched along the gutter; I caught the first snatches of a tongue that sounds

Tim Moore
@mrtimmoore

Yeah, yeah.

like drugged Italian. Most of the youngsters gave me a wave, and most were arrestingly rotund, the fattest kids I'd seen since leaving home. A legacy, I deduced, of all those food-free towns in 1990: it must be very hard for parents reared in famished deprivation to resist the reactive reflex to stuff their own children's faces.

But the towns, starting at Moldova Veche, were simply dreadful. Their streets were entirely bereft of the culture and history that had ennobled Serbia's larger settlements, and didn't converge on any definable centre: Ceauşescu couldn't build his towns around a victory-over-fascism memorial plaza, as his neighbours generally did, because Romania spent most of the war fighting with the Nazis. Instead, there were just rows and rows of degenerate grey tenements that looked as if they'd been strafed by light artillery. Every lay-by and bus stop was an open-plan skip and the dead-cat count ticked sharply upwards. Mono-browed idlers gave me looks that had my hands tightening around the bars. The European Union is a rich tapestry; here I was at its tattered seams.

Then the cars and buildings vanished, I rounded a gravelly corner and there was the Danube, smooth and green and impossibly broad, stretching out like the sea with Serbia a misty suggestion on its opposite coast. What an Amazonian beast, the EU's longest watercourse – with a drainage basin of almost a million square kilometres, swelled by the rain of eighteen nations, it's the closest we have in Europe to an Old Man River. An old man's river, too: the broad, gravelly foreshore was here and henceforth speckled with topless anglers of pensionable age. I would follow the Danube all the way down the Romanian border, with one titillating fantasy always lurking in my thoughts: if I strapped the MIFA to a lilo and clambered on, after an effortless day or two we'd be bobbing out together into the Black Sea.

I stayed at an upscale but unfinished hillside guest house, sharing my first swimming pool and a majestic overview of the Danubian

sunset with a fat family and two JCBs, very loudly excavating a
terrace ten feet from our heads. The vista was timeless, but my
company and surroundings captured the essence of a bipolar new
Romania. Medieval hayricks and stooped peasants dotted the
sloping, gold-green pastures; my poolside companions were an
unappealing vision of plump and gaudy entitlement, flumped on
sunloungers with brown-domed bellies, wrists weighed down with
precious metal, periodically clicking fingers for more beers. From
time to time the prostrate paterfamilias would lazily swivel his
massive bald head and fix me with one open eye, a look that spoke
of a fortune made through nefarious means. It was Russia all over
again. I felt so sorry for the nervous young waiter that after dinner I
left him a sixteen-quid tip. Admittedly I might not have done had I
got to grips with the exchange rate, and refused some of the umpteen
complimentary shots of slivovitz that punctuated my meal.

In the late Sixties, during a rare moment of Yugo-Romanian harmony,
Tito and Ceauşescu agreed to build a hydro-electric dam across the
Danube, near a pinch-point known as the Iron Gates, which lay at
the end of a long gorge. Doing so submerged hundreds of villages,
amongst them the extraordinary Ada Kaleh – a Turkish enclave that
had held out on a river island for almost a hundred years after the
Ottoman Empire's collapse. (In this part of the world you often get
the impression that everyone is still doing their best to forget the
centuries of Ottoman rule: Vršac was part of the Turkish empire for
200 years before the mid-Victorian era, but the only surviving record
of this period is a single account left by a passing diplomat in 1662,
who described it as 'a little town of Oriental type, with three
mosques, a public bath and a courthouse'.)

The Danube's damming also required Romania and Yugoslavia to
build new roads above the waterline, a challenging assignment given

the steepling walls of rock that hemmed in this stretch of river. The light of a hot new day allowed me a clear assessment of each nation's approach. Over on the opposite bank, Serbia as is, the road speared impressively and very expensively through the cliffs or between them: tunnel, bridge, gallery, bridge, tunnel. Here on my side, the engineers had been compelled to take the economy option, and national route 57 meandered apologetically around the foot of the towering canyon wall, close to the Danube's ever more urgent waters. Even at this range – despite the narrowing gorge, the river was never less than a kilometre wide – Yugoslavia flaunted its relative prosperity, a land of civil-engineering extravagance that was a self-evidently better place to live. No surprise to learn that hundreds of tantalised Romanians drowned here; the few who made it across endured a four-hour battle with a current so strong that larger ships had to be pulled through with the help of locomotives.

I've often wondered why anyone bothers with those tumbling-rock warning signs. How are you expected to moderate your driving style to account for the imminent possibility of a granite cascade? I guess closing the sunroof might be an idea. These signs infested the N57, a major transnational route whose mysterious emptiness was explained when I swept around a bend and found the carriageway interrupted by a boulder the size of a shipping container. The effect was comical rather than sobering: I half-expected a condensed Dick Dastardly to totter out from under it, just a pair of shoes under a flat hat. That night I was told that the N57 had been thus blocked for six weeks, condemning road-users unable to carry their conveyances around large obstacles to a 190km detour. Other than a little red reflector stuck to the boulder itself I hadn't spotted any advance notification, and there was no evidence of an attempt to clear the road.

I approached the Iron Gates through a circuitous and punishing route that wandered distantly away from the river and wound upwards, through the sometimes inhumanly grim hilltop towns built by Ceaușescu to replace the submerged villages. Then the road twisted down, the granite flanks pressed in and the green waters began to surge and billow. The Iron Gates of Kladovo sound like the setting for a Spinal Tap live album, and look it too, with those walls of rock and the mighty water. For good measure, one rearing granite promontory was embellished with the monumental head of an ancient Dacian king, commissioned by an eccentric Romanian

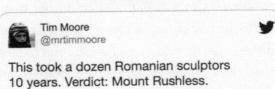

Tim Moore
@mrtimmoore

This took a dozen Romanian sculptors 10 years. Verdict: Mount Rushless.

billionaire in the 1990s. It's apparently the tallest rock sculpture in Europe, but I fear my reaction was out of line with expectations: the overall suggestion is Brian Blessed in a wizard's hat.

In Berlin I had acquired two aerosols of police-grade pepper spray, principally to ensure that my friends cried when I left, but also for later use in taking the fight to the famously excitable dogs of rural Eastern Europe. No-nonsense weaponry seemed a lot more appealing than the favoured 'three S' defensive tactics revealed by my online research: stand your ground, shout, throw stones (in the Moore-ish translation: scream, sob, surrender). Since leaving Austria, unchained rustic yapping had steadily progressed from occasional irritant to regular menace; even in kindly Slovenia, a mad old collie had chased me for the best part of a kilometre along a mercifully downhill road. The farm hounds of Croatia had upped the ante, and ever since I'd been packing double-barrelled heat,

one little can of 'Pfeffer KO Jet' tucked under the front luggage strap and the other stuffed in my rear jersey pocket.

Romania, as I feared and had been severally warned, was in a barking class of its own, top dog, Peak Cur. Nowhere else would man's worst friends play faster or looser. By far the stupidest, chasiest aggressors were the shop-dogs that lay in wait outside every grocery in every godforsaken concrete settlement. Once my CamelBak was dry and my breakfast burned off, I would approach those tantalising awnings and alfresco fridges with a thwarted sigh and a clench of foreboding, knowing that if I even thought about stopping, and frankly even if I didn't, a howling mass of fur and fury would fly out at me from some unseen shady recess between crates. I would then be closely escorted with the most intense enthusiasm to the edge of town, in a dusty ball of frenzied barks, fast legs and the very reediest profanity.

Only once, when a squat half-breed got his jaws into my right-hand pannier, did my juddering, fearful fingers flip the safety lid off the Pfeffer KO Jet; the vicious little shit instantly disengaged at the simple sight of that nozzle of maximum distress, and dived under a parked lorry before I could offload liquid fire into his filthy yellow face at the recommended point-blank range. But however dearly I wished to damage these ghastly animals, it was probably as well that I never did. The long, lonely hours in the saddle offered ample opportunity to play out relevant scenarios in my mind, and these imaginary confrontations never ended in the right sort of tears. A shopkeeper who chose to repel all passing trade with bestial assault had, I reasoned, already proven himself an irrational man of violence; if such a man discovered his furry charge in whimpering, stricken distress with half the Danube frothing out of his face holes, one might expect him to launch a prompt and vengeful investigation. As a conspicuous witness with two cans of

Pfeffer KO Jet visibly about his person I might plausibly be invited to assist with this inquiry, and there would only be one way of excusing myself. Don't Mace the dog if you can't Mace the man.

Banished from groceries I was forced into a Proper Sit-Down Lunch: the regional omeletty institution that is ham and eggs, pronounced ha-man-dex, consumed on a lofty, vine-shaded terrace. On the spangled Danube below, a pair of enormous, low-slung bulk-commodity barges struggled manfully against the current, and I wondered how the Romans had managed to span this vast bastard just upstream (Trajan's Bridge was well over a kilometre in length; no one would build a longer arched rival anywhere on earth for more than a thousand years). The Romans were only here for a century and a half, yet exerted a disproportionate and durable influence on Romania, as you may cunningly deduce from its name. The native language is in no small part derived from the military Latin slang spoken by the legionaries who came, saw, conquered and quite swiftly buggered off, which means Romanian still boasts a one-word command to thin trees in order to facilitate their collapse on an invading army. I'm not telling you what it is, though, in case you spoil my plan.

Romania's endgame was a trial of Russian proportions, played out on an undersized road that overflowed with heavy vehicles, all rejoining my route at the end of their monstrous diversion around that boulder. Lorries strained and ground up the bottle-green hills, then barrelled thunderously down the other side, buffeting the MIFA up against the threadbare ridge of shin-high Ceaușescu cement that separated me from the Danube seething distantly beneath. It was sultry in the extreme, and more than one truck swept by with its me-side cab door held wide open, providing a passenger with welcome ventilation and an unhindered, close-up view of the top of my helmet. On occasion the edge of the road was interrupted by deep, jagged arcs, as if some giant beast had taken bites out of it. About this time I stopped wondering why I hadn't seen a single bicycle in Romania.

Looking back, I fear that I may have exhausted my reserves of national compassion. As a veteran of Romania's properly dreadful past I was better placed than most to forgive the country its manifold present failings. But in the event, all attempts to muster some farewell empathy were shouted down by a simple, profound desire to get the hell out of there. As a bonus, doing so involved crossing EV13's most extraordinary border: I rode back into Serbia over the Danube-spanning Iron Gate dam, a mighty, rushing turbine roar thrumming up through my wheels from far, far below.

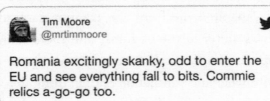

Tim Moore
@mrtimmoore

Romania excitingly skanky, odd to enter the EU and see everything fall to bits. Commie relics a-go-go too.

16. SERBIA II

ROMANIA

Kladovo

SERBIA

Zaječar

BULGARIA

It would be wrong to suggest that my days now spooled by in a blur – very wrong, an injustice both to the captivating, sunbathed hillscapes that increasingly defined EV13, and to my heroic endurance in repeatedly conquering them. But with seventeen nations under my wheels and just three ahead, I was infected for the first time with something that felt like confident expectation, and which sometimes spilled into impatience. I began to tug EV13's multi-stranded, squiggly string a little more tightly: when the route guide and my maps offered a choice between pushing for an hour down a wandering sandy track or a direct main road, I didn't agonise. With well over 1,000km left this was one hell of a finishing straight, but I'd wound up some momentum and couldn't bear to let it slip.

From here on I rarely knocked out fewer than 120km a day, and the marker-pen line I traced on my laminated EV13 map, which for long, dispiriting weeks had seemed barely to progress, now squiggled eagerly towards its conclusion. As it did, so the Iron Curtain narrative seemed ever more muted and distant: Yugoslavia and Romania were just two rogue Commie states in a desultory sideshow face-off, and my remaining nations – Bulgaria, Greece and Turkey – hardly reeked of the Cold War. Whole days went by without a single old watchtower troubling the horizon.

I was at that stage of a long trip where everyone starts falling out with each other, but the MIFA didn't argue back and, despite my very best efforts, nor did the route guide. Whoever had compiled this last section was an absolute maestro of the maddeningly superfluous.

'Be careful to avoid potholes!' Woah, let's get this straight: you're telling me to steer *around* craters in the road?

'TIP: beware of lorries on this highly travelled section!' Are you sure? Are you absolutely certain that as a cyclist I should be paying attention to heavy goods traffic?

'And after a long day, why not enjoy an ice-cold local beer?' Of *course*! And to think of all those hot evenings spent rubbing gravel into my gums.

My spirit was eager, but both bike and body had long since settled into a state of grumbly resignation, obeying orders without enthusiasm and reminding me at regular intervals what an unreasonable bully I was being. The Duomatic hub rattled like a tin of tacks in low gear, and occasional flare-ups of third-degree Brinelling kept me on the straight and narrow when I least wanted to be. But this seemed like small beer in the big picture. I was, after all, asking the MIFA to do something it had never been expected to do: work properly without immediately falling to bits.

Every morning my ankles carried me gingerly down to breakfast, raw and tender and all but creaking like old doors; riding a bike all day seemed an improbable remedy, but after a couple of hundred wincing revolutions they piped down. In the evenings my thigh muscles were prone to a cramp so severe that when I crossed my legs, as I invariably seemed to when sitting back in my restaurant chair after dinner, both hands and many loud gasps of agony were required to uncross them. The endless quantity of roads did for my legs; my arms were ravaged by their jarring, potholed quality. A palsied numbness crept across my hands, eventually disabling the outer three fingers of each. My enfeebled wrists began to fall distressingly foul of Lycra's tensile strength while yanking the front of my shorts down behind trees. One morning, saddling up the MIFA before a coach party of pensioners outside a hotel reception, the front carrier's elastic strap whiplashed from my frail grasp, and its hefty clasp thwacked me square in the nuts.

My buttocks came closest to mutiny. They'd been spoiled soft by all those weeks riding on grey German velvet, and the pebble-dashed Balkan roads came as a bruising wake-up call. I spent the morning shifting about in search of a bearable perch, but by mid-afternoon just sat down and took it, the saddle a cluster of hard and complex protrusions. It was like squatting on a typewriter for nine hours. I felt strangely betrayed by a mass of flesh that had always served me well, a faithful, uncomplaining servant in those long rides around France and Italy; to conjure an image we can all fruitfully savour, my bum stood on the burning deck, while all about it burned. Only now do I grasp a causal connection with drastic weight loss: by this stage I was literally down to the bones of my arse.

Serbia brought shopping bikes back to the roads, and bright little homes in place of Romania's soiled and crumbling hutch-stacks. Tortured yowling and electro-accordions serenaded me through every town; ripe red cherries embellished the roadsides. I dined splendidly – kebabs, Greek-style *shopska* salad, refreshing gumfuls of gravel – and as the bills were laid down, came to a belated understanding of why so many people in this part of the world whinged on about the EU: Romania, a starkly inferior nation, had been significantly more expensive.

As a more ambivalent courtesy, during our second spell together Serbia accommodated me in some truly arresting socialistic-era crap-holes – a useful last perspective on the centralised-economy guest lifestyle, with one overarching lesson: any Briton over forty-five who has ever shared a house with fellow students could probably have coped with Communism. Rooms were frailly illuminated by a single bare bulb that dangled from a battered false ceiling alive with scuttling badness; my feet parted with sickly reluctance from carpets blotted with complex stains and ingrained wodges of vegetable matter. The horridest hotel didn't even have bedclothes. A less exhausted man would have baulked at taking his ease on a grimy towelling under-sheet covered with a car blanket. A more sensible one might have troubled himself to investigate. In the morning, my flesh sticky to the touch, I opened the wardrobe and found a full set of ironed bedding stacked neatly inside. It was a curious DIY system, doubtless some collectivist hangover, and one that lingered sporadically, deep into Bulgaria.

The people, though, were unfailingly kind and courteous – clearly determined on an individual level not to embody their nation's unfortunate reputation, in a way that almost every Russian so proudly had. Yes, Serbs were lethally terrible drivers – on the busier roads, every blind bend and hill crest was crowned with a thicket of death-shrines, often commemorating multiple simultaneous victims (typically two or three young men, sometimes alongside a dedication to a much older motorist who one presumed was the hapless third party). And yes, they were not a painstakingly ethical bunch, or so I deduced from the incredibly detailed passive-aggressive 'price lists' of fixtures and fittings that graced every superior hotel room: moving boldly beyond the usual haul of coat hangers and bath robes, previous guests had by implication scuttled out through reception with their suitcases full of wall lights, telephones and bedspreads.

But above and beyond all that, these were people who knew how to grill meat and brew beer and show the weary shopping cyclist a restrained good time. Hotel receptionists would lead me halfway across town to the door of their favourite restaurant. When I waved, everyone waved back. Tito fed his people on Communism Lite, and Serbia retained an almost moreish hint of its flavour. There was a refreshing absence of global chains on the high streets, and on the shelves: after months of sustaining my afternoons with a couple of Mars bars or Snickers – they even had them in Russia – I was now refuelling with Eurocrem Blok. By name and nature this brown and white slab should by rights have been laid under laminate flooring, but I found its appearance pleasingly functional, and whatever the hell it was made of had a usefully higher melting point than cocoa solids.

I didn't see any of the black-glazed king-of-the-roadmobiles or razor-wired executive compounds that betrayed a miserably divided society. Tickets at the national theatre in Kikinda were a quid a pop. Whole days went by without a policeman in sight, and the mood was always wonderfully laidback. If the GDR came closest to mastering the cold logistics of centralised state control – the science of old-school Communism – then Serbia offered a glimpse of an artier, more relaxed side we might have seen if the socialists had survived and learned from their mistakes.

On my final hours beside the Danube, wobbling along a remote water's-edge trail, a woman ran yelling out through her front door and flagged me down with the desperate intensity of Jenny Agutter halting that locomotive in *The Railway Children*, making it wordlessly plain that I should turn around at once. I did so and was later told by a hotelier that she had spared me a 20km round trip to the foot of a vast landslide and back. In most countries I'd been through, nobody would have bothered. In one, I'd have been pushed into the river.

In Zaječar, where I watched the Champions League final in the courtyard of a Tolkien-themed Irish pub and could have purchased the air-conditioner remote control in my hotel room for 5,000 dinars, I finally met some other touring cyclists. They were New Zealanders of about my own age, a cheery and indefatigable couple

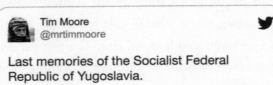

Tim Moore
@mrtimmoore

Last memories of the Socialist Federal Republic of Yugoslavia.

who were riding from Spain to China – a journey that knocked mine into a cocked hat, then sat on it and farted. ('But we've got proper bikes,' the husband modestly insisted.) It was the first time I had been required to explain myself and my MIFA to native speakers of English since leaving home. How very glad I was to be having this conversation now, with the end nigh, to an audience who in consequence appeared gratifyingly impressed, indeed almost astounded. If I'd met them near the start they'd have nodded indulgently, thinking: You're riding that all the way to the Black Sea? That's right, sonny, of *course* you are.

17. BULGARIA AND MACEDONIA

The last time I entered Bulgaria, tears of relief welled in my hollow eye sockets. A few hours later they rolled copiously down grimy, lined cheeks, as my wife and I stood before a restaurant buffet, bony hands locked together, and understood that food did exist after all, in crisp and colourful, freshly harvested abundance. Our holiday in Romanian hell was at an end, and Bulgaria unfolded before us like some post-Soviet Arcadia, a land of milk and honey, not to mention wine, salad, chicken and passers-by who would help push-start a crappy old Saab in return for nothing more than a wave and a nod of gratitude. In a heady mood of convivial reck-lessness, we made friends with every Bulgarian we met, such firm friends that after a few months they began to turn up at our door in London. One couple stayed with us for the whole summer. On their first day we took Nikolai and Angyela to Sainsbury's and they burst into tears in the exotic produce aisle. Watching them sob on the pineapples I wondered if Bulgaria might have been slightly less idyllic than it had seemed at the time, if our own buffet break-down was more a reaction to leaving the very worst place in Europe, rather than the merits of the land we had left it for.

A part of me has been wondering ever since, and that part – let's call him Doug – rode pillion as I rolled away from Dimitrovgrad, Serbia's last outpost and even late on a Sunday a riot of fun and colour, the pavements dense with noisy promenaders and alfresco café patrons. 'A lot of Bulgarian number plates,' noted Doug. 'Bad sign.'

Doug chuntered dismally through the border post, and along a truck-heavy highway that wound between the rocky and desolate green hills. 'No houses for miles,' he muttered. 'Classic Soviet-style

 Tim Moore
@mrtimmoore

Old border police control points. Whole area was once an exclusion zone. They really didn't trust the Yugoslavs.

border exclusion zone.' The sun had gone down by the time I free-wheeled creakily up to a motel in Dragoman, a transit town as grim as it sounded, defined by heavy goods vehicles and even heavier goods trains, Richter-scale trundlers that would shake my bed through the night. The motel was new and comfortable, but lay at the dusk-fringed edge of a forlorn straggle of *Khrushchyovka* tenements and gravelly wasteland. Doug didn't need to say anything. He smiled significantly at me half an hour later, when the waitress in the motel restaurant slapped a menu in front of me like a poker player throwing down her twelfth crap hand in a row. I opened it and saw Cyrillic dishes with their weight in brackets.

'Tomorrow-breakfast-ten-o'clock,' she intoned robotically as I left, under-fed on 90g of chips and a 120g kebab. Ten?! I told her I needed to leave before nine, procuring a shrug. 'For you no breakfast.'

'Back in the USSR,' sang Doug, fatuously, and with that he was gone.

Fuelled on an emergency stash of Eurocrem Blok and Strong Hell (my taurine carrier of choice with Magic Man absent from the shelves), the western Bulgarian borderlands I now struck deep into presented a lonesome, ageless panorama, locked in by thousand-metre, pine-topped hills. This was the Balkan landscape of my imagination: steep and dark green, cleaved by gorges, a dramatic horizon that reared and plunged under a cloudless sky. The dustiness of rural Serbia seemed long gone. There just wasn't sufficient human activity here to stir up the earth, nothing but the odd swaddled smallholder bent double with a hoe. For hours I was alone on a sinuous, frail road scarred by frost and heat, weeds stealthily creeping in from both sides and sometimes meeting in the middle. The steepest and most profoundly forsaken stretches were occasionally overlaid by a toppled tree, its fall arrested just above head height by some sturdier rival on the opposite side. Rolling terrain and decrepit roads made an unhappy combo: I would slalom wildly down a bumping descent and suddenly find my front wheel spoke-deep in gritty sand. The ensuing battles for control desecrated a dozen empty valleys with girlish shrieks and awful words, but I never learned to take it easy, and quite miraculously never paid the price.

Sometimes I would pass a memento of times past trapped in three decades of overgrowth, a colossal acclamation of socialism in lichen-streaked concrete, or a yellow-tin border-patrol checkpoint. Every so often, which wasn't often at all, I would wheeze through some decaying hamlet, all rusty hand-pumps and roofless barns. The only signs of habitation were glass bottles of moonshine lined up to cure on sunny window sills. Those and the dogs. The New Zealanders had met an American cyclist whose companion had been repatriated after a Bulgar farm hound made off with most of her right calf in its jaws; as soon as I spotted a cluster of tiled roofs ahead, the Pfeffer KO Jet came out in preparation. (I only had one can left: after the Kiwis told me that story, I gave them the other.) Yet again the mere sight of chemical retribution in my quivering grasp seemed deterrent enough, accompanied by some of the daftest threats ever to pass human lips. 'Go ahead, Shep,' I once heard myself rasp, 'make my day.'

The first town I went through was Tran, marooned way up in the hills and full of very dark-skinned gypsies who stared as if I had ridden by on an emu. Some had made their homes in dented old shipping containers, and the wearing of shoes seemed optional. I wasn't astonished to discover that Tran ranks amongst Europe's poorest municipalities. An oncoming Moskvich pick-up bounced through a pothole at intemperate speed, ejecting a number of rusty tools from its load bay, amongst them a cold chisel that flew past my face and hit the wall of an apartment block with a heavy chink. As with so many Romanian settlements, there was no architectural evidence of life before 1950. For the first time in months I was beyond the reach of the great old empires – the Russian, the Prussian, the Habsburg – that had washed across central and Eastern Europe and then receded, leaving castles on hilltops and stately edifices around every town square.

I bought a plaster-casted forearm of bread in a bakery with a bare concrete floor, and ate what I could of it on a bench behind some bronze hero of moustachioed collectivist toil. Doing so required the final drops of my Tabasco, the dear, dear friend who had been making bad food better since the middle of Finland. In the days ahead I would regularly dredge some fossilised comestible from my panniers and consider, with ratcheting seriousness, bringing it back to life with just the teensiest squirt of Pfeffer KO Jet.

Civilisation returned grudgingly, the villages more frequent and less desperate, the roads busier, the wild landscape tamed by active agriculture. I stayed in Kyustendil, a town surrounded by the first snow-veined peaks since Finland, at a humble guest house whose proprietor showed me to my room in total and very stony silence. This meant I didn't dare ask why he was wearing a miner's-lamp helmet, a mystery that troubled me for eleven long minutes until the power went down. It returned soon afterwards, but he still had the helmet on when I returned at ten full of bacon and beer, the only two items I had been able to identify with any confidence from the Cyrillic menu.

'Good man,' I said, giving him a thumbs-up, because it isn't every night you come back and find your host painting his garage door by the light of a miner's lamp, and the least I could do was acknowledge the dedication. He turned to me in silence and for a while I stood dazzled; then the beam moved slowly from side to side before sweeping back to the shiny, wet metal. Only when I was in bed with the door double locked did I understand: I had just been reacquainted with the no-means-yes Bulgarian head-shake, a gesture that had wreaked havoc in our dealings with that parade of house guests who pitched up on our doorstep back in 1991 ('You're not seriously intending to stay for the whole summer are you, Nikolai?').

I later wondered if that headshake – more accurately a sort of *comme ci, comme* ça shimmy, the international sign of meh – was an expression of evasive restraint, a Russian-reared reluctance to commit yourself to something you may later regret. My dealings with Bulgaria's border guards, receptionists, shopkeepers and waiting staff were all coolly infused with sidelong glances and a standoffish anti-banter. And motorists, once they returned in numbers, exerted a recognisably Russian indifference to their own continued survival and mine. The steadily uphill road south out of Kyustendil was a colon-clenching stampede of hot and heavy metal, massed with thundering lorries that duked it out all over the tarmac like Ben Hur chariots. After the third near miss I wobbled cravenly onto the railway-ballast verge, crawling for miles through supersized gravel and the giant thistles that sprouted from it, slashing exposed flesh from ear to ankle. Down in the valley floor, workmen were putting the final touches to a smooth and sinuous motorway, which by now will doubtless have lured away all those multi-wheeled maniacs, making life much easier, and indeed longer, for future generations of endurance shopping cyclists.

Focused on self-preservation, I had barely noticed the craggy eminences that stared down at the road from both sides, until EV13 hung a sharp right and threw me straight up them. The traffic vanished, the sun blazed, the lonely tarmac weaved and tilted ever steeper. How I toiled to regain the rhythm that had seen

 Tim Moore
@mrtimmoore

Kyustendil really Commied out as I left it this morning.

me up the mist-wreathed brows of Bavaria, a synchronised grand alliance of rasped respirations, pedal revs and Garmin-reported altitude: nine forty-five, *puff, crank, huff, creak*, nine forty-six . . . The shrubs gave way to scree and bleached rock, my limbs burned and shone, a hornet the size of a humming bird droned waywardly past. At a thousand metres it was still over 30 degrees; I clamped my seared fingertips, hand by hand, around the MIFA's shaded, blissfully cool seat post. One thousand one hundred and twelve . . . *fuff, thunk, ptthh, screeek* . . . one thousand one hundred and . . . twelve and a half . . . This was the highest I had yet climbed, but of all the agonies endured in getting there, that sheer, dredging sloth was the most torturous. Speed and its association with accumulated distance hadn't bothered me in the slightest when I'd been slithering pitifully down frozen Finland, not just taking each day as it came but each minute, every tenth of a click. But now with the end so tantalisingly near and yet so steeply far it really was an appalling frustration, chewing painfully on gristled uphill kilometres when I wanted to wolf down great tender chunks of them.

The road flattened, I rounded a final broiled bend and there at the head of the pass, flapping above a clutch of booths and barriers in my smeary, sweat-stung field of vision, flew my eighteenth flag. A geometric red and orange starburst, like something a kamikaze pilot might have wrapped around his brow before take-off: what a splendidly mad departure from all the dreary, homogenous stripes of red, white and blue I had ridden under of late. What on earth had persuaded Slovaks, Slovenes and Croats to celebrate their release from the state-socialist yoke by rallying under a national pole-topper almost indistinguishable from Russia's?

I knew almost nothing about Macedonia beyond the fact that it was previously part of Yugoslavia, and had since independence been locked in a furious row with Greece over its name – a fantastically Balkan badge-kissing, no-surrender stand-off that hinged on the triangular ambiguity between the new nation, the ancient kingdom of Macedon and the adjacent Greek region of Macedonia. (I never enquired about the current state of play, wary of having my chest prodded deep into the night by moustachioed mountain men wearing ammo bandoliers.) This aside, my ignorance was shamefully complete. Did it have its own language? Was it in the EU?

Were its people as miserable as Bulgarians? Would I sleep in a monastery full of plastics executives? Down I swept into a valley filled with soupy heat and donkeys, where the answers lay in wait.

Macedonia won a bloodless independence from Serbia, and maintains friendly – almost fraternal – relations with the Yugoslavian rump state. Their native languages are almost indistinguishable and so too, I found, were the respective country-folk and their contented, approachable demeanours. The country I rode into seemed like a more venerably bucolic version of the land north of the border, its people far removed from the dour and silent types who lived east of it. Beetle-browed ancients cheerily cajoled livestock and shouldered bundles of sticks across the rich, red earth of a plateau ringed by plump hills. A man with a grey moustache in a double-breasted Al Capone suit bounded out of a cherry orchard with a bunch of wild flowers in his hand and leapt into a waiting Yugo. There were mule-drawn haywains and a billion butterflies. I waved at everyone I passed, largely to acknowledge that most of them were having a visibly harder afternoon than I was. From horseback and hillside and the top rung of a cherry-picker's ladder, they all waved back.

The villages were a bit of a mess – every other wall had bare patches of wattle and daub – but at Berovo I lucked-in miraculously, accommodated in the cloistered, comfortably modernised splendour hinted at in a nearby paragraph. Here, via a kindly manager, I learned of Macedonia's thwarted efforts to join the European Union (the Greeks have a veto). Then I went out on to the colonnaded terrace and watched the Balkan sun go down over a table groaning with defiantly unweighed comestibles, soothed by dense, dark local wine and the stultifying discourse of paunchy executives conversing in their thickly accented lingua franca.

'Any advance in laminate, we must all be aware. But I am not having a good success with my new thermal moulding.'

I couldn't begin to imagine what had brought such people all the way out here, but I was very glad of their presence. Though I may never understand what on earth possessed me to take a university degree course in Business Studies, it is moments like this that remind me how sensible I was not to take in a single minute of it.

Macedonia's schools were breaking up for summer and I inched out of Berovo through alarming scenes of juvenile excess: at 9 a.m., the main street was full of empty beer bottles and staggering young brass-band trumpeters, some no more than twelve or thirteen. One kid tried to high-five me as I weaved through, with such enthusiastic imprecision that he almost fell over in the process. These were the people who in a few years – perhaps a few hours – would be going up the silent mountain pass I now effortlessly conquered, daubing angry-looking slogans on the ironstone rock and letting every road sign have it with both barrels.

The broad, flat valley ahead and a thousand metres below seemed to shimmer with flood water, but after a terrific, tooth-loosening descent I found myself rolling between several thousand shoddy plastic greenhouses. The peppers and tomatoes skulking towards ripeness under sickly yellow roofs brought my stomach to noisy life, as everything even passably edible did by now. An hour or two later, when I stopped at the last restaurant in Macedonia to offload my dinars, the unfortunate proprietor could hardly make himself heard above my gastric orchestra of fizzing squelches. I gathered he was trying to tell me that the dish I had ordered, helpfully pictured in the menu as an earthenware pot of cheese-topped stew, was of such overwhelming

stand-alone substance that I should think again about my supple-
mentary request, which I had effected by pointing at a neighbouring
photograph of a plate of chips. I thought again, and amid a reprise of under-jersey percolations, additionally ordered six slices of
bread.

I was alone on the street-side front terrace, and the final stages
of my feat were witnessed through the window by the boss and a
woman I took to be his wife. I think money might have been riding
on it, because the minute I wiped the last wodge of bread around
the emptied stew-pot's interior and folded it into my sauce-rimed
mouth, the wife shook her head and shuffled briskly away. Then a
young man with lavishly tattooed arms emerged through the fly
curtains, introduced himself in English as the owner's son, and
told me I was dirty fat Greek pig who bring great shame to family
and Republic of Macedonia. Actually, he didn't. Instead, he asked
many questions about my so-small bicycle and where we had been
together, widening his eyes gratifyingly at my every response,
before revealing that he was back home on holiday from his job as
a van driver in Switzerland.

'Here in Macedonia, nobody can bring home 250 euros in one
month, even in police.' We shook our heads at the trundling
border-bound traffic. 'Life is not easy here. In next month will be
45 degrees in temperature, in January can be 15 minus. And
always big problems with, you know, with other peoples.'

I nodded, and against my better judgement made reference to
the proximity of national enemy number one: Greece was looking
down on us from the right-hand mountain-tops.

'What you try to say?' His expression made me dearly wish I
hadn't. 'Greece, no problem, here we are many with Greece blood;
Bulgaria, no problem, I have also Bulgarian passport; gypsy people,
no problem, they like to have many horses but that is OK.'

Anyway, it was the Albanians. Apparently they expect always something for nothing. As this personable young man ranted on at baleful length I wondered if there was any hope for this part of the world. The Balkan jigsaw had a thousand pieces, but every time someone joined together a hopeful corner section, someone else would dash the whole thing angrily to the floor.

'*Meistari, meistari!*'

The Macedonian border guards saw me off with transparently ironic cries of acclaim, but when you're on 250 euros a month you deserve a perk, and I smiled indulgently. It was certainly more fun than the glazed indifference that welcomed me back into Bulgaria. For many long miles thereafter the road gently descended the wide Strumica valley, a land of maize and shepherds backed with leering, mighty slopes. By Petrich I was freewheeling all the way, down now below 100m, but with the giant hills closing in on all sides I prudently called it a day. Along with not having any more children and buying a cordless long-reach hedge trimmer, this proved to be one of the few truly wise decisions I have made in middle age.

The route guide, still witlessly preoccupied with how the long-distance cyclist might entertain and refresh himself at point B, was displaying an ever looser interest in describing the journey there from point A. I had to find out myself that I was currently approaching the route's lowest point since the Baltic coast, and, more crucially, that within a few dozen kilometres EV13 would be levelling out at 1,408m, its loftiest peak to date. Ahead of me lay what would be, and by a gigantic margin, the most gruelling vertical challenge along the entire Iron Curtain Trail.

This was a prospect that needed blotting out, and an hour or two later a Petrich waitress handed me a multilingual restaurant menu, which along with 'sham peanuts' and 'hotch-potch up masters' thoughtfully offered 'bulk wine'. This and the balmy night air allowed my postprandial ruminations to blunder far and wide as I sat out on my fourth-floor hotel balcony, hands locked behind head, gazing blearily across at the misted, moonlit hills and below at downtown Petrich's grubby roofs and busy nightfolk.

How different would this scene have been under Communism? Fewer cars and fewer lights, maybe fewer people on the pavements at . . . well, at ten past nine (to ride a bike all day is to exist in a separate time zone: if you're still awake at 10 p.m., it feels like four in the morning). But the dead hand of centralised planning remained on dominant display in the gloomy ranks of apartment blocks, and thirty years back the night breeze would have been just as warm, the wafts of pee rising up from the alley beneath just as pungent, my belly just as full of bulk wine.

On my way out to the restaurant I'd popped into the Petrich Lidl to stock up on dependable Latin-alphabet sandwich fillings. (More than one village grocer had bagged up my mystery cheese and meat selections with a disconcerting nod of impressed approval: 'Horse-lung sausage *and* pickled sow's whey? Fair play, son.') The aisles had been packed, and after a while I noticed that very few people were carrying baskets: this was a barebones discount supermarket, yet the locals had come to browse its shelves and raw wooden pallets in unworthy wonder. I saw a young couple cradle a packet of Lindt chocolate, faces aglow with longing, before placing it tenderly back in place. At the time it seemed pitiful, a shaming level of consumer deprivation here in the EU. But now, more expansively, I wondered if this pimped-up semi-socialism – bread and milk from your local grocery, push-the-boat-out 70 per cent cocoa from the uptown Lidl – could be the future: a compromise between Soviet-empire food queues and the overwhelming purchasing decisions that are such a draining feature of modern west-European existence. I thought about this and suddenly felt a wave of righteous outrage wash boozily over me: what foul forces had conspired to build our twenty-first-century consumerist society, a soulless, hateful world where a good man such as I was compelled to spend his every waking hour trying to find a slightly cheaper online source of AA batteries?

I stooped recklessly over the balcony and at length focused on the MIFA, a muddy glint far below in the hotel's side return. I wasn't at all sure what I was trying to ask myself, but the bike seemed part of the answer: it was a bit rubbish, but it did the job. What more could you ask? And, in fact, what more did I need? What else did anyone need? I had my trusty little runabout, two packets of mechanically recovered Lidl meat slices and the clothes I stood up in. And then I looked down at the clothes I stood up in, the trousers that shone with the accumulated after-hours dribbles and stains of eighteen countries, and with one of those abrupt cogitative twists of a drunken mind, thought: This is not the evening look I was hoping for at the age of fifty-one. What has become of me? I eat stolen breakfast rolls in bus shelters and wear fingerless gloves. I pee in lay-bys and crap behind trees. My nose is a bruised plum and I'm wearing filthy old tramp's trousers, like the filthy old tramp that I am.

18. BULGARIA II

EV13 would throw everything at the MIFA and me in the 123km that separated Petrich from Dospat, a trial of topographical and meteorological mercilessness that felt like some final, crowning test of our mettle. The first climb into the Rhodope Mountains was what is known in sporting circles as a reducer, a brutal, humid haul through aged villages that blew my hangover to bits, but was cruelly undone at once by a plunging, back-to-square-one descent. Then it was up to the foot of a vast green wall, past a lorry driver filling his radiator in preparation, and a poor old nag hauling a trailer with an elderly couple in the box seat. As I toiled by, the wife cried out in a tone of scolding exasperation. 'That's it, Dimitar,' she almost certainly said, 'we're getting a car.'

The hairpins came thick and slow, and sweat was soon pooling in the usual crevices. Man and MIFA creaked and groaned; somewhere beneath us an unseen cowherd berated his charges, bawling in rage above the weary lowing and clonking of bells. The trees thinned, offering views of the conquered slopes below and – oh, take them away – the balding, rocky Rhodope brows so very far above. How grateful I was for the trickling springs that some patron saint of under-prepared travellers had erected in tiled road-side shrines at thoughtful interludes: first I sipped from their mossy faucets, then suckled and glugged; after three hours and 800 metres I plunged my smouldering skull into the falling water with an almost audible hiss.

The road began to dissolve at the edges, its threadbare asphalt scattered with fallen rocks; at one point half the hillside had come down, and I pushed the bike over a metric shitload of crudely bull-dozed red earth. And all the while the air grew thicker and my shadow more frail, as the puffy clouds clumped and darkened and came down to meet me.

Every morning since day one had begun with an obsessive weather check, which in the increasing absence of wifi meant flicking through fuzzy TV channels for long minutes until I blun-dered across someone standing in front of a map. I'm not entirely sure why I ever bothered. It wasn't as if I could take a detour or a day off, or ask the man in the shiny blue suit to stick some different symbols over southern Bulgaria: 'Come on, Georgi, you can do better than that.'

Anyway, that morning's Georgi had made it clear that I would be getting very wet, and he wasn't wrong. Without even the slightest drip-drop build-up, at 1,000m the leaden heavens abruptly shed their mighty load. I was soaked in a second, like the victim of a slapstick routine; in thirty more the tarmac was submerged and the world around screened out by heavy wet curtains. The road-side culverts boiled and frothed and spat out a year's worth of accumulated pine cones and beer cans. Brown water surged spoke-high through the MIFA's little wheels. I was barely moving by now, but I didn't stop. Nor did the rain. I have never, at first hand, experienced such intensive and relentless precipitation. Clumps of mountain, some as big as house bricks, were sluiced across my path. Somewhere amid the layers of exhaustion and sodden hardship, I felt a small, fearful thrill at finding myself engulfed by such elemental ferocity.

A bronze socialist partisan stood guard at the head of the pass; I dropped the MIFA at his feet and staggered towards the tiny orthodox chapel on the other side of the road. The door was locked so I crouched under the domed porch and began pushing damp wodges of bread and sausage into my mouth, rain clattering the tin tiles like popping corn. Then, beneath God's roof and at EV13's highest and heaven-most peak, I clicked open a Strong Hell and the world fell silent. As suddenly as it had begun, the storm departed. I looked up through the dripping pine trees and saw blue sky; by the time I picked the MIFA back up, steam was rising off the road in wispy coils.

The rain was done for the day, but the Rhodopes absolutely were not. For hours and hours I was always doing something agonising or lethal on an extremely steep road. The climbs broke my body and the descents blew my mind. It became ever more difficult to maintain the requisite concentration and dexterity, and by stages a terrible, fuck-it fatalism set in: when you feel half dead, finishing the job doesn't seem such a biggie.

My right calf cramped up while stamping down on the coaster brake at 60kmh. I shot through an asteroid belt of armoured green insects with an abysmal mastery of flight, copping one in the teeth and welcoming another through a vent in my helmet, the first act of a flappy, flailing farce. The asphalt was savagely potholed, and I routinely careered round a bend along some scree-flanked eternity to find my side of the road annexed by a crater-avoiding motorist.

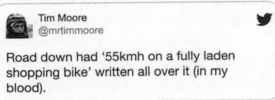

Tim Moore
@mrtimmoore

Road down had '55kmh on a fully laden shopping bike' written all over it (in my blood).

I couldn't understand how I had yet to witness even a single road accident on this trip, but I didn't have long to wait: at the apex of a demanding hairpin, an ancient Transit van that had passed me very noisily an hour before was wedged upside-down in the bushes, with a police car beside it. As I swept by I saw three men in the back seat, all cradling heads in hands. It struck me that if I died in such an incident, it would at least be a tragic hero's death – a haunting fear at this stage, with the finish line almost in sight, was that I might fatally choke on Eurocrem Blok in a bus shelter, or slip down a ravine while having a poo behind a mountain pine, or suffer some other form of ignominious, legacy-soiling demise. 'It is not yet clear why Moore, who was apparently on some sort of bike ride, had wandered into the forest, though for his family's sake let's pretend the boars attacked him with his shorts up.'

The settlements were few and desolate, introduced by a monumental, granite-sculpted son or daughter of Communist toil fixing the mountaintops with a thousand-yard stare. However daftly overblown, these always stirred the soul: imagine the tingle of driving home past some massive concrete postman astride a 10-foot EALING. There was usually just one shop, selling everything from milk to tractor tyres, with a plump and grumpy proprietress who never met my eye. Nobody seemed to notice the hollow-faced man on the strange little bike: not the gangster types in black Mercs, filling jerrycans at the village spring; not the masons who squatted in their hundreds among roadside heaps of sandstone tiles; not the Del Boys and Rodneys flogging brooms and buckets out of Lada boots in the muddy squares. Rural Bulgaria was lost in its own dour little world.

Dospat had cows wandering its steep, cracked streets. Dospat had minarets and old ladies in hijabs. Dospat seemed strange and different, but my brain was dead and my body empty, hollowed out like a Halloween pumpkin, and I couldn't be entirely sure of anything. One minute I was riding very, very slowly past a domed mosque; the next I was punch-drunk in front of a hotel reception desk, grasping it with both hands for support. In the morning, the curly-haired young man behind the desk would have to help me find my bike – I had no idea where I'd left it.

'Is your first time in Dospat?'

At some point in the addled late afternoon, I had graced the receptionist's home town with a nickname that had thereafter burst from my throat every time it appeared on a signpost. Reflexively it now emerged in a broken whisper.

'Tosspot.'

He tilted his head, put a room key on the desk and looked at me with the sort of kind-hearted condescension I shall have to get used to when I'm struggling to dress myself.

'Tosspot,' I mumbled again, and weaved off down the wrong corridor.

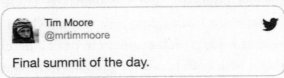

Tim Moore
@mrtimmoore

Final summit of the day.

It was mid June, halfway through a year that I had largely spent riding a shopping bike across a continent. In the early stages there had been moments of profound misgiving, some of them up to eleven days long. But I was now locked into an automatic Stakhanovite routine, the unquestioning repetition of hard toil. My parents and my two daughters had hatched a plan to meet me at my journey's end, and my wife forwarded a related email she had sent to our youngest's head teacher with a view to securing permission for absence. 'Her father has been working abroad since the middle of March,' I read, and as daft as that sounded, I had. Riding a little bicycle all day and every day was no longer an absurd and monstrous self-inflicted punishment. It was just what I did; it was my job.

In the days ahead I developed an ever more intimate working knowledge of the Rhodope Mountains, now creaking up through a moribund ski resort, now plummeting into a hollow clustered with terracotta roofs and the blue-tipped rocket of a minaret. Sometimes I grovelled across plump hillsides that offered a cruelly benign backdrop for suffering; sometimes I shot impressively through stupendous gorges, the road squeezed in beside a river that tumbled along between cliffs of cork-like rock. I hit EV13's ceiling at 1,679m, but the ensuing terrain still undulated fiercely. The endless climbs had now engorged my legs to worrisome dimensions, the calves swollen and rippled, big double chins of muscle overhanging each kneecap. It somehow felt as if the MIFA should have bulked up too, but instead I just looked ever more wrong on it, a physically over-engineered bully. This seems as good a place as any to reveal that the MIFA 900 was briefly marketed in West Germany as the Everest.

Women in woven shawls and plastic macs herded sheep down hillsides or split logs on their garden walls. I passed a cemetery stone embedded with two photographs, one of a husband who had died in 2008, the other of his extant wife above her date of birth and a blank space. Terrific nocturnal thunderstorms wrought fearsome havoc amongst dogs and livestock, and one night blew up my phone charger. They took the edge off the daytime heat but brimmed the extravagant potholes I battered and splashed through, each one testament to the 'extreme *mañana*' approach to road maintenance that had set in over recent weeks. How had I not suffered a single puncture since Finland? It made no sense.

The fields in this forgotten world had a tentative, pioneering look, dwarfed on all sides by great stands of pine trees, a landscape newly claimed by man. Old horseshoes glinted in the gutter; one morning I saw three mules dragging ploughs across the valley before I passed my first motorised vehicle. Like half the cars round here it was a Moskvich, most hopeless of all the Soviet crock-mobiles: older than me and still somehow moving under its own steam. All through Germany and Austria I had lived in fear of a serious mechanical mishap, knowing how hard it would be to persuade any Teutonic technician that the MIFA was worthy of their professional consideration. But now I was reassuringly deep into the land of make-do-and-mend: if my crappy old bike fell apart, these people would put it back together.

By mid-afternoon, as more and more of my body and soul was siphoned away into those distended legs, I would dependably run out of food on some giant empty hillside and burrow light-headedly through my panniers for sustenance. By some shameful miracle these searches always turned up a few biscuit shards or an extremely forgotten slice of cheese. Then, by stages, I all but nodded off in the saddle. Riding all day up big hills with little wheels is tiring in the most literal sense. By 6 p.m. I could easily and quite happily have curled up in a pothole waterbed and slept. Instead, I motored vacantly onwards, through a shaded cleft and up to the foot of another stack of hairpins, the dread sound of a labouring lorry echoing down from the heavens.

My day would end at a dog-eared socialistic-era hotel, as the low sun was blotted to a smudge by those dark clouds that crept in from the horizon towards twilight. For long and empty-headed minutes I slumped against broken tiles under a tiny bathroom's curtainless shower, water and road-filth splashing all over the toilet and crusty towels; then it was down to another deserted restaurant, and another Cyrillic bill of fare that swam before my eyes.

'*Frytki, salat shopska, chleb, shashlyk.*'

These days I just put the menu down and ordered chips, Greek salad, bread and kebabs in a garbled mash-up of Polish, Russian and Serbo-Croat. It was lazy and very possibly offensive, but if I repeated myself enough it always did the job. An hour later, sunk in the mid-mattress imprint left by distant generations of tubby party officials and tractor-factory managers, I would listen to the first clatters of rain against glass and dwell on my foreign prede-cessors, those who had stared up at this stained polystyrene ceiling in decades past, their pulses quick and their mouths dry.

In 1970, the GDR installed 60,000 trip-wired anti-personnel mines along the inner German border, obliging more rational would-be escapees to seek a softer underbelly in the Iron Curtain defences. Some East Germans tried their luck in Hungary; some in Romania. But most, at least 4,500 of them, were drawn to the Bulgarian-Greek frontier.

Pedalling across those remote hills and valleys, I could easily understand why so many Trabants had congregated down here, purportedly on holiday tours. Of course the all-seeing, all-knowing Stasi understood it too, and invariably knew well in advance which travellers weren't planning to come home. They tipped off the Bulgarian border authorities with habitual efficiency: more than 80 per cent of runaways were arrested in the 15km exclusion zone, and returned to the GDR for sentencing.

Nearly all of these were subsequently ransomed to the western Federal Republic of Germany for hard currency, and lots of it. Amid all those tales of heroic, death-defying cross-curtain escape bids, it's easy to forget – particularly if like me you didn't know in the first place – that once the Wall went up in 1961, the vast majority of East Europeans who made it to the West were prosaic- ally, though very secretly, sold by their cash-strapped overlords. Ceaușescu's regime kept itself afloat by flogging 424,000 ethnic Germans to the Federal Republic, receiving a more than handy 11,000 deutschmarks for each of them by the late 1980s. For the GDR, the trade was a win-win means of getting paid to ship out potentially dangerous dissidents. Twice a week, a fleet of buses with James Bond-style revolving number plates – GDR for the first leg of the trip, FRG for the second – would ferry political prisoners and recidivist runaways over the border. In the 1980s, for every East German who escaped, ninety-nine were surrepti- tiously exported: by then whole trainloads were being shipped out, bought by the West Germans for 100,000 deutschmarks a head, equivalent to around 25,000 pounds.

As their foreign debt mushroomed, the East Germans grew more desperate, and much cheekier. Once they demanded a ship- load of bananas be thrown in as part of the ransom deal. Noting that the state earned nothing from citizens who secured visas to visit relatives across the wall, the GDR took to arresting them by the thousand on fictitious charges, then selling them to the West, rebranded as political prisoners. Over 34,000 East Germans were thus traded, swelling the state coffers by an estimated eight billion DM. 'It was the kind of sum without which the country could not survive,' concludes Victor Sebestyen, in his pannier-bulging trea- tise, *Revolution 1989*.

But enough of the lucky ones. South of Chepintsi, in the deepest, darkest Rhodope borderlands, I passed close – as close as a bicycle allowed – to a mossy-trunked birch that some locals call the Bone Tree, others the German Woman. For weeks the scent of the Iron Curtain Trail had been slowly fading, but now, at EV13's southernmost extremity, I caught a potent whiff of its grisliest relic. Officially, thirteen GDR citizens were shot dead along the Bulgarian–Greek border, but many more than that disappeared in the area, and an academic study has suggested an accurate toll would nudge into three figures. All fell victim to a cruel and very deliberate deception: having cleared a raked sand-strip and a 3m fence, they believed they'd made it to Greece. In fact, the border proper lay 2km away, and in crossing the fence the escapees had tripped a detection wire that alerted the nearest border post. Its guards reacted promptly and with only one thought in mind.

A 1974 'friendship agreement' between the GDR and Bulgaria not just allowed but required the native border patrols to shoot East German escapees on sight, and recent investigations have unearthed detailed evidence that the GDR embassy in Sofia offered guards a bounty. Kill an East German in the death-strip and you would be rewarded with between ten and fifteen days' leave for 'neutralising a traitor', plus a bonus of up to 2,000 leva and a Glashütte wristwatch. Thus incentivised, border patrols became execution squads. An autopsy found that Michael Weber, a nineteen-year-old student from Leipzig killed near the Greek border in July 1989, had been shot at close-quarters in the top of the head. A month later, he could have wandered freely into the West from Hungary.

But the forensic and investigative diligence that followed Weber's death was conspicuously absent in the 1970s and early '80s. East Germans killed in the death-strip back then were relieved of their documents – you needed proof to claim your bounty – and dumped in shallow forest graves. These were routinely dug up by scavenging wildlife, and Chepintsi locals spoke grimly of remains left strewn across no man's land. But it was only in 2014 that a German TV crew confirmed the darkest rumour of all: a tree, deep in the old killing zone, decorated with human bones nailed high up the trunk. A warning to other escapers? A trophy shrine? It's a fair bet that the truth will never be known, though analysis of a shoulder blade and fibula showed they belonged to a woman born around 1955. This, along with the tree's more ominous nickname, suggests that whoever put them there tells the time with a Glashütte.

With Greece looming on my forward and right-hand horizons, everything began to look hotter and crispier. The balding brown hillsides were dotted sparely with tufts of gorse and the sky was a stern, hard blue. Hens darted out for a roadside dust-bath; cows hid from the sun in bus shelters. I baptised myself at every life-saving water shrine and squeezed breakfast jam sachets into my hot gob, like rubbish energy gels. EV13's route from here to its conclusion was agonisingly dilatory – so much so that as I wended my very weary way over the Rhodopes' scorched foothills, I never once bothered to consult the wind forecast. Long gone were all those due-south and due-west weeks, when a day could be made or ruined by having half the Beaufort scale in my face or up my arse.

I passed a fat man riding a donkey, and a Moskvich straining desperately up a gentle hill with a sofa on its roof. Two gangs of village kids throwing stones at each other interrupted hostilities to jog alongside the MIFA, whooping like over-excited spectators on a Tour climb. Their elders, hoes in hand out in the dusty fields, tracked me with familiar stares of amused bewilderment; work-weary, weather-beaten labourers who would never, ever understand why anyone would do what I was doing in the name of fun.

Late one day I barrelled into Ivaylovgrad with the weary negligence that always infected the final descent, avoiding a twilight tortoise but not half the potholes, to the great detriment of my liver and testes. A snake coiled up on the central white line reared up and struck cobra-style in my general direction as I shot past; a speed-trap policeman at the town-limits sign waved his little lollipop stop-stick at me in jest. I freewheeled to a halt outside a glitzy new hotel just beyond the town's scabby tenements, and found that my right shoe had melted fast to the pedals. Or so at first it seemed; after 144 baked and rolling kilometres, even the most basic physical task demanded a deep breath and a focused effort. Then one more alarmed and faintly disgusted receptionist; one more stairwell sleep for the MIFA; one more vacant congress with my blistered reflection above a sink full of frothing, laddered Lycra: 'You did it. You did it again.' Days like this seemed a month long, a ten-volume saga of hot hills and peasants, of flaky concrete partisans with their inscriptions crowbarred off, of grumpy grocers and Strong Hell. But with the lonely Rhodopes now behind me, those days were at an end.

19. GREECE, TURKEY AND BULGARIA

Nation number nineteen barely troubled the scorers. A brand-new little border crossing, just two Portakabins and a couple of uniformed smilers, allowed me to trim an irksome 50km loop off EV13, leaving no more than a cloudless, three-hour corner of north-eastern Greece to traverse. It was flat and arable and utterly deserted. I saw my first ripe peach, and because there was nobody around, stole and ate it. For the first time in a month, Sunday felt like Sunday: in the godless ex-Communist countryside I'd ridden through since Austria, these fields and orchards would have been generously dotted with hunched toilers. The empty farms were vast and well-maintained, every sleek new barn fronted with a rank of shiny machines; I had seen my last beast of burden. The villages, when at length they came, seemed equally trim and prosperous: a parade of white concrete homes with roller shutters and wrought-iron balconies, like mid-range Spanish holiday villas.

This Greece seemed to share very little with the one I recalled from my admittedly distant previous visit. As a student Interrailer, I had trundled lethargically through the scraggy realm of walnut-faced goatherds, in an airless carriage full of black shawls and grey stubble. It was, in fact, very reminiscent of the country I had just left behind, and with a small internal sigh I realised that quite soon, perhaps after another two decades of EU membership, rural Bulgaria would look like this: an agro-industrial landscape free of donkeys and sickles.

Yet this Greece also seemed nothing like the desperate, angry nation depicted in so many news reports over the previous half-dozen years. I had half expected to find people gnawing the bark off trees or auctioning elderly relatives in the street, but the only evidence of national strife was an unusual preponderance of political graffiti and some angrily ripped election posters. Kastanies, the first and only town I would go through, was thronged with well-presented Sunday moochers, crisp-shirted husbands clustered convivially under one café awning, crisp-bloused wives under another. The Turkish frontier's flags and barriers stood in plain sight at the end of the road, but even the startling proximity of two of the world's worst enemies hadn't put a damper on the mood.

Indeed, when I rolled up to the border gates, I found no man's land clogged with joggers wearing numbers on their vests: a cross-frontier fun run was apparently in progress, and the guard told me to go away and come back in an hour. Thus I joined the ouzo-loosened husbands, spending my forgotten euros on feta and chips, and leafing through yet another alien menu. For the last time I marvelled at little Europe's astonishing diversity: in a 10-mile radius from my shaded seat, three separate alphabets were in use. And the only wholly familiar letters would shortly,

Tim Moore
@mrtimmoore

Into country 19/20. Spot a stork & a watchtower & win all my leftover Serbian dinars.

though not that shortly, be welcoming me into the Asia-straddling nation that was last on my list.

'What dis?'

It was my second encounter with the Turkish border guard in the mirrored sunglasses. The first had ended an hour before with a demand for a visa fee that required more euros than I had left; I'd ridden back across no man's land and returned with the fruits of a Greek cashpoint. Several passages through back-to-back gauntlets of automatic weaponry and menacing stares had put me straight on the fraternal co-existence implied by that feet-across-the-border mini marathon. And now a man with a big gun and a sweaty top lip was asking me about the police-grade anti-personnel weapon I had inexplicably left on open display, threaded through the elastic strap of my front carrier.

'Pfeffer KO? It's incredible stuff. Pop those shades off and I'll give you a demo.'

I didn't say that, of course. In fact, every explanation that now scrolled rapidly through my head, not least the true one, seemed open to the sort of misunderstanding that might land me in a window-less cell with a dozen sobbing joggers, so I didn't really say anything.

'Well, it's for . . . ah . . .'

'For bicycle, yes?'

I looked up but he'd already lost interest, waving me through and looking past my shoulder at the long queue of cars I had pushed in front of. Once again the MIFA's childlike innocence had saved me a strip-search. And so, after paying my visa fee at one window, and queuing for my change at another, and standing at the last for a full half-hour while my passport was stamped and returned, I entered my twentieth and final country. What a terrible pity, from the perspective of narrative progression, that my journey's end lay back in the seventeenth.

On the Turkish side they were clearing up after the fun run. There was a water station just inside the border, and beyond it the road was carpeted with plastic bottles. Young men were sweeping these into giant bin-liners, knotting the tops and gaily tossing their harvest over a fence into the wasteland behind. An old man was burning stuff on his doorstep, beside a cabbage patch fenced off with barbed wire. Muscular wafts of human waste swept across the road. The thought that I would stay in Turkey for just a single night seemed steadily less dismal. Until, that is, I rattled over an ancient, many-arched bridge into Edirne, and at once found myself engulfed by chaos and colour and towers and domes and very restless decibels. I pushed the MIFA through a log-jam of horns, chatty pedestrians streaming between hot metal: in two minutes flat, this drive-through *Game of Thrones* marketplace in the one-time Ottoman capital out-bustled anything I had yet experienced. But it took me an awful lot longer than that to break through into the calm of Edirne's mirror-glassed commercial outskirts, and as thrilling as it was to find exhilarating novelty still being flung at me 8,381km down the line, on those thronged and manic streets a dream died.

For three months, I had been painfully hauling my overall average speed back up from its ignominious Finnish depths: 9.9kmh after two days, 10.5 after two weeks, 11.9 by the Russian border. Those hateful little digits goaded me all day, the cad's moustache on my Garmin's info-slathered face. All I wished for, and it didn't seem much to ask, was a final average speed of 16.0kmh, better known to those of a certain age and with any sense of basic human pride as 10mph. When I rolled into Germany with 14.5 on the clock, imperial double-digits seemed inevitable, but as I'm told is generally the way with long-term averages, the numbers grew ever harder to shift. My fitness reached a plateau but the roads did not; I wondered what speed a man of my age might be reasonably expected to maintain riding up mountains all day on a shopping bike. The Czech Republic, 15.2; Hungary, 15.4; Croatia, 15.6; Romania, 15.8. Through a superlative effort that will forever be spoken of in hushed tones whenever men gather to discuss feats of small-wheeled endurance, in the mighty Rhodopes I had somehow endeavoured to bring up the 15.9. But a mere 150km now remained, and shuffling through the Edirne crowds I sensed that decimal place being anchored for good. I'm sorry to break the news just like that. It must be harder for you than it was for me.

*

The road out of Edirne led me across a bare, beige landscape that seemed to have been bullied flat by the sun. It was so brutally hot that the tarmac began to boil, swelling into little bubbles which popped and crackled beneath my tyres like space dust. Pick-up trucks shimmered up out of the heat haze and flew past at crazy speeds, parping horns and trailing yelps of raucous derision. Such at least was my assumption before I rode into a dusty little town, and was borne past the concrete shacks and bus shelters on a wave of exuberant but very genuine encouragement. Children ran alongside, whooping and clapping. 'Hello mister!' cried one. 'HELLO MISTER!' chorused a dozen more. A woman in a glittery headscarf and a smart red trouser suit held out a tray of pastries she was mysteriously crossing the road with. Three young men by the petrol station pointed me to the horizon in stirring unison, like Soviet sculptures: 'Go forth to your destiny, hero cyclist.' Turkey meant me well. In fact, it meant me better than anywhere else I had been, and in doing so brought a premature tear to my eye.

My final staging post was considerably larger than I had expected, but Kirklareli only had one hotel and I couldn't find it. After a circuit of its lively principal thoroughfares, I squeaked to a halt at the edge of the main square, a fittingly totalitarian public space accessorised with giant military statues, fighter jets on plinths and a mural of flag-planting soldiers that filled the side of a facing apartment block.

I didn't have any native money and the blue sky had begun to darken at its edges. It was a predicament I had regularly endured on this journey, and with unfailing distress. But this time I didn't panic. Indeed, I barely cared. Perhaps, now that it had come down to it, I didn't really want to find my last bed, because that would mean this – all this, my purpose on earth, life as I knew it – would be over. The French once called Tour cyclists 'convicts of the road'; my sentence was almost served. Like an institutionalised old lag finally given parole in *The Shawshank Redemption*, I wasn't at all sure how to deal with that eventuality, though ideally not by hanging myself from a doorframe. Or perhaps I just knew that if I stood here long enough, helmet unbuckled by a taxi rank, Turkey would sort me out.

'You make EV13, I think?'

The first and only cyclist I met in Turkey was also the first and only cyclist I met anywhere who expressed familiarity with the Iron Curtain Trail. My journey's final Samaritan was a sprightly chap of about my own age, riding a smart new tourer that he would, the very next day, be sticking in a plane bound for Prague. 'With three friends I make EV4, we ride to Paris.' It all seemed fairly extraordinary. When I asked about the hotel, he hopped back on his bike and beckoned me to follow him; several mad rounda-bouts later we pulled up outside a big new box on the ring-road. I offered him my heartfelt gratitude and we wished each other luck.

'Tomorrow EV13 for you is Istranca Mountains,' he said, as we shook hands. 'Not easy, I think, on this bicycle.'

I smiled, thinking that even on downhill velvet the day would overwhelm me. My parents and daughters had already landed in Bulgaria; we had arranged to meet for lunch at Malko Tarnovo, close to the Turkish border. It was 50km from Kirklareli to there, and another 56 onwards to Tsarevo, EV13's Black Sea conclusion.

I went through the last rites with a light head and a strangely heavy heart. The toothpaste I had cracked off in frozen chunks on my first night oozed blood-warm onto the brush. The fear-blanched, frosted face I had stared at in that Finnish motel mirror was now the chestnut head of a very odd lollipop. I'd shed 10kg and striped myself silly, an unusually shy stickman who went for a mahogany spray-tan in his pants, vest and socks. Somehow it didn't seem plausible that this figure before me would never again drape wet kit all over a hotel bathroom, or sluice out a CamelBak with a sachet of shower gel, or shuffle off down strange streets in a town he would never see again, on the hunt for mysterious life-giving calories.

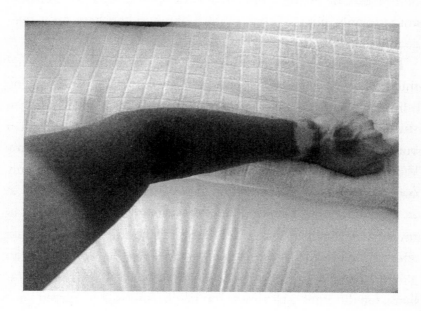

I ate on the garden terrace of what was clearly Kirklareli's premium eaterie, served by expressionless young women in dark waistcoats who glided up bearing small bowls decorously filled with salads, meats and vegetable paste. The night air hung warm and lazy, infused with pine resin, sticky tarmac and grilled meat. Crickets and cicadas trilled and squeaked. A tall glass of beer, appealingly beaded with condensation, stood on the glossy black table before me, and for once the stars were out. I took it all in, every sloth-inducing holiday sensation, then thought: Please, not now. Not just yet.

The mournful, off-key tremolo of native wind instruments struck abruptly forth from a function at the garden's distant fundament, presently accompanied by tortured calls to prayer crackling out of a PA speaker atop the mosque down the road. Could somebody, anybody, please explain how I had come from the silent, barren tundra to this sultry realm of wailing imams? Sensible answers only, none of that rubbish about riding here on a two-geared children's bicycle.

I spooned toothsome pepper pulp into my mouth and trawled through a murky ocean of memories. Was that really me, watching a little white bike slide down a big white hill with one eye frozen shut? Eating smoked trout in a bank and pink eggs at a Russian bus stop, reading *Pravda* in a KGB ghost town, falling asleep in my shorts by a fishmonger's stove? It seemed fanciful. I could only convincingly picture myself from about Serbia onwards, placed in an environment of heat and kebabs that bore tangible relation to my current surroundings. Everything before that, the *postipanki* and schnitzels, the wanking gnomes, the bagging-up and garden gloves, the Bon Jovi and mulleted miners . . . It was all too far back, too different, just simply too much. And so I wandered back to the hotel through loud traffic and roach-scuttle, lay down on my last bed, cleared my mind and waited for an enlightened perspective to settle over this sprawling endeavour. Then I closed my eyes and at once fell into a dreamless coma.

Nine hours later I took my place behind the suits in the buffet queue, just another man with a job of work to do, a job that would require three plate-piling visits to those silver troughs. I raised the last with a sigh of pleasure and regret. Chips for breakfast! The all-day cyclist's Holy Grail, right at the death. Back at the table I automatically ran through my routines, checking the weather, slyly pocketing rolls, and parting the ring-bound route guide on the relevant page. What a strange thing to see the little red line I had been following over these maps for most of my adult life wiggle briefly north into Bulgaria, then across to the Black Sea and stop dead.

The MIFA had slept with two real bikes in a storage room full of wedding decorations. When the receptionist opened the door for me, there it was, safe and sound amongst the white satinette and plastic flowers. An endgame phobia evaporated. In these latter stages I had been haunted by the sorry anticlimax that cut short Colin Martin's trailblazing small-wheeled adventure: in 1970, having nearly circumnavigated the globe on a Moulton Marathon, Martin walked out of a guest house in Kalgoorlie, Western Australia, and found that his little bike had been pinched in the night. (He abandoned the trip and settled there, finally completing the last leg of his ride thirty-eight years later.)

'The small one? It's really yours?'

I turned to the receptionist and saw the look I had come to know so well. Yes, it really was mine. But, and I could say it now: what a bike. My MIFA 900 had taken me through snowdrifts and sand dunes and a million bone-cracking craters, slow and steady up 60 vertical kilometres, fast and loose back down them. Its destiny as a museum exhibit – though unfulfilled at the time of writing – seemed much less foolish now. This so-small Commie campsite wobbler, this jerry-built underbike, had somehow conquered a continent.

As I portentously clipped on the panniers, outside in the sharp sun, the automatic doors hissed ajar and the receptionist trotted through them with a half-litre bottle of mineral water.

'Please,' he said, placing it down in the MIFA's shade. 'Good luck to you my friend.'

I thanked him, and when he was gone bunged it into the front bag, alongside the two I had smuggled out of the breakfast hall.

The roads were eerily quiet for a Monday morning: with Ramadan about to commence, I guessed everyone was gearing up for its associated upheavals to the working routine. Through the outskirts of Kirklareli it was just me, the odd cheery shopkeeper sweeping his threshold ('Hello, welcome!') and those amplified ululations that poured maddeningly from every minaret. Then, as my local cyclo-chum had warned me, the broad, vacant asphalt began to tilt and weave, winding itself up for the big stuff. EV13 wasn't going down without a fight.

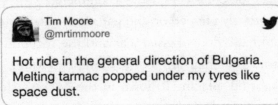

Tim Moore
@mrtimmoore

Hot ride in the general direction of Bulgaria. Melting tarmac popped under my tyres like space dust.

I clicked the Duomatic back into low, eased myself up in the saddle and got to work. It was wiltingly hot, hotter than it had ever been at this hour, and in its more exposed sections the road surface began to soften and liquefy. The under-wheel slurps and slithers seemed distantly familiar; at length I remembered hearing these exact sounds just prior to every slo-mo spill in the traction-free slush of middle Finland. And look, here they came again: the spindly pine battalions, marching back to the roadside to see me off. Cut me and I'd bleed resin.

My hotel water bottles were empty by 500m; after that it was tepid, soapy suckles from the CamelBak. Strange new pains began to pulse from obscure zones, desperate to make a name for themselves before it was too late. Both elbows began to creak and the crimson tips of my ears, laid bare to the sun by that moonshine barber, throbbed like silent klaxons. My scrotum had clearly been waiting for its time to shine: having gone quietly about its business for ninety days, it now agonisingly inveigled itself between the saddle and the top of my right thigh every time I sat down.

But the propulsive essentials, my legs and lungs, kept quiet and applied themselves uncomplainingly to this latest challenge. Back in the Serbian dog days, I had spent half an airless afternoon calculating the pedal revolutions required to propel a Duomatic-powered MIFA 900 from Kirkenes to Tsarevo: those hairy, copper knees had now risen and fallen 1.7 million times. I looked down at them and wondered what on earth I would do with all this flabbergasting physical resilience. Please, I urged myself, please carry the torch forward. Take home the good habits, and leave the bad behind. Yes to regular aerobic exercise, goal-oriented achievement and focused discipline. No to 3,000-calorie breakfasts, public urination and bellowing offensive adaptations of popular hits for hours on end.

'Eight five hundred up.'

I had counted out every centenary kilometre aloud, but this one, delivered to the brown hills and the pliable tarmac, would be the last. In the hours ahead I filled my camera's memory card with commemorative on-the-move video; the wobbly footage makes poor viewing, but the soundtrack is remarkable. Below my respirational huffing runs a fusion of mechanical dismay: a stick-along-the-railings thrum, competing clonks and creaks, the pea-in-a-can rattle of agitated aerosol paint. The net effect suggests a rusty tombola filled with bottle tops. It is truly awful to hear, yet at the time I filtered it all out. And presumably had done so for weeks, for these sounds carried the weariness of a well-worn orchestra. My poor little MIFA was begging for mercy, but all I heard was the hot, mountain silence.

Above, through the pine trees, stood the concrete gantry of a border watchtower. Euro Velo 13's final frontier; I was about to cross the Iron Curtain for the last time. I thought back to the first, cycling into Russia with dread knotting my innards. It was twenty-five years since the Cold War fizzled out, but veterans on both sides still bore the scars. Those childhood nights hunched up by a short-wave radio, twiddling through crackly, haunting Soviet jingles, had clearly left their mark on me. The Finns were distant and drank to forget. So did the wary, bitter Russians. Germany was still two nations, as were the Baltic states, each of them pumped half-full of Russians by Stalin. A thread of glum detachment lingered stubbornly on in so many border zones, an expression of the late Václav Havel's assertion that 'two new generations will have to grow up to wash away the footprints of Communism'. Was it coincidence that the only consistently cheerful people I had met – the Serbs and Turks – had played no more than bit-part Cold War roles?

The Iron Curtain's fall was inarguably a good thing for all

concerned. And yet part of me missed it. I missed the simplicity of a clear-cut, them-and-us divide, and the heady, high-stakes history it fostered. You just don't know where you are today with all these shape-shifting terrorist splinter cells and tangled geo-political alliances. Yes, the Cold War was a colossal waste of everybody's time and money, and left three global generations with an ingrained terror of nuclear annihilation. But, you know, it drove us all forward, gave both sides a goal, something to prove, someone to better. It was why we put men in space and invented the microchip. Look at the giant strides the world took from 1945 to 1989, and its apologetic shuffles since then. Take mobile phones and the internet out of the picture, and in technological terms we have barely evolved. And I sometimes wonder if the balancing influence of an alternative economic system, one based at least nominally on fairness and equality, helped put a brake on the polarising excesses of capitalism. During the Cold War years, the share of all income earned by the richest 1 per cent of Britons fell steadily; since the curtain went down, it has trebled. 'Money didn't matter in the GDR,' an old East German artist told a BBC reporter recently. 'Now everything depends on it. Yes, we now have the freedom to travel, but what good is that if you're on the dole and can't afford it?'

'Where you go?'

The Bulgar in the epaulettes thumbed idly through my passport; there would be no incredulous snorting this time.

'Tsarevo,' I said, jabbing a thumb over my shoulder in the general direction of the proximate Black Sea coast. 'Then, um, home.'

He flicked back to the photo page, compared it briefly with my frankly unrecognisable face, then handed the passport back through the window of his hot little booth. 'Have nice day, Mister Timoteya.'

Back in 1990, our Saab spluttered up to the Bulgarian Black Sea coast at Varna, a resort town ruled by seagulls so vast and fearless we watched one fly off from a restaurant terrace with a whole roast chicken in its beak. After three months, we'd run out of cash and exhausted our wanderlust; it was the end of the line. How strange that this journey, the longest I had ever been on since, should be wending towards the same terminus.

The finale would not be the serene and pensive victory parade of my imagination: between the imminent familial rendezvous at Malko Tarnovo and the Black Sea sand lay 56 savage, vibe-harshing kilometres. The lonely road would rise and fall and crumble into Russian disrepair. I would be chased a very long way by a very big dog, battering desperately through the potholes. I would run out of fuel, succumb to the cold sweats and go a little bit mad, in fact so mad that I attempted to deliver an elegiac voice recording into my CamelBak mouthpiece. I would be welcomed into Tsarevo's half-built holiday apartments by forked-lightning fireworks and a ticker-tape parade of rain. And at bruised and woozy length, with 8,558.4 kilometres on the clock and a face creased in bemusement, I would stumble through damp, shingled sand and unattended sunloungers and part the Black Sea with my little MIFA's filthy front wheel, the tepid, gently lapping brine as grey as the Arctic Ocean I had squinted at through bullets of iced sleet in some previous life.

But all that lay ahead. For the moment, I sat on a bench outside a grocer's shack in one last semi-derelict borderland hill-town, a can of Strong Hell warming in my hand, and waited for a car full of half-forgotten faces.

 Tim Moore
@mrtimmoore

The final curtain.

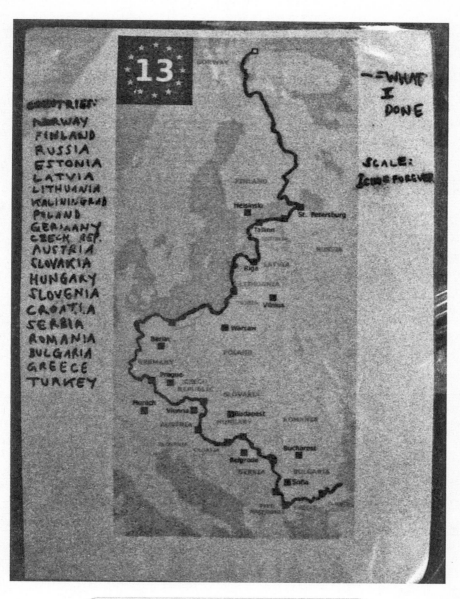

Tim Moore
@mrtimmoore

Last entry in the Progressometer.